Ken Thomson

CROSSOVER

The new edition

1

Ein Lehrwerk für berufliche Gymnasien

KLASSE 11

Cornelsen

Crossover 1 – The new edition wurde geplant und entwickelt von der Redaktion Moderne Fremdsprachen des Cornelsen Verlags, Berlin.

Verfasser:	Ken Thomson, Berlin
Beraterinnen:	Marilyn Clifford-Grein, Stuttgart Dorothee Gräter, Schwäbisch Gmünd Gabriele Holtermann, Ludwigsburg Petra Lehmann, Kehl
Kritische Durchsicht:	Regine Ziegler, Görlitz
Projektleitung:	Jim Austin
Verlagsredaktion:	Andreas Goebel
Redaktionelle Mitarbeit:	Stefanie Heimann, Leah Holroyd, Kate O'Brien Oliver Busch (Wörterverzeichnisse)
Bildredaktion:	Gertha Maly
Layout und technische Umsetzung:	Petra Eberhard, Berlin
Umschlaggestaltung:	Klein & Halm Grafikdesign, Berlin
Titelfoto:	Fotosearch RF
Illustrationen:	Oxford Designers & Illustrators (S. 17, 41) Marcin Nowakowski (S. 13, 62) Mariusz Zabdyr (S. 72, 82)

Erhältlich sind auch:

Workbook	ISBN 978-3-06-020480-9
Vocabulary Practice Book	ISBN 978-3-06-020500-4
Audio-CDs	ISBN 978-3-06-020481-6
Handreichungen für den Unterricht mit CD-ROM	ISBN 978-3-06-020482-3

www.cornelsen.de

Die Links zu externen Webseiten Dritter, die in diesem Lehrwerk angegeben sind, wurden vor Drucklegung sorgfältig auf ihre Aktualität geprüft. Der Verlag übernimmt keine Gewähr für die Aktualität und den Inhalt dieser Seiten oder solcher, die mit ihnen verlinkt sind.

1. Auflage, 2. Druck 2010

Alle Drucke dieser Auflage sind inhaltlich unverändert und können im Unterricht nebeneinander verwendet werden.

Druck: CS-Druck CornelsenStürtz, Berlin

ISBN 978-3-06-020479-3

Inhalt gedruckt auf säurefreiem Papier aus nachhaltiger Forstwirtschaft.

Vorwort

Crossover 1 – The new edition ist ein Lehrwerk für Klasse 11 an beruflichen Gymnasien. Es ist in vier Hauptthemenbereiche aufgeteilt, die von der Lebenswelt heutiger Jugendlicher über Aspekte der englischsprachigen Welt und moderne Medien bis hin zu Staat und Regierung in Großbritannien und den USA reichen. Voraussetzung für die Arbeit mit dem Buch ist der Mittlere Schulabschluss. Das Lehrwerk deckt die grundlegenden Anforderungen der Stufe B1/B1+ des Europäischen Referenzrahmens ab; Band 2 führt zu Stufe B2 und teilweise C1.

Crossover 1 – The new edition bietet eine Fülle von Materialien, die es den Lernenden ermöglichen, ihre Kenntnisse aus der Mittelstufe zu festigen und zu erweitern. Die authentischen Texte verschiedener Herkunft, denen *Warm-up activities* als Einstieg vorangestellt sind, behandeln aktuelle und relevante Themen. Die Erarbeitung geschieht über vielfältige Textverständnisaufgaben, die unter der Rubrik *Working with the text* zusammengefasst sind.

Andere Rubriken sind dem Aufbau des Wortschatzes (*Working with words*), der Festigung grammatischer Strukturen (*Looking at language*), dem Umgang mit dem einsprachigen Wörterbuch (*Working with the dictionary*), der Entwicklung mündlicher Sprachkenntnisse (*Discussion, Role-play*), der Sprachmittlung (*Mediation, Translation*), den Schreibfertigkeiten (*Writing*), dem Hörverständnis (*Listening*) und anderen Schlüsselfertigkeiten gewidmet.

In der Randspalte des Buches finden sich durchgehend Querverweise zum Anhang:
- Der Buchstabe **L** verweist auf den Teil **Lernstrategien**, der einen handlichen Leitfaden mit Lernhilfen zu allen wichtigen Fertigkeiten enthält.
- Der Buchstabe **G** verweist auf die **Grammar summary**, in der die wesentlichen Bereiche der Grammatik übersichtlich zusammengefasst sind.

Zum Nachschlagen stehen umfangreiche Wörterverzeichnisse zur Verfügung.
In der **Unit word list** bietet die mittlere Spalte Gelegenheit zum Lernen englischer Umschreibungen und Synonyme.

Nicht zu vergessen: die hintere **Umschlagklappe**. Im Unterricht lässt sie sich für den mündlichen Gebrauch ausklappen, die eingeklappte Seite hilft bei den Hausaufgaben.

Wir hoffen, dass die Arbeit mit dem Buch Freude bereitet und in motivierender und herausfordernder Weise auf Begegnungen mit der englischsprachigen Welt vorbereitet.

Inhalt

TOPIC 3 The Media Today

TOPIC 4 The State We're In – USA and UK

ANHANG

TOPIC 1 Young People in Britain and America

TEXT 1 Spare Time – Making the Most of it

WARM-UP

1 Complete the questionnaire about what you do in your spare time. Then work with a partner and tell them about what activities you do and why.

Spare time – What do you do to make the most of it?

1 How often do you spend time in the following ways:

a meeting friends
b going to the cinema
c playing computer games
d chatting with friends on the internet
e watching sport
f playing music
g going dancing
h reading

2 How often do you take part in the following sports?

a handball
b running or jogging
c inline skating
d football
e badminton
f skateboarding
g gymnastics
h tennis
i other: …

3 How often do you take part in activities to help the community such as:

a helping to organise activities for children
b working with old people
c working on environmental projects
d helping to organise a youth club
e training children in a sports club
f other: …

regularly	sometimes	occasionally	never
☐	☐	☐	☐

WORKING WITH THE TEXT

The Duke of Edinburgh's Award is an award for personal achievement for people between the ages of 14 and 25. People taking part in the award programme choose a personal interest, such as a sport, which their award will then be focussed on.

L ▸ Lesen schwieriger Texte: Grobverständnis (p. 108)

2 Read the text on the opposite page and match the four headings to the sections A–D.

1 Why you should do the Award
2 Who can do the Award
3 How long the Award takes
4 What the Award is

The Duke of Edinburgh's Award

A The award is a programme of activities to do in your spare time. There are three Awards: Bronze, Silver, and Gold. Gold takes the longest and is the hardest – usually, people start on the Bronze Award.

You have to choose one activity under each of these headings, and do it for a set length of time:

Service: Help the community or the environment, or train to save a life …

Skills: Whether you fancy yourself as a fine artist or a trapeze artist, we've got something that will suit you …

Physical Recreation: Any sport, dance or fitness activity can count towards the Award.

Expedition: Go on an expedition and find yourself. Plan an adventurous journey in the countryside on foot, on horseback, by boat or by bicycle …

Residential Project: Work as a team on a conservation or activity-based project for five days.

It's fun and a real challenge … so take the plunge!

B A Bronze Award takes at least 6 months, a Silver at least 12 months and a Gold Award at least 18 months. If you already have one Duke of Edinburgh's Award, the next may take you less time.

It certainly won't wipe out your studying time or your social life!

C Firstly, it's a great laugh! It's about trying something new or improving your existing skills.

You'll discover how achieving personal goals can change your life. It's proving popular – over 225,000 young people in the UK are now doing the Award.

Since many employers regard the Award as an extra qualification, it could even benefit your career.

D The Award is for anyone aged 14–25. Male or female, whether able-bodied or not and regardless of religion or background, the Award is for you.

If you're 14 (or nearly 14), you can do the Bronze Award.

If you're 15, you can do the Bronze or Silver Awards.

If you're 16 or over, you can do the Bronze, Silver or Gold Awards.

All Awards must be completed by the time you're 25.

You obviously fit the bill … so take the challenge! (340 words)

Source: www.theaward.org

CD 1 Track 2

award *Auszeichnung, Preis*
6 community *Gemeinschaft*
7 fancy oneself as sth *sich für etw halten*
13 residential *mit Übernachtung*
15 take the plunge *den Sprung wagen*
19 wipe sth out *etw zunichte machen*
25 benefit sth *etw nützen, zugute kommen*
26 able-bodied *gesund, tauglich, nicht behindert*
27 regardless of *unabhängig von*
32 fit the bill *der/die Richtige sein*

3 Decide whether the following statements about the text are true or false. Correct the false statements. You may need to read the whole text for some of the statements.

L ▸ Lesen schwieriger Texte: Suche nach Einzelinformationen (p. 108)

1. Although the Silver and Gold Awards are more difficult, it is possible to start on them as soon as you feel ready.
2. It is possible to do any sport or fitness activity as part of the Award.
3. It is possible to complete one of the Awards in less than the usual time.
4. While you are doing the Award you will not really have time for any other spare time activities.
5. You can only do a sport or activity which is new to you as part of the Award.
6. Over 225,000 young people have completed the award programme so far.
7. Doing the Award could help you with jobs when you leave school or college.
8. The Award is open to anyone between the ages of 14 and 25.

L ▶ Mediation (p. 122)

L ▶ Gruppengespräche und Diskussionen führen (p. 122)

MEDIATION

4 **Explain in German what the Duke of Edinburgh's Award is. Then summarise sections A–D in German.**

DISCUSSION

5 **In groups, discuss whether you know of a similar award scheme in Germany. Would you do a Duke of Edinburgh's Award if you had the opportunity?**

WORKING WITH WORDS

6 **In which of the sentences are the phrases from the text used correctly?**

1 set length of time

a There's no set length of time for completing an Award. You can take as long as you need.

b Can you tell me the set length of time? I have to meet my mum at 5 o'clock.

2 residential project

a I'm working on a residential project next week but I'll be coming home every evening.

b Ben's taking part in a residential project in Warwickshire. He won't be back home until next Tuesday.

3 it's a great laugh

a You should come camping with my friends and me. It's a great laugh – we have a lot of fun.

b Wait till you hear this new joke. It's a great laugh.

4 able-bodied

a Able-bodied people sometimes find it hard to understand how difficult life is for people with physical disabilities.

b Clare is very fit and strong because of her swimming. She's really able-bodied.

5 fit the bill

a This shirt is too big for me. It doesn't fit the bill.

b Sara applied for a job in the supermarket but they said she didn't fit the bill. They are looking for people who can work longer hours than she can.

7 **Rewrite the sentences using the verbs or nouns which are related to the underlined words. The first sentence has been done for you.**

1 I chose to do an aerobics course first, but it was full so I had to do something else.
My first choice was an aerobics course, but it was full so I had to do something else.

2 I'm going to train to be a football coach during the summer.
I'm going to do some …

3 Gordon plans to do a Bronze Award next year.
Gordon's …

4 The aim of the project is the conservation of green areas in the city.
The aim of the project is to …

5 I discovered that I really love camping last summer.
Last summer, I made the …

INFO

Extra-curricular Activities in British and American Schools

Although the school day in Britain and North America is longer than in Germany – it generally goes on until around 3.30 p.m. – many students stay at school at the end of the day to take part in extra-curricular activities. These are clubs and societies which are run with the help of teachers who often give up their time without getting paid for it. Sport is a key element of extra-curricular activities in many schools. Schools in Britain often have football, netball and cricket clubs. In America after-hours sports activities are generally focussed on things like American football, basketball and baseball. In both countries schools frequently compete in inter-school sports competitions.

Sport is not the only thing on offer. Many schools have clubs and societies which focus on computing, science, history, geography and so on. Such after-school activities not only offer students a structured environment in which to follow their hobbies and interests, but also benefit their school work in these subjects.

However, the main aim of most extra-curricular activities is to be fun for the students. Many teachers also see them as a way of helping students to identify more positively with school and to see it as more than just a place where they have to work hard.

6 netball *Korbball*
8 compete *gegeneinander kämpfen*

LOOKING AT LANGUAGE

8 Put the verbs in brackets into the simple present or present progressive.

G ▸ The simple present and present progressive (p. 125)

1. Stephen … (have) too much school work to do to think about doing an award programme.
2. Alison … (plan) her expedition just now.
3. Normally I …(spend) most of my time working on my Duke of Edinburgh Award.
4. But I …(work) two evenings a week in the supermarket this month to earn some extra money.
5. I … (do) my homework right now but … (watch) television at the same time.
6. Craig usually … (come) to football training on Saturdays but he … (prepare) for a residential project at the moment and can't come this Saturday.

LISTENING AND ROLE-PLAY

HANDS-ON TASK

CD 1 Track 3

9 Listen to the dialogue and do the following tasks.

1. You are going to listen to a conversation between Sarah, who wants to do a Duke of Edinburgh's Award, and an award advisor who will ask Sarah for some basic information about herself. Make a list of the information you think the advisor may ask for. Then listen to the dialogue. How many of the things on your list were mentioned?
2. Now listen again and make notes on the information that Sarah gives the advisor.
3. Use your notes to complete Sarah's application form for the award.
4. Now work with a partner and take turns to role-play the dialogue you have heard in the listening exercise, giving your own personal details and information about your hobbies and interests.

L ▸ Das Hörverständnis üben (p. 111)

Name ....
Address ....
Date of birth ....
Information about spare time activities
Personal aims in doing the Duke of Edinburgh's Award ....

TEXT 2 The School Uniform Debate

WARM-UP

1 a Work with a partner and read the following statements which are often used as arguments in favour of school uniform. Which do you find plausible?

School uniforms help …
1 to prevent gangs forming in schools
2 to make pupils better behaved
3 to prevent students feeling that they have to buy trendy clothes
4 to make it clear if an outsider is in a school
5 to make economic and social differences between students less obvious
6 to make students feel proud of their school
7 to improve attendance at school

b Would you be for or against the introduction of a uniform at your school? State your reasons.

2 Quickly read the text and match three of the headings to the correct paragraphs (A–E). Two of the headings do not correspond to a paragraph in the text.

1 What do studies say about school uniforms?
2 Are school uniforms too expensive?
3 How have education staff reacted to this research?
4 How common are school uniforms?
5 What is the future of school uniform?

L ▸ Lesen schwieriger Texte: Grobverständnis (p. 108)

CD 1 Track 4

The Debate over School Uniforms

By Marian Wilde, GreatSchools.net Staff

Recent data indicates that 23% of elementary schools in the U.S. have a school uniform, but a new book makes the case that uniforms do not improve school safety or academic performance.

A In *The School Uniform Movement and What It Tells Us About American Education: A Symbolic Crusade*, David Brunsma offers a comprehensive look at the studies conducted to date on the effect of uniforms on academic performance.

B In his research Brunsma finds that uniforms have no effect on school safety or academic achievement. Put simply, there is little difference between schools with and without a uniform in terms of violence and students' examination results.

C "I'm generalizing here," says Brunsma, "but I feel stronger support and understanding of the results from teachers who are working every day in the classroom. School principals, on the other hand, seem to have more of a problem with the results and arguments presented in my work. Principals want to simply disregard rigorous, scientific study of the issue."

D The school uniform movement has now spread to about a quarter of all elementary schools. Experts say that the number of high schools with uniforms is about half the number of elementary schools.

1 indicate *besagen*
2 make the case *die These vertreten*
3 performance *Leistung*
5 crusade *Kreuzzug*
comprehensive *umfassend*
6 conduct *durchführen*
to date *bis heute*
7 research *Studie, Untersuchung*
8 achievement *Leistung*
12 principal *Schulleiter/in*

E Uniforms are supposed to curb school violence and improve academic results. Why are they not more prevalent in high schools then? These goals are just as important there as they are in elementary schools. Because, notes Brunsma, "It's much more difficult to introduce uniforms in high schools. The student resistance is much, much higher. Of course, this uniform debate is also about whether children have rights!" (262 words)

Adapted from: www.greatschools.net

18 curb *eindämmen*
19 prevalent *gängig, verbreitet*
21 resistance *Widerstand*

WORKING WITH THE TEXT

3 Answer the following questions about the text.

L ▶ Fragen zum Text beantworten (p. 114)

1 What information did David Brunsma use to write his book?
2 What does his book show about the relationship between school uniform and academic performance?
3 Compare the reactions of teachers and school principals to Brunsma's book.
4 How many high schools have a uniform?
5 What does Brunsma say about introducing uniforms in high schools?

4 Look back at exercise 2. With a partner, find headings for the two paragraphs that do not match.

MEDIATION

5 You have been asked to write an article about the school uniform debate for the next issue of your school magazine. Work with a partner and take turns to summarise the three following points about the text in German.

L ▶ Mediation (p. 122)

a the results of Brunsma's study
b the reaction to his study
c the situation in the US regarding school uniform

WORKING WITH WORDS

6 Rewrite the sentences in your own words, replacing the underlined expressions with the corresponding expressions in the box. Be careful to use the correct form of the expressions in each context.

argue | complete | examination results | contain | show | widespread

1 The chairman of the Head Teachers' Association <u>made the case</u> in favour of school uniform in a newspaper interview.
2 Norford High School's <u>academic performance</u> has improved since the school stopped having a school uniform.
3 We want to make a <u>comprehensive</u> study of the effect of school uniform on pupils' behaviour.
4 Schools need to do more than simply have a uniform in order to <u>curb</u> violence in schools.
5 The <u>prevalent</u> idea that pupils do not like wearing a uniform is not true.
6 The study <u>indicated</u> that most students preferred to wear a school uniform.

7 What are the opposites of these words and phrases from the text?

1 difference **2** stronger **3** more **4** curb **5** more difficult **6** higher

L ► Mind Mapping (p. 114)

8 a Read the text again and make a mind map of all the vocabulary and expressions which are specifically about school. Add any other words you know.

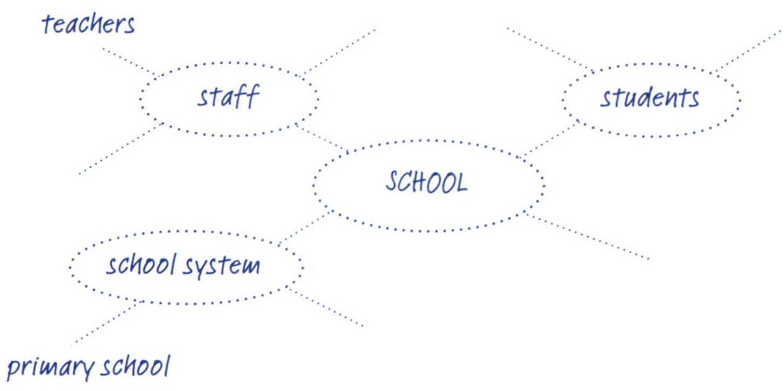

b Now read the info box below and complete your mind map with words and expressions from the box.

c Work with a partner. Make a poster comparing the school systems of the US, Britain and Germany in a table.

Age	USA		UK		Germany	
18–19	–		–		grammar school / vocational college	Class 13
17–18	high school	12th grade	sixth form	Year 13		Class 12
16–17		11th grade		Year 12		Class 11

INFO

The British and American School Systems

In England, Wales and Northern Ireland pupils begin primary school aged 5 in what is referred to as Year One. Their primary education continues until the end of Year Six: they leave primary school at the age of 11. Next comes secondary school. This either takes the form of a comprehensive school where children of all abilities are schooled together, or grammar school where pupils are selected on the basis of their academic performance. Pupils are required to remain in secondary school until the age of 16 at the end of Year Eleven. If they choose to go on and do their 'A' Levels they enter sixth form for two years. They will then leave school at the end of Year Thirteen aged 18.

Due to the fact that individual states have responsibility for shaping education in the US, it is hard to generalise about the school system there accurately. However, it is generally the case that children start elementary school at the age of five in a school year which is referred to as kindergarten. At age six they move into first grade and remain in elementary school until they have completed the fifth grade at the age of 11. They then go on to middle school. This lasts for three years: pupils leave at the end of eighth grade aged 14. Four years of high school come next: high school students graduate and leave school at the age of eighteen.

6 be required to *es wird von jdm erwartet*
9 shape *festlegen*

SPEAKING

9 **Below is an excerpt of the dress code from Edlington Comprehensive School, outlining what students are not allowed to wear. Read the excerpt and say which of the school students in the cartoons are breaking the dress code and in what way.**

overly *übermäßig*
baggy *ausgebeult, herabhängend*
scarf *Kopftuch*
dog collar *Nietenhalsband*
stud *Piercing*

Dress Code

for Edlington Comprehensive School

All students are expected to look smart in school. The following are not allowed:

- overly large or baggy clothes
- clothes with holes in
- sweatbands or scarves (exceptions are made for religious clothing)
- visible underwear
- bare stomachs, low-cut necklines or bare backs
- cycling shorts, swimsuits or pyjamas
- visible piercings, except in the ear
- dog collars, tongue rings and studs, or chains that connect one part of the body to another

LISTENING

10 a **Listen to the three students from Edlington Comprehensive School being asked about their views on school uniform for a radio programme. Which of them …**

CD 1 Track 5

L ► Das Hörverständnis üben (p. 111)

1 supports school uniform?
2 is against school uniform?
3 is uncertain about school uniform?

Mike

Bill

Gordon

CD 1 Track 5

b **Listen again and choose the most appropriate ending for each sentence.**

1 Mike says that …
a there are some difficulties with school uniform.
b there are no problems with school uniform.
c school uniform causes problems.

2 Mike also says that uniforms …
a stop violence in schools.
b don't stop violence in schools.
c cause violence in schools.

3 Bill says uniforms …
a stop people creating their own identity.
b help people create their own identity.
c don't stop people creating their own identity.

4 Bill also says that uniforms make school students …
a targets for bullies.
b less easy for bullies to identify.
c turn into bullies.

5 Gordon says that uniforms …
a help you to be an individual.
b help the team atmosphere in schools.
c don't help the team atmosphere in schools.

LOOKING AT LANGUAGE

G ▶ Simple present (p. 125)
Simple past (p. 126)
Present perfect (p. 126)

11 **a** **Ask David Brunsma questions in English about his work and ideas. Use the German questions to help you.**

1 Seit wann interessieren Sie sich für dieses Thema?
2 Haben Schuluniformen auch positive Auswirkungen?
3 Warum haben Uniformen keinen Einfluss auf schulische Leistungen?
4 Welche Kleidung sollte in Schulen nicht erlaubt sein?
5 Warum sind Schulleiterinnen und -leiter für Uniformen?
6 Mussten Sie in der Schule eine Uniform tragen?
7 Würden Sie Ihre eigenen Kinder auf eine Schule mit Uniform schicken?
8 Sehen Schülerinnen und Schüler in Uniformen nicht besser aus?

b **Work with a partner and role-play an interview with David Brunsma using the questions from Part a. Then swap roles.**

GIVING A PRESENTATION

HANDS-ON TASK

L ▶ Die Arbeitsergebnisse präsentieren (p. 119)

12 **Follow the steps below in order to prepare a presentation about school uniforms and dress codes to give to your class.**

1 Make a list of the advantages and disadvantages of school uniform.
2 Now work in a group. Your school is making a move towards having either a uniform or dress code but will allow students to decide which they would prefer. Hold a vote to find out which option the group would prefer.
3 Now decide what the uniform or dress code should consist of.
4 Present your group's ideas to the rest of the class.

TEXT 3 Teenagers are Trouble?

WARM-UP

1 **Match the correct captions (1–4) to the photographs.**

1 1960s mods
2 1970s hippies
3 1980s punks
4 1990s hip-hoppers

2 **Look at the photograph on the right. Does the teenager, who is wearing a hoodie, look frightening or just cool? Say why.**

3 **a** **Which of the German expressions (a–c) is the correct translation of the English expressions?**

1 fashion statement
a *Modenschau*
b *Ausdruck eines modischen Stils*
c *modische Behauptung*

2 be up to no good
a *nichts Gutes im Schilde führen*
b *zu viel des Guten sein*
c *sich auf und davon machen*

3 vicious circle
a *Nahrungsmittelkette*
b *Teufelskreis*
c *Zirkeltraining*

4 This is down to the media.
a *Daran sind die Medien schuld.*
b *Da unten geht es zur Medienabteilung.*
c *Dafür muss man sich an die Medien wenden.*

5 climate of fear
a *Angst vor dem Klimawandel*
b *Klima des Grauens*
c *Klima der Angst*

b **Now scan the text on the following page to check your answers.**

CD 1 Track 6

British Adults Fear Teenagers Wearing "Hoodies"

Who would want to be a British teenager? These supposedly hard-drinking, drug-taking and violent young people have never had a worse reputation. So, is something going horribly wrong? Or has it always been this way? Could we be overreacting to problems that have always been part of youth behaviour?

Teenagers who wear hoodies personify the "problem teenager" in Britain. Hoodies, which were originally designed for sport, are the number one garment for many teenagers, especially boys. Most teenagers wear them as a fashion statement. But people fear that they are worn by gangs and that teenagers use the hoods to hide their faces when shoplifting or doing something else illegal.

This has led to many shopping centres banning hoodies. The Elephant and Castle shopping centre in south London is one of these. Centre manager, Brian Turnbull said, "Young people who wear hoodies are often up to no good. That's why we banned them. This has made our shopping centre more pleasant for other people." Many teenagers feel insulted by such bans, says Lance, 18. "The hoodie has become, in adult minds, a criminal garment. When adults see teenagers wearing them, they become afraid. This angers and frustrates young people," he says.

"A woman who walks past clutching her bag will be more of a target than if she walked by in the normal way because she is insulting young people in her assumptions. This may provoke young people to taunt and intimidate her. It's a vicious circle." Lance added: "This fear is down to the media and the way young people are shown. Teenagers wearing hoodies are portrayed as criminals."

"People are afraid when they see teenagers in groups. There is a real climate of fear," says Dr Juanjo Medina, lecturer from the University of Manchester's School of Law with a research interest in youth crime, who also blames the media for creating fear about young people.

Every generation seems to think that it has the worst youth problem — so it may be worth remembering that historically the behaviour of teenagers was often seen as problematic.

As Professor George Rousseau of the Centre for the History of Childhood says: "There are examples of such thinking from Ancient Greece through to the 17th century and beyond."

(375 words)

1 supposedly *angeblich*
2 reputation *Ruf*
6 garment *Kleidungsstück*
7 fashion statement *Ausdruck eines modischen Stils, Statement*
9 shoplifting *Ladendiebstahl*
12 be up to no good *nichts Gutes im Schilde führen*
14 insult *beleidigen*
17 clutch *umklammern*
target *Ziel*
18 assumption *Annahme*
19 provoke *provozieren*
taunt *verhöhnen*
intimidate *einschüchtern*
vicious circle *Teufelskreis*
20 be down to sth *an etw liegen*
21 portray *darstellen*
24 blame sb for sth *jdm/etw die Schuld an etw geben*

WORKING WITH THE TEXT

L ▸ Lesen schwieriger Texte: Suche nach Einzelinformationen (p. 108)

4 Are these statements true, false or not clear from the article? Correct the false statements and explain those which are not clear.

1 British teenagers have a good reputation.
2 The first hoodies were made for people doing sport.
3 Most teenagers who wear hoodies are potential troublemakers.
4 Many teenagers who wear hoodies stole them from shops.
5 Many shopping centres no longer admit teenagers with hoodies.
6 Adults' attitudes to teenagers wearing hoodies can have a negative effect on the behaviour of young people.
7 Many people in Britain are frightened of teenagers.
8 The behaviour of teenagers was worse in the past.

5 a List all the arguments in the text which say that teenagers wearing hoodies is a bad thing and all the arguments which say that adults overreact to teenagers who wear hoodies.

b Look at the cartoon and describe it.

c Which of the arguments about hoodies do you think the cartoonist agrees with? State reasons for your answer.

L ▶ Interpretation von Bildern und Karikaturen (p. 119)

6 a **Read the following news article. What do the words "thugs" and "upstanding" mean? Use the context they occur in to help you decide.**

L ▶ Umgang mit unbekannten Vokabeln (p. 109)

A school has made hooded tops part of its uniform in a move that could help to save the reputation of "hoodies".

Richard Haigh, Head Teacher of Coombeshead College, Newton Abbot, Devon, has criticized "hysterical" stereotyping of 'hoodie' wearers as thugs.
"Most young people are fine, upstanding citizens, and some of them wear hoodies. Why should they be thought of as bad?" he said.
Bluewater shopping centre, Greenhithe, Kent, last week banned hooded tops.
"It's the behaviour that's the problem, not the clothing," Mr Haigh said on Thursday.
He added: "If you know how young people's minds work, the best way of encouraging them to do something is to ban it."

Source: www.bbc.co.uk (abridged)

b **Do you think it is a good idea to use hoodies as school uniform? Give reasons.**

L ▶ Eine Stellungnahme schreiben (p. 115)

WORKING WITH WORDS

7 **Match the words from the text on page 16 (1–8) to the synonymous words and expressions (a–h).**

1 violent (line 2)	a an item of clothing
2 overreact (line 4)	b depict
3 personify (line 5)	c annoy (someone) into doing something
4 garment (line 6)	d be an example of
5 shoplifting (line 9)	e aggressive
6 ban (line 10)	f respond in an exaggerated way
7 provoke (line 19)	g stealing from shops
8 portray (line 21)	h prohibit

3 widespread *weit verbreitet*
6 despite *ungeachtet dessen*
8 survey *Umfrage*
9 offender *Straftäter/in*
10 regarding *bezüglich*
13 claim *behaupten*
14 binge *Sauforgie*

INFO

Crime and Anti-social Behaviour among British Teenagers

Crime and anti-social behaviour among teenagers is the subject of heated public debate in Britain. The British media often publishes stories about criminality among teenagers and the idea that teenage crime is widespread and increasing is common.
Some people argue, however, that this idea is not based on hard facts. According to official statistics, the number of known young offenders has fallen over the last two decades. Despite what the statistics say, the British public at large continues to believe that crime among the young is on the increase. 75% of the people who took part in a recent survey carried out by the Home Office believed that the number of young offenders was rising.

Regarding anti-social behaviour, a study by the Institute for Public Policy Research (IPPR) suggests that British teenagers are among the most badly behaved in Europe. The report says that they drink more alcohol and are more violent than teenagers in the rest of Europe. The report claims that in 2003, 38% of British 15-year-olds tried cannabis. It also says that in the same year 15-year-old Britons were the third worst binge drinkers in Europe. The IPPR blames this on British teenagers not spending enough time with adults to learn social skills. For example, while 93% of Italian teenagers eat regularly with their families, only 64% of British teenagers do so.

Based on: *Why UK teenagers struggle to cope*, www.bbc.co.uk

DESCRIBING A GRAPH

L ▸ Interpretation von Grafiken (p. 121)

8 a **Describe the trends shown in the graph. Use the expressions on the right to help you.**

Crime figures	increased climbed rose went up	slightly slowly steadily considerably suddenly sharply
	went down decreased fell	

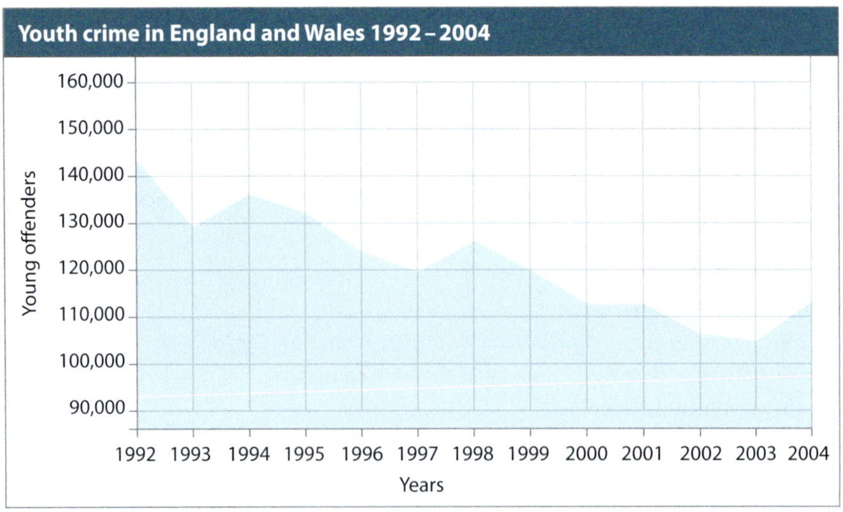

Source: Nacro (National Crime Reduction Charity), *Youth Crime briefing March 2006*

b **Now compare the information given in the graph with the info box above.**

LOOKING AT LANGUAGE

9 **Put the verbs in brackets into the simple past or the present perfect.**

G ► Simple past (p. 126)
Present perfect (p. 126)

Another North London Shopping Centre Bans 'Hoodies'

A north London shopping centre ...[1] (ban) teenagers wearing hoodies from its premises. The Arnlee Centre, in West Hampstead, last week ...[2] (join) the increasing number of shopping centres which ...[3] (impose) hoodie bans in the last year.

Centre manager, Nick Horford, ...[4] (say) yesterday, "We regret this ban but, in our view, it's necessary. Last year, hundreds of our customers ...[5] (complain) that they feel intimidated by teenagers wearing hoodies. Since March this year, the shops in the premises ...[6] (report) a 12% increase in shoplifting. We believe that much of this is down to hoodies. That's why we ...[7] (decide) to take this step last week."

The police are not altogether happy with such bans. "Although there ...[8] (be) more and more reports of trouble in shopping centres associated with 'hoodies' in the last few months, we believe that banning teenagers with hoodies is not the answer. For one thing, not all of them are troublemakers. And bans only push the real troublemakers onto the streets where they will commit petty crimes elsewhere," ...[9] (comment) a spokesperson for the Metropolitan Police at the end of last year. The Met ...[10] (not issue) a statement since Arnlee ...[11] (announce) its ban last week.

Shoppers at Arnlee ...[12] (appear) to be happy about the ban when we ...[13] (speak) to them yesterday. Claire Gordon ...[14] (say), "A little thug in a hoodie stole my handbag in this shopping centre last October. I ...[15] (not be able to) to identify him because he was wearing his hood up. Since Christmas, three of my friends ...[16] (be attacked) in a similar way. It's about time something was done about this problem."

WRITING

10 **The conflict over hoodies highlights the fact that people of different ages often have different ideas and attitudes. Can you think of other examples of this "generation gap"? Write a comment on these conflicts between young and old people. Try to think of reasons for such differences.**

L ► Eine Stellungnahme schreiben (p. 115)

ROLE-PLAY

HANDS-ON TASK

11 **Role-play a discussion between a parent and a son or daughter.**

1. Work in pairs. Student A takes the role of a parent, who does not like hoodies. Student B takes the role of a teenage son/daughter who wants to wear a hoodie to school. Think of as many arguments as possible for both sides of the discussion. Note these down.
2. Study the role cards on page 106. Note other words and expressions that you may want to use – for example, from the text.
3. Now role-play the discussion. Try to find an answer to the problem that you are both happy with.

TEXT 4 Part-time Jobs

WARM-UP

1 a **Work with a partner. Which of the following are advantages and which are disadvantages of the type of part-time jobs that school students often do? Think of further advantages and disadvantages.**

1. Part-time work is often poorly paid.
2. Young people with part-time jobs can develop their time-keeping skills.
3. Working and earning money gives young people some financial independence.
4. Part-time jobs often involve tasks that are boring and repetitive.
5. Young people doing part-time work develop a sense of responsibility.
6. Working part-time means that there is less time for schoolwork.
7. Having a part-time job is an opportunity to make new friends.
8. Young people who have part-time jobs have less time for hobbies and socialising.

b **Do you find the type of work shown in the photograph attractive or unattractive? Which of the advantages and disadvantages from above do you think apply to this type of work?**

c **Now read the poem on the opposite page and say whether any of the additional advantages or disadvantages you thought of are mentioned.**

WORKING WITH THE POEM

L ▸ Fragen zum Text beantworten (p. 114)

2 **Answer the following questions about the poem using your own words as far as possible.**

1. How does Patti feel when she gets in her car to go to work?
2. When she arrives at the parking lot outside McDonald's, Patti's feelings are different from a customer's. In what way?
3. What is the only positive thing for Patti about arriving for work?
4. When she goes to the grill area, what does Patti see which a customer would probably rather not see?
5. In which verse of the poem does Patti come closest to describing hell? What language and imagery does she use to achieve this?

3 **Put the statements describing the parts of Patti's working day in the order mentioned in the poem.**

Patti …

a goes to the area where food is prepared
b greets her colleagues
c has something to eat before starting work
d thinks about the point of working
e has a messy problem with a customer order
f prepares to travel to work
g officially starts her working day
h starts to feel unwell as she nears her workplace
i feels trapped by being at work

Working – I Work In Hell

by Patti S., Glasgow, MT

When I get into my car
I dread knowing that I have to spend
the next six to eight hours at McDonald's.
I work in hell!

When I get to the parking lot
my stomach starts to churn & I can feel myself getting sick
from the stench of the food in the air.
I work in hell!

When I walk into McDonald's I walk into my dungeon, where I
know I am a prisoner, unable to escape and be free.
I know McDonald's is like the sixth circle of hell.
I work in hell!

Working there the people know you too well so
I almost never get a cheerful hello. I order
a Big Mac w/out lettuce and pickles, the only thing that
sounds remotely good at the present moment.
I work in hell!

Now time to clock on: out of my chair, around the corner,
down to the grill area.
I can see the greasiness of my surroundings.
By the grills, I can hear the sizzling and crackling of the
cooked brown meat on the hot metal surface.
I work in hell!

By the time clock I wonder what I always wonder.
Why am I still working here?
Clocked in and washed up and out front to do my job.
I work in hell!

With all of my luck I'm asked to make an ice-cream cone.
Of course, the machine breaks and ice cream comes gushing out
as if vomiting all over my hand.
I work in hell!

McDonald's is a horrible place to work and yet
I really like the job. Jobs are one of the basic
essentials we all must live with.
But all the same …
I work in hell!

(285 words)

Source: www.teenink.com

CD 1 Track 7

2 I dread *mir graut es vor*
6 my stomach churns *mir dreht sich der Magen um*
7 stench *Gestank*
9 dungeon *Kerker*
10 escape *entfliehen*
15 lettuce *(grüner) Salat*
16 remotely *entfernt*
18 clock on *(den Arbeitsbeginn) stempeln*
20 greasiness *Schmierigkeit, Öligkeit*
surroundings *(pl.) Umgebung*
21 sizzle *brutzeln*
crackle *knistern*
29 gush out *herausschießen, heraussprudeln*
30 vomit *erbrechen*
34 essentials *(pl.) Notwendigkeiten, das Wesentliche*

4 Read between the lines.

1. In what way is Patty a "prisoner"?
2. What do you think Patty means when she says, "Working there the people know you too well" (line 13)?
3. Why do you think Patti says that "of course" the ice cream machine breaks down (line 29)? What does this say about her attitude towards her job?
4. If Patti "works in hell", why does she stay there?

WORKING WITH WORDS

5 **Look at the poem again and find as many expressions as you can which Patti uses in a negative way to describe how unhappy she is with her work.**

WORKING WITH THE DICTIONARY

L ▸ Umgang mit unbekannten Vokabeln (p. 109)

6 a **Match the words in the box, some of which are not in the text, to the appropriate headings. Use your dictionary to find the meanings of any words you do not understand.**

chilled | chocolate sauce | cones | crackle | dessert | french fries | fry | grease | oil | sizzle | strawberry sundae | wafers

Ice-cream machine	Grill area
chilled	

b **Each of the words *vegetable*, *ice-cream* and *spoon* combines with a different word from the box above to make a new expression. Write down these three expressions and then use your dictionary to find more expressions containing the words from the box.**

INTERNET PROJECT

L ▸ Grafiken, Diagramme und Tabellen (p. 121)

L ▸ Suche nach Informationen im Internet (p. 112)

7 **Read the info box below and follow these steps.**

1 Present the information about the different areas in which US high school students work in a pie chart.

2 Find corresponding information about Germany on the Internet and compare it with the US.

INFO

The Culture of Part-time Work among High School Students in the US

There is a common stereotypical view that most high school students in the US hold down part-time jobs after school. This, however, is not the case: only a minority of high school students in the US are involved in part-time work. In 2006, just 2,767,000 – or around 27% of high school students in the US – had jobs outside of school.

Another popular view is that most of those high school students who do work are employed by fast food restaurants and in shops. It is true that significant numbers work in these areas – a recent survey found that 29% of 15-year-old students with part-time jobs worked in food outlets and 16% in shops. However, 31% worked in service sector occupations, 12% in construction and manufacturing, 6% in agriculture and 6% in other types of occupation. Indeed, the fact that many high school students work in occupations usually reserved for adults worries some people in the US. They fear that many of the jobs done by young people are too hard and dangerous for them and that they receive lower rates of pay than adults carrying out the same work.

Source: US Bureau of Labor Statistics

[1] hold down a job *einer Arbeit nachgehen*
[8] food outlet *Imbiss*
[9] occupation *Tätigkeit*

WRITING

L ▸ Einen Text sinnvoll gliedern (p. 118)

8 **Write an article about Patti's job and how she feels about it for the school magazine.**

TEXT 5 Calorie Countdown

WARM-UP

1 a Describe the photographs.

L ▸ Interpretation von Bildern und Karikaturen (p. 119)

b Compare the two photographs using the adjectives in the box.

attractive | healthy | fit | natural

c What effect do the photographs have on you?

d Are young men and women under the same pressure to be thin? Is it more acceptable for a young man to be a 'little bit rounder' than it is for a young woman?

e Read the text on the following page quickly. Is the author a man or a woman? What evidence can you find in the text to prove this?

L ▸ Lesen schwieriger Texte: Grobverständnis (p. 108)

WORKING WITH THE TEXT

2 Now read the text on the following page closely and do the following tasks using your own words as far as possible.

L ▸ Lesen schwieriger Texte: Detailverständnis (p. 108)

1 Explain the reasons behind the author's decision to lose weight in this way.
2 Analyse the author's feelings about hunger.
3 Explain why the author's doctor advised her to start eating properly again.
4 Describe the author's feelings after she found out how much weight she had lost.

CD 1 Track 8

Counting Down the Calories

The recent "super thin" fashion seems to have caused a frightening increase in young women developing eating disorders, as they associate "skinny" with "success". How could I show the many young girls what starving themselves actually means; that the short-term "gain" of a stick-thin frame had long-term harmful side effects? I decided not just to write about it but to do it. I did the unthinkable, and road-tested the super skinny lifestyle myself. Eight weeks ago, I introduced a totally new concept of eating into my life, that being – not eating. I would eat an absolute maximum of 500 calories a day.

When I decided to take on the gruesome task of a starvation diet, I was wrong to believe that hunger would be my only challenge. Depression, loneliness and chronic insomnia were the side effects of my dangerously low calorie intake. Hunger actually became a sick comfort to me, a reassurance that I was doing the "right" thing. Even on day one I was having headaches, mood swings and demonstrating weird obsessive behaviour … and that was before lunch! By day two I was even more moody and groggy.

The hunger never goes. But you begin to enjoy and trust it. When your goal is to be thin, hunger is your best friend. It's the only thing that assures you that you are working hard enough.

My weekly assessments with my doctor revealed my magnesium and potassium levels plummeted to worrying levels, as did my white blood cell count, and my antioxidant levels. I had increased my chances of contracting serious conditions such as tuberculosis, and dangerously increased my risks of getting cancer. Despite my doctor's advice to eat properly, I continued.

Most worrying was how my confidence got so low. As the project went on, I felt more and more self-aware and hated the idea of anyone looking at me. I looked at my body in the mirror and hated it because it was the cause of me feeling so down. I couldn't look at the weight loss as an honourable achievement because I was disgusted in what it took to achieve it. I think it was then that I truly understood the pressures so many models are under, and how miserable their lives must be trying to keep up with the super skinny look that their industry demands.

When I began this journey I was 67 kilos. In just 8 weeks, by my final weigh-in, I had lost 8 kilos. After everything I had been through, this disappointed me. I felt like I had not achieved what I set out to do. That's exactly what this is about: normal women, with normal bodies set on unachievable goals. And when they don't meet them, they feel like failures. I hope to God that my experience puts anyone else off trying the same thing. The body needs fuel. Food works, eat it.

(484 words)

Adapted from bbc.co.uk

2 eating disorders *(pl.)* *Essstörungen*
skinny *mager, dürr*
3 starve oneself *hungern*
4 short-term *kurzfristig*
gain *Zugewinn*
stick-thin *spindeldürr*
9 gruesome *grausig*
11 insomnia *Schlaflosigkeit*
12 sick *krank, pervers*
comfort *Trost*
reassurance *Bestätigung*
13 mood swing *Stimmungsschwankung*
14 weird *seltsam*
obsessive *zwanghaft*
19 assessment *Beurteilung, Prüfung*
reveal *offenbaren, verraten*
potassium *Kalium*
20 plummet *fallen*
21 contract *sich zuziehen*
25 self-aware *seiner selbst bewusst*
27 honourable *ehrenhaft*
28 disgusted *angewidert*
29 miserable *elend*
36 failure *Versager/in*
put sb off *jdn abschrecken*
37 fuel *Treibstoff*

3 Use suitable words from the text to complete the gaps.

Many young women are being influenced by the …[1] for being skinny and some are dieting in a way that is unhealthy. The writer decided to think the …[2] and try out an extreme …[3] to see what it would feel like.
…[4] was one of the problems she experienced but since her …[5] was to be thin, hunger let her know that she was coming closer to it.
In the end the author was …[6] by the results of her hard dieting. She felt that after so much hunger she should have lost more weight.

4 a **Make a mind map of the negative effects of the extreme diet described by the author.**

L► Mind Mapping (p. 114)

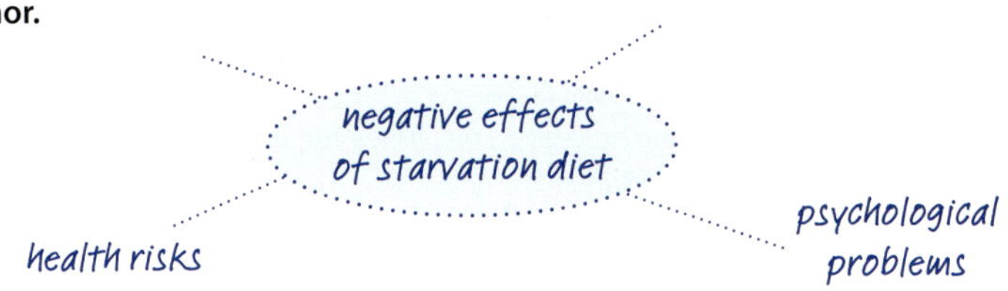

b **Use the mind map to summarise the unpleasant effects of not eating enough, as experienced by the author.**

WORKING WITH WORDS

5 **Use the words in the box to form common two- or three-word phrases. Check your answers in the text.**

conditions | disorders | effects | harmful | new | starvation | swings | task | totally | unachievable

1 eating …
2 … side …
3 … … concept
4 gruesome …
5 … diet
6 mood …
7 serious …
8 … goals

6 a **Use the phrases to complete the sentences.**

1 You should only have aims which you can achieve and not set … for yourself.
2 What? You're only going to eat 700 calories a day? That's a … .
3 I really did not enjoy preparing for my final examinations. It was a … .
4 If you smoke, you can get … such as heart disease.
5 When I was dieting I had a lot of … . You know, one minute I was happy, the next I was angry.
6 Young people who worry too much about their weight can develop … .
7 Sport is good for you. But one of the … can be that you injure yourself.
8 A few years ago, the Internet was a … for most people. They'd never seen anything like it before.

b **Now note down the equivalents of the phrases in German. Then translate the sentences 1–8 into German.**

L► Übersetzung (p. 123)

7 **Rewrite these sentences using your own words and replacing the underlined expressions with the phrasal verbs in the box.**

go through sth | keep up with sth | put sb off doing sth | set out to do sth | take on sth

1 When I started trying to lose weight, I thought the results would be different.
2 I decided to accept this challenge even if it put my health at risk.
3 I hope my experiences will discourage young girls from going on dangerous diets.
4 My sister is still trying to follow the latest fashion trends.
5 Looking back now I can't believe how much I suffered just to look thin.

INFO

A Short History of Physical Beauty

We might believe that ideas about physical beauty are 'natural' and, therefore, do not change over the years. This, however, is not the case. We can see this particularly clearly in the case of female beauty. Our current ideas about what an attractive woman looks like – tall and thin – are only the latest version of a view of beauty which has developed throughout history.

In Europe in the Middle Ages someone like Kate Moss would not have been considered attractive: rather she would probably have been seen as underfed. While Moss's face is thin, pale and long, the medieval idea of beauty was that attractive women had well-rounded faces and broad foreheads. In fact, when women were depicted as thin and pale, this was generally done to show their suffering; for example, in the case of paintings of the Virgin Mary.

Indeed, even in our own recent past, this was the case. Actresses in the 1950s, such as Liz Taylor, generally had fuller figures. Their male admirers were far more interested in them than in skinny women, who were thought to be too girl-like. In our own times, different cultures see beauty differently. In parts of the world where food is less plentiful than in the West, some cultures regard well-rounded women as most desirable because they are seen as healthy and well-nourished. The view, then, that beautiful women are tall and skinny, is by no means an unchanging idea of female attractiveness.

9 underfed *unterernährt*
10 medieval *mittelalterlich*
11 forehead *Stirn*
14 Virgin Mary *Jungfrau Maria*
21 desirable *begehrenswert*
22 well-nourished *gut genährt*
23 by no means *keineswegs*

WRITING

L ▸ Eine Stellungnahme schreiben (p. 115)

8 **Read the information box above and comment on the three pictures. Use the following phrases to help you.**

I am going to comment on …
I will start by looking at … / To start with then, I would like to …
Then, I will turn to … / Next, I'll consider … / Finally, I would like to look at …
In conclusion, I think that … / To summarise, I have …

LOOKING AT LANGUAGE

G ▸ The future (p. 128)

9 **Use the sentence parts and either the simple present or present progressive to make sentences about the future.**

1. Jennifer / plan / to go on a diet / after Christmas.
2. I / meet / my mum / to go to a fashion show / on Wednesday.
3. When / you / go on / your country cooking course?
4. London Fashion Week / start / on Monday / next week.
5. Sarah / not / come / out for a meal / weekend / because she is on a diet.
6. Is it true that Pete / start / a food and nutrition course at college / autumn?
7. Happy Hour at Pizza Paradise / begin / 5.30 / every weekday.
8. What time / they / come back / from their visit to the Chocolate Museum / Sunday?

ANALYSING AN ADVERTISEMENT

HANDS-ON TASK

L ▶ Interpretation von Bildern und Karikaturen (p. 119)

L ▶ Gruppengespräche und Diskussionen (p. 122)

10 Look at the advertisement below and follow these steps.

1. Describe the advertisement.
2. Work in a small group and discuss how you feel about the message of the advertisement. Do you think it encourages responsible and healthy weight loss? Which elements of the advertisement play unfairly on women's fear of being overweight?
3. Design a poster aimed at young women telling them of the harmful side effects of losing too much weight too quickly. Look back at the text on page 24 for points to include in the poster.

Do you hate looking at yourself in the mirror?

*"Before I started taking **SlimGirl** tablets, I used to hate looking at myself in the mirror. All that horrible fat! I always found losing weight difficult and hated going shopping for clothes because none of the nice things would fit me. But thanks to these slimming tablets I've lost an amazing **63 pounds**! Now I feel prettier and younger and I have so much energy. I can wear fashionable clothes again and now when I look in the mirror I see an attractive, happy woman. I recommend **SlimGirl** to anyone who wants to lose weight quickly."* – Jodee Palmer, Miami, FL

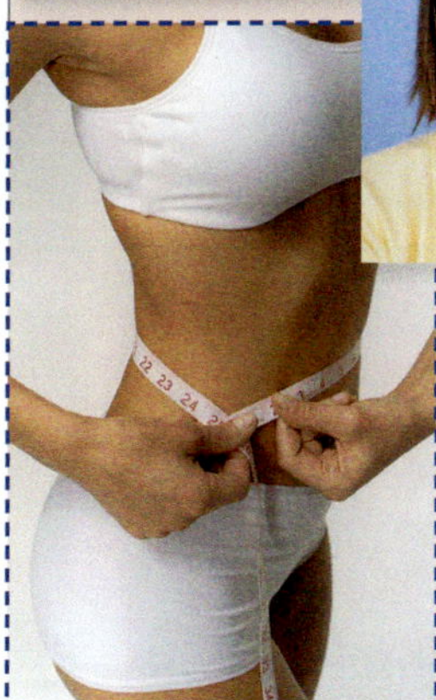

SlimGirl has helped thousands of women across America and it could help you too! Even top celebrities, from models to musicians, have used ***SlimGirl*** to make them look great. Research shows that ***SlimGirl*** slimming tablets really do work. Not only will they get rid of all that ugly fat but they will also give you lots of energy, all day, every day. Whatever your reason for wanting to lose weight, ***SlimGirl*** is the way to do it. Order ***SlimGirl*** today and you will see the fantastic results for yourself!

It works!

*"As a doctor, I have recommended **SlimGirl** to all my overweight patients. It's 100% natural so it's completely safe. It's the most effective slimming product available today."*
Dr George Bellevue

TEXT 6 Intercultural Relationships

WARM-UP

L ▸ Gruppengespräche und Diskussionen führen (p. 122)

1 **Work with a partner and discuss the following questions.**

1. When two people from different cultural backgrounds decide to have a relationship, what problems might they have (with their families, for example)?
2. What is more important: love between two people or being faithful to your cultural background by being with a partner from the same background?

2 **The pictures show scenes from the film *Ae Fond Kiss* and provide an outline of the story. (*Ae* is a Scottish word meaning 'a' or 'one'.) Read the info box and match the four texts (a-d) to the correct scenes from the film.**

INFO

Ae Fond Kiss

The film *Ae Fond Kiss* (2004) is set in Glasgow. The two main characters are Casim, a young Pakistani Muslim man, and Roisin, a young Catholic woman from Ireland. The film tells the story of their relationship which is troubled by its intercultural nature.

a Casim expresses his doubt about the relationship to Roisin. He tells her that, although he loves her, he does not want to hurt his family by continuing it.
b Casim and Roisin meet by chance and fall in love.
c Casim's family find out about his relationship with Roisin. They try to stop the couple being together.
d While on holiday in Spain Casim tells Roisin that his parents have arranged for him to marry Jasmine, a young woman from Pakistan. Roisin is angry at the news and breaks off their relationship. Soon after, however, the couple get back together.

L ▸ Lesen schwieriger Texte: Grobverständnis (p. 108)

3 **Read the two excerpts from *Ae Fond Kiss* on the opposite page and say which two pictures above show these scenes from the film.**

Ae Fond Kiss

CD 1 Track 9

Scene 1

CASIM I'm not coming.

ROISIN Eh?

CASIM I'm not coming up.

ROISIN What do you mean? Why not? Did you talk to your folks?

CASIM I tried to tell them last night. I just couldn't think of the words. I feel so strong when I'm around you. But it'll break their hearts. It'll destroy them.

ROISIN What about your heart? What about my heart? Jasmine? Do you love her?

CASIM You don't understand. It's ... It's not about love. It's much more than that.

ROISIN So are you just gonna sit back and let your parents make all your choices for you? Or are you gonna actually do something about it and say something to them?

CASIM I'm their only son. I can't let them down. I can't.

ROISIN Casim ... We're good together, you know? I mean ... it's easy. It feels right, you know? And I think that we can ... If we want to, we can make it work.

CASIM For how long?

ROISIN I don't know, but who knows that? Does anybody ever really know that? You just ... You just take a chance.

Scene 2

RUKHSANA Excuse me. Are you Miss Hanlon?

ROISIN Yeah.

RUKHSANA My name's Rukhsana Khan. I'm Casim's older sister.

ROISIN Hi.

RUKHSANA Erm ... is it possible to have a chat with you?

ROISIN Yeah, sure. Do you want to come up?

RUKHSANA Could we go elsewhere? *(Roisin and Rukhsana go into a café.)*

ROISIN Tea?

RUKHSANA Thanks. Roisin, you must be wondering why I've asked to ... Well, I've come to see you, I suppose. You must think this is very odd, but ... basically, I feel that I had to talk to you because of what's going on just now with my family. Erm ... Casim's left home and he's living with you. And erm ... as far as my family's concerned and my community's concerned, it's brought a great deal of shame on all of us. You see, we have this concept called "izzat", which I guess is family honour, and that's really, really important to people. And my parents, all their life, have worked very, very hard to maintain that, to keep that. And they've built up respect and trust in the community. And what Casim has done has basically taken that away. And not only that ... I don't know if Casim told you, but I met Amar through my family and we got on really well, our families got on really well. We were very fond of each other. In the short time that we've known each other, we feel very strongly. And we both want to get married. But because of what Casim's done, his mother phoned up and cancelled the wedding.

ROISIN I love your brother. Why can't you accept that?

RUKHSANA For how long?

ROISIN I ... I don't know.

RUKHSANA When will you know? When everybody's lives are fucked up? Can't you understand what's going on? Can't you understand that, because of your ... love, that so many people's lives are being destroyed? You clearly don't understand, do you? Roisin, I'm just going to ask you straight. Will you leave my brother? Please will you leave my brother?

(489 words)

13 let sb down *jdn im Stich lassen*

28 odd *seltsam*
30 as far as sb is concerned *was jdn betrifft*
34 maintain *bewahren*
37 get on with sb *sich gut mit jdm verstehen*
38 be fond of sb *jdn gern haben*
40 cancel *absagen*
47 straight *offen, direkt*

WORKING WITH THE TEXT

L ▶ Fragen zum Text beantworten (p. 114)

4 Answer the questions about the two scenes from the film in your own words.

1 Why could Casim not tell his parents about his relationship with Roisin?
2 What reasons does Roisin give for thinking that her relationship with Casim could be successful?
3 Why can Roisin not say how long she thinks their relationship might last?
4 Why does Rukhsana want to talk to Roisin?
5 What effect does Rukhsana say Roisin and Casim's relationship has had on her family?
6 What was Rukhsana's relationship with Amar before he heard about Roisin and Casim?

L ▶ Eine Stellungnahme schreiben (p. 115)

5 Read between the lines.

1 Explain what Casim means when he says that his relationship with Jasmine is about more than love.
2 Comment on the significance of the fact that Casim is his parents' only son.
3 Rukhsana says that Roisin must think it strange that she wanted to talk to her. Explain why.
4 Both Casim and Rukhsana ask Roisin "for how long?" when talking about the relationship. Comment on this question.

DISCUSSION

L ▶ Gruppengespräche und Diskussionen führen (p. 122)

6 Discuss the following questions.

1 Loyalty to your family or to the person you love: what would you do if you were in Casim's position?
2 Rukhsana asks Roisin to leave her brother. What do you think Roisin will do?

WORKING WITH WORDS

7 Use the verbs in the box in the correct form to complete the sentences. The expressions are all in the text on page 29.

break | build | concern | let | sit | take

1 Jean is extremely upset because her boyfriend broke up with her last night. It has … her heart.
2 Tom never acts or makes any plans. He just … back and takes things as they come.
3 Jeff didn't come to football training. He has … the team down.
4 I think I'll … a chance and try to catch the next bus. It leaves in five minutes but if I hurry, I'll catch it.
5 As far as Leslie's …, Michael's an idiot for not going to university. But I think she's being too hard on him.
6 When Pakistanis first came to Britain they had to work hard to … up respect among British people.

8 **a** **Match the following expressions to the expressions you have completed in Exercise 7. The first one has been done for you.**

a chance it *Sentence 4 – take a chance*
b disappointed
c doesn't do anything
d from her point of view
e gain
f made her very sad

b **Rewrite the sentences in your own words, using the new expressions.**

Example (sentence 4): *I think I'll chance it and get the next bus if I can. I've only got five minutes but I should make it if I'm quick.*

LOOKING AT LANGUAGE

9 **a** **In which of these sentences can the relative pronoun be left out and why?**

G ▶ Relative clauses (p. 136)

1 There are around 2,800,000 British Asians in the UK, whose parents started coming to the country in the 1950s.
2 Steve heard music at the multicultural festival that he had never heard before.
3 Hasim manages a supermarket which is part of his father's chain of local shops.

b **Join the following using *who*, *which*, *that* or *whose* where necessary. Where possible, leave out the relative pronoun.**

1 Have you been in that new Asian shop? It opened last week.
2 Muslim parents often can't accept their children's choices. They cannot understand the way western teenagers think.
3 Jim bought some food at an Asian shop. He had never tried it before.
4 Ali's parents live in Norwich. They come from India.
5 Most of Gordon's friends are Asian. He goes to college with them.
6 Clare's dad wants her to stop seeing her boyfriend Hamid. He is, to be honest, a bit of a racist.
7 Aurindum's family want him to work in their shop. They own their own business.
8 I was talking to a gorgeous Asian lad at the disco last night. I had never seen him before.
9 Indian Bangra is Blair's favourite music. It is very fast and rhythmic.
10 Young Muslims sometimes have problems with the expectations of their families. Their parents came to Britain over thirty years ago.

GIVING A PRESENTATION

HANDS-ON TASK

10 **Read the short text and follow the steps on the following page.**

L ▶ Die Arbeitsergebnisse präsentieren (p. 119)

National Identity in the UK

National identity is strongly related to country of birth. People from all religious groups who were born in the UK were more likely than their foreign-born counterparts to identify themselves as British. Almost all (99 per cent) UK-born Jews, Christians and people with no religion had a British national identity. Nine out of ten UK-born Buddhists (93 per cent), Sikhs (93 per cent), Muslims (91 per cent) and Hindus (89 per cent) gave a British national identity.

L ▶ Grafiken, Diagramme und Tabellen (p. 121)

L ▶ Die Arbeitsergebnisse präsentieren (p. 119)

1 Work with a partner and decide what sort of chart (pie chart, bar chart, etc.) would best illustrate the information contained in the short text on p. 31.

2 Design the chart on a large sheet of paper, using different colours.

3 Read the info box below and compare the information given in the box with your chart.

4 Prepare a short presentation about your chart, using the info box as background information.

5 Give the presentation to the other students in the class. Use the chart to illustrate the points you make.

INFO

Immigration to Britain

Though Britain has opened its doors to immigrants from all over the world for centuries, the main waves of immigration into the country came between 1945 and the early 1980s. During this period, people from former British colonies were given the right to come and live in the country. However, changes in the law in 1983 led to fewer immigrants settling in Britain. Nevertheless, the years of large-scale immigration ensured that Britain now has a large and diverse multiracial population. For example, in 2001 the total Black population was 1.2 million or 2.2% of the total population. In 2004, it was estimated that there were 2,799,700 British Asians. Other ethnic groups are also represented in some numbers in the country. For instance, there were 247,403 British Chinese people living in Britain in 2001.

One likely reason for the success of British multiculturalism is that it has been possible for ethnic communities to combine being British with aspects of their own ethnic culture. The way that cultural identity can be shaped by individual people is illustrated by Casim's younger sister's description of herself at the beginning of *Ae Fond Kiss*: "I am a Glaswegian Pakistani, teenager, woman. Woman of Muslim descent who supports Glasgow Rangers in a Catholic school … I'm a dazzling mixture and I'm proud of it."

Casim's sister Tahara giving a speech at her school in which she describes the many sides of her identity

However, at the level of relations between individuals – for instance, within families – there can be tensions. The children of first generation immigrants often find themselves caught between their needs as young people growing up in a western society and their parents' expectations. However, later generations often go back to their ethnic roots in search of their identities and reject parts of being British which they do not feel comfortable with.

However, although the integration of immigrant communities into British society is not free of tension, the result of the process is that Britain is now a stable multicultural country.

5 large-scale *in großem Umfang*
6 diverse *vielfältig*
27 dazzling *schillernd*
29 tension *Spannung*
32 feel comfortable with *mit etw gut zurechtkommen*

TEXT 7 A Gap Year in the US

WARM-UP

1 a **Work with a partner and match the gap year jobs to the photographs.**

L ▸ Gruppengespräche und Diskussionen führen (p. 122)

1 working on an organic farm
2 working as a summer camp counsellor
3 working with old people
4 working for a company

a

b

c

d

b **Which of the qualities in the list below would you need to do each of the gap year jobs mentioned above? You can add your own ideas.**

- enjoy working with young children
- able to work as part of a team
- interested in the environment
- enjoy working outdoors

c **Discuss which gap year job you would most like to do. Explain your reasons.**

INFO

What is a Gap Year?

It is now quite common for young people in the English-speaking world to spend a year travelling or working between finishing school and starting university. This is referred to as a 'gap year'. The idea behind the gap year is that young people gain experience of the world before their busy university lives begin.

2 a **Work with your partner and make a list of the benefits you think someone might get from working as a summer camp counsellor during their gap year.**

L ▸ Lesen schwieriger Texte: Grobverständnis (p. 108)

b **Now read the text on the following page quickly. Were any of the points on your list mentioned?**

CD 1 Track 10

Camps and Outdoor Education: A Volunteer Story

***Philip Denton** volunteered at Camp Becket in Massachusetts during his gap year*

Before working my gap year at Becket I suppose I had led a sheltered life. But I took the chance of going there so that I could develop myself. When I arrived, I began to realise how different my life was going to be during my gap year. I faced the complete unknown as I had never really been interested in outdoor adventure programs and didn't know how to instruct them.

It was a great experience. We taught and were taught canoeing, high ropes, teambuilding, challenge courses, winter survival, arts and crafts, kayaking, nature walks, pond probes and even pretzel making.

Though the experience was fantastic for me personally, I also felt a sense of pride for all the help we gave to other people. After my friend Craig and I had been there for two weeks we were joined by two other gappers, Hollie and Leann. The four of us worked with groups ranging from ten-year-old kids to multi-millionaires that came with corporate groups. Each group faced a different challenge and each had its own reward. These challenges could be helping a twelve-year-old girl to climb a sixty foot tower or a fifty-year-old chief executive overcome his fear of heights. And the reward was clear – seeing that look of achievement and success on a person's face and knowing you have helped them get there. It really is the best feeling to do a job that you know is making people's lives better or at least getting them to try something they felt they would never do.

After I completed my initial placement, I was offered a position as a camp counsellor for the summer. I jumped at the chance. As a camp counsellor, I lived in a log cabin with an assistant counsellor and nine boys, aged between twelve and fifteen. What made this so different was the fact that you didn't say goodbye to the kids at 5pm, but they stayed for four weeks. Basically, I was a parent, friend, older sibling and counsellor for the boys. The days were so energetic, fun-filled and rewarding. I had to organise two activities a day for my cabin and teach two program areas.

I suppose the one bit of advice I'd offer to a prospective gapper is just throw yourself in at the deep end. Never has the saying "You only get out what you put in" been so true than in your gap year. For me, there is nothing more rewarding than the summer I spent at Becket. I acquired so many new skills there. I have grown up a lot and can now take responsibility for myself and other people.

(442 words)

Adapted from: www.gap.org.uk

1 sheltered *behütet*
3 face sth *vor etw. stehen*
6 high rope *Hochseil*
8 pond probe *Teichuntersuchung*
13 corporate *Firmen-*
14 reward *Belohnung, Lohn*
15 chief executive - *Vorstandschef/in*
16 height *Höhe*
20 initial *erste(r, s)*
placement *Praktikum*
21 counsellor *Betreuer/in*
22 log cabin *Blockhütte*
25 sibling *Bruder*
28 prospective *zukünftig*
throw oneself in at the deep end *ins kalte Wasser springen*

WORKING WITH THE TEXT

L ▸ Lesen schwieriger Texte: Suche nach Einzelinformationen (p. 108)

3 Read the text again and decide which of the people mentioned in it could have said the following things.

a I had a great time working at Camp Becket. My friend Hollie and I are really happy to have met Philip and Craig. They're great guys and working with them was a lot of fun.

b My job is tough and I have a lot of responsibilities. But overcoming my fear of heights was much tougher than anything I have to do at work. Philip and Leann really helped me with this. They're fine kids and I told them that if they are ever looking for a job they should just call me.

c Philip is a brilliant camp counsellor. Me and the eight other boys who lived in our cabin had the best time with him. I want to go back to Becket next summer. I hope Philip is my camp counsellor again!

4 Answer the following questions about the text.

L ► Fragen zum Text beantworten (p. 114)

1 In what way did Philip think the camp was going to change his life?
2 Why did Philip find his work at the camp rewarding?
3 What was the best feeling that Philip got from his work?
4 How did Philip's relationship with the children change when he became a camp counsellor?
5 What does Philip mean when he says you should "throw yourself in at the deep end"?

5 Read between the lines.

1 Speculate on what Philip's life may have been like before the camp.
2 Why do you think Philip was offered a place as a camp counsellor after his initial placement?

6 Copy and complete the flow chart to show Philip's personal development.

Philip is unsure of himself

Philip is proud of ...

...

WORKING WITH WORDS

7 Find German equivalents of these English expressions from the text.

1 lead a sheltered life
2 face the complete unknown
3 feel a sense of pride
4 jump at the chance
5 you only get out what you put in

8 Complete the sentences using the words in the box. Take care to put them into the appropriate tense.

acquire | complete | face | feel
offer | overcome | take

1 Nora ... the chance of doing a gap year because she did not want to go straight to college after finishing school.
2 Sue loved being a camp counsellor because she had to ... a new challenge every day.
3 Nigel could not ... his fear of heights so he could not do any of the climbing activities.
4 Ross came home after he ... his initial placement. He was so homesick.
5 Let me ... you a piece of advice. Don't do a gap year: just go straight to university.
6 Gordon loved his gap year job because he ... so many new skills while doing it.
7 When she finally reached the top of the climbing tower, Michelle ... a real sense of achievement.

WRITING

9 **You are working at a summer camp in the US. Use the model email and information from the text to write an email to your friend telling them about the camp.**

E-Mail

Hi …
I'm having a great time at the summer camp. We spend a lot of time …
The kids are great and …
My favourite activity is …
It's really rewarding working here because …
Looking forward to seeing you again soon.
Love from
…

L ▸ Mind Mapping (p. 114)

10 **Read the info box below and summarise the information about gap year activities in a mind map.**
(You can add other ideas from the websites given in the box.)

INFO

Gap Year Activities

Young people do gap years for a variety of reasons. Many take the chance to pursue an interest which they will no longer have time for when university begins. Others get experience of a type of work they want to do in the future or of one they know they will never do again later in life.
Whatever the reasons for taking a gap year, there is a wide range of different activities on offer. Sport is always popular and many young people take the chance to train other youngsters in a sport in a distant part of the world. Another gap year favourite is going on an expedition of some sort. This might be boating hundreds of kilometres down a river in Africa or walking across a mountain range in South America.
But gap year activities can also focus on work. Nature conservation work in distant countries is currently popular and can range from helping to conserve forests to protecting endangered species of animals.
Many gap year programmes, which are put together by specialist travel companies, combine elements of work and adventure: for instance, four months of work on a conservation project followed by an expedition. Of course, not everybody goes abroad for their gap year and there are also lots of options for people who wish to spend their gap year in their own country. There are several websites on the Internet which can help you make your gap year choices. For example, check out:
http://www.realgap.co.uk/
http://www.gapyear.com/

1 a variety of *eine Vielzahl von*
pursue *verfolgen*
5 range *Spektrum*
9 mountain range *Gebirgszug*
11 range *reichen*
17 abroad *ins Ausland*

LOOKING AT LANGUAGE

11 **Brenda has just returned from working at a summer camp in the US. Her friend Craig is asking her about her experience. Complete his questions.**

G ▸ Simple past (p. 126)

CRAIG Hi Brenda. Great to see you again. How was the summer camp?
BRENDA It was brilliant. I had the best time.
CRAIG What ...
BRENDA We did lots of things. Went swimming with the kids. Taught them to cook. Played baseball.
CRAIG Sounds good. ...
BRENDA My favourite activity? Climbing. It was great. I'd never done it before.
CRAIG ...
BRENDA No, I wasn't frightened at all. I've lost my fear of heights.
CRAIG ...
BRENDA Yes, I made lots of new friends.
CRAIG ...
BRENDA Yes, the kids were really nice. I liked them a lot.
CRAIG ...
BRENDA Well, I did have one bad experience. I took the kids forest walking and we got lost!
CRAIG ...
BRENDA We just kept walking until we came to a road. Then we asked for directions back to the camp.
CRAIG ...
BRENDA Yes, I was really happy to get back to camp. We had a big meal and all went to bed early.

GIVING A PRESENTATION

HANDS-ON TASK

12 **Work with a partner and complete the following tasks.**

1 Look at the websites mentioned in the information box on page 36 and plan a gap year. Put together an interesting and mixed programme. Consider the following points:
- your interests
- travel and accommodation
- insurance
- local transport
- activities offered on site
- any equipment you need

2 Write a short presentation about the gap year programme you have designed.

3 Give your presentation to the class. Think about the following:
- What do you want to say?
- What's the best way of saying it?
- How well are you saying it?
- Are you looking up and not just reading from your notes?
- Are you using visual aids as well as you can?

L ▸ Die Arbeitsergebnisse präsentieren (p. 119)
L ▸ Suche nach Informationen im Internet (p. 112)

TOPIC 2 Regions in Britain and the US – and a Changing City

TEXT 1 Robbie Coltrane's Glasgow

WARM-UP

1

1

2

3

Test your knowledge about the United Kingdom

1 Match the flags to the countries.
a Scotland b England c Wales

2 In 2007 the population of the United Kingdom was
a 112,980,397 b 60,776,238 c 24,305,934

3 Which country uses the euro?
a England b Ireland c Northern Ireland

4 When did England win the football World Cup?
a In 1966. b In 1990. c England have never won the World Cup.

5 Cardiff and Swansea are cities in
a England b Wales c Scotland

6 Which of these cities is in the west of Scotland?
a Edinburgh b Glasgow c Aberdeen

7 Which statement about Northern Ireland is true?
a Northern Ireland is part of the United Kingdom.
b Northern Ireland now has its own assembly and is independent of the United Kingdom.
c Northern Ireland and the Republic of Ireland are now one country which is part of the United Kingdom.

8 Which statement about Scotland is true?
a Scotland has a different legal system from the rest of Great Britain but the same currency.
b Scotland has a different legal system and currency from the rest of Great Britain.
c Scotland has the same legal system and currency as the rest of Great Britain.

L ▸ Lesen schwieriger Texte: Grobverständnis (p. 108)

2 Scan the text about Glasgow on the opposite page quickly and match the photographs to the most appropriate sections.

a

b

c

d

My Bit of Britain

CD 1 Track 11

Robbie Coltrane

Robbie Coltrane, a famous Scottish actor, tells us what he loves about the Scottish city of Glasgow.

Don't ask me to be objective about Glasgow. I can't – I'm a Glaswegian. It's a great city with a little bit of everything. I love the way it looks. It was originally laid out in a grid system like New York, and they managed to save all the best Victorian buildings, which is tremendous.

There are lots of things to do. If you are interested in art galleries, we have the Burrell Collection, which is visited by more people than almost anywhere else in Europe. Then there is the Kelvingrove Museum and Art Gallery which is once again open to the public, having undergone massive refurbishment.

Glasgow has a very European feel these days. Twenty years ago you had the choice of eating a cheese roll, a cheese roll with onion or a cheese roll with tomato and if you asked for mustard, people would think you were some sort of weirdo. Now, on sunny days you can see most of the pavements filled with people eating outdoors. There are so many great restaurants, it's a worry for a man of my size! There's every sort of food imaginable and the best curry. Of course, I can't say where exactly, which is a shame because I'd probably get free curry for life!

Transport has improved over the years; we have a fantastic underground or 'Clockwork Orange' as it is known because The trains are orange, go round in a small circle and stop everywhere you need to go in Glasgow – it's an extraordinary bit of work.

Coltrane as Hagrid in the Harry Potter films

The trouble with being brought up in Glasgow is that you start taking it for granted. I think Glaswegians need to be more vocal about how beautiful Glasgow is. It really is an astonishingly beautiful city and you can stand and stare at it all day long.

And Glaswegians these days are notoriously stylish – much more so than people from Edinburgh. Glasgow people dress to the nines. When Glaswegians go out on a Saturday night, they look astonishingly glamorous. Woe betide you if you go out in shabby clothes!

There are fabulous pubs in Glasgow. In the West End there are lots of pubs where you can get good pub grub as well as a drink nowadays. On Sundays we have the Barras open-air market, a great Glasgow institution, which hasn't changed much over the years. It's still full of scallywags trying to flog you things!

Next to the Barras is the "Barrowlands" where you are still allowed to dance when a band is on instead of being told to stay seated and behave. Glasgow has always been a rock and roll city and has produced great bands – real bands not just ones invented by old farts my age to please people's mums, but proper rock and roll from disaffected youth – music that's a bit scary! That sums up the whole city really. It can be a little rough and hard, but very exciting. (486 words)

Slightly adapted from *In Britain* magazine, April/May 2005

5 grid *Gitternetz*
7 tremendous *großartig*
12 refurbishment *Renovierung*
13 feel *Atmosphäre*
14 roll *Brötchen*
15 weirdo *komischer Kauz*
26 take sth for granted *etw für selbstverständlich halten*
27 be more vocal about sth *etwas lauter sagen*
28 astonishing *erstaunlich*
31 notorious *berüchtigt*
stylish *elegant*
33 dress to the nines *sich in Schale werfen*
35 woe betide you *wehe dir*
38 grub *(umgs.) Essen*
40 scallywag *Schlingel*
flog *verhökern*
44 old fart *(umgs.) alter Sack*
45 disaffected *desillusioniert*

L ▸ Lesen schwieriger Texte: Suche nach Einzelinformationen (p. 108)

The Kelvingrove Museum and Art Gallery

WORKING WITH THE TEXT

3 Choose the most suitable answer.

1 Glasgow …
a was designed by the same people who designed New York.
b was set out in the same way as New York.
c was designed after New York.

2 The Kelvingrove Museum and Art Gallery …
a badly needs to be refurbished.
b is now open to the public after a small refurbishment project.
c is now open to the public after a large-scale refurbishment project.

3 Twenty years ago the food in Glasgow was …
a quite boring and basic.
b better than it is now.
c always served with mustard.

4 The problem with growing up in Glasgow is that …
a you forget how beautiful the city is.
b you spend your time telling people how beautiful the city is.
c you get bored with the city.

5 People from Glasgow …
a don't care about the clothes they wear.
b care less about the clothes they wear than people from Edinburgh.
c are well known for dressing very fashionably.

4 List the ways in which Glasgow has or has not changed over time. Then compare your list with a partner.

WORKING WITH WORDS

5 Complete the sentences using the following adjectives from the text. Two of the adjectives are not used.

beautiful | fantastic | glamorous | massive | objective | proper | rough

1. Some parts of Glasgow are still quite … . It's not all trendy restaurants and museums.
2. People in Glasgow wear very … clothes to go out in the evening. They like to get dressed up.
3. Glasgow is the biggest city in Scotland. It really is … .
4. Our holiday in Scotland was … . We had a great time.
5. Glasgow is not really a … city. Some parts don't look very nice.

6 Match the expressions from the text (1–5) with their definitions (a–e).

1 grid system
2 take it for granted
3 dress to the nines
4 woe betide you
5 a great institution

a a place, building or organisation with a long tradition
b put on very fashionable clothes
c you better be careful
d a way of planning a city where streets are laid out to form squares and rectangles
e be so used to it that you don't admire it any more

CARTOON ANALYSIS

7 a Describe the cartoon.

L ▸ Interpretation von Bildern und Karikaturen (p. 119)

b Now read the info box below. In what way does this cartoon illustrate a point made in the info box?

INFO

Glasgow

Glasgow is the largest city in Scotland with around 1 million inhabitants. In the past, the city's wealth was based on industries like iron and steel and shipbuilding. By the end of the century, Glasgow was a major shipbuilding town with shipyards lining the River Clyde to the west of the city centre.

However, in the second half of the 20th century, shipbuilding, as well as iron and steel production, went into decline and by the early 1980s Glasgow had become a depressed city with little industry, high unemployment and poverty. Then, during the 1980s, the redevelopment of the city, marked by a series of landmark events, began. In 1988 Glasgow hosted the Garden Festival on land beside the Clyde which had been previously derelict. And in 1990 Glasgow was named the European City of Culture. These events marked a turning point in the city's fortunes which have continued to go from strength to strength up until the present time.

Glasgow is now often seen as a city characterised by thriving shopping streets, much light industry and a booming entertainment sector. However, critics of the 'new Glasgow' say that the city remains a centre of poverty and social problems and that the glossy image of Glasgow just covers up an unpleasant reality. They point to unemployment, poor housing, drug abuse and crime in the city's East End and say that money has been invested in entertaining wealthy people and not in reducing poverty.

3 shipyard *Schiffswerft*
line *säumen*
6 decline *Rückgang, Niedergang*
7 poverty *Armut*
8 mark *prägen*
landmark *wegweisend*
9 host *ausrichten*
previously *zuvor*
10 derelict *heruntergekommen*
11 fortune *Schicksal*
13 thrive *florieren*
15 glossy *glänzend*
17 abuse *Missbrauch*

LOOKING AT LANGUAGE

8 Use the phrases and words to write passive sentences.

G ▸ The passive (p. 132)

1. The Burrell Collection / open / in 1983.
2. The Glasgow Garden Festival / visit / by hundreds of thousands of people from around the world.
3. The Glasgow band, Franz Ferdinand / form / in the city in 2001.
4. These days, many Glaswegians / employ / in service industries like retail and entertainment.
5. Now, as in the past, most poverty / concentrate / in the east end of Glasgow.
6. The development of Glasgow / influence / by New York.
7. Glasgow / change / a lot by redevelopment in the last 20 years.
8. Glasgow's city centre and the west end / connect / by the 'clockwork orange' underground system.

HANDS-ON TASK

PROJECT: PLANNING A CLASS VISIT

9 Work in a small group and do the following task.

1. You are going to plan a two-day class visit to Glasgow. Look on the Internet to find out the cheapest way of travelling to Glasgow and to find suitable accommodation.
2. Use the Internet to find information about places to see and things to do in the city.
3. Try to find a museum, theatre, restaurant and pub not mentioned in the text to visit. Also, try to find some other interesting things to do.
4. In your group, work out a programme of activities for your two-day visit using the information you have found in your research.
5. Prepare a short presentation about the travel and accommodation options you have chosen and your planned programme. Give the presentation to the rest of the class using pictures you have found on the Internet.
6. Once all the groups have given their presentations, decide which programme for two days in Glasgow is the most interesting.

LISTENING AND ROLE-PLAY

10 Now work with a partner and do the following tasks.

CD 1 Track 12

1. Listen to two telephone calls: the first booking flights to and from Glasgow; the second booking hotel rooms in the city. Which of the following expressions do you hear – a or b?

	a	b
1	I'd like to book a flight between Stuttgart and Glasgow for the 16th of September.	I want to book a flight between Stuttgart and Glasgow for the 16th of September.
2	There will be nine of us in total.	There will be a total of nine of us.
3	Can I book these seats, please?	I'd like to book these seats, please.
4	Do you want my customer number?	Would you like my customer number?
5	I'd like to book some rooms with you.	I'd like to book some rooms for three nights.
6	Can you tell me what the cost of that will be, please?	Can you tell me how much that will cost, please?
7	Is there breakfast included in that price?	Is breakfast included in the price?

2. Your teacher will give you the two telephone dialogues cut up on strips of paper. Separate the dialogues and put them in the correct order. Listen again to check your answer.
3. Take turns to read the roles in the dialogues. Then take turns to role-play the dialogues without reading.

CD 1 Track 13

4. Now listen to the announcements made at the airport. Take turns to explain to a friend who does not understand English what the announcements mean in German.

TEXT 2 Poor Diet in Glasgow's East End

WARM-UP

1 What do you know about healthy eating? Before you read the text below, answer the questions and discuss your answers with the rest of the class.

1 You should eat five servings of fresh fruit and vegetables per
a day. **b** week. **c** month.

2 Which statement about fast foods is true?
a You should never eat fast food if you want to be healthy. Every burger you eat damages your health.
b Eating fast food occasionally is fine as long as you have a healthy, balanced diet.
c Regularly eating fatty fast foods, which are rich in calories, is fine as long as you don't eat too many other foods which are rich in calories.

3 Which foods are rich in unhealthy fats?
a Burgers, sausages, pizzas
b Bread, potatoes, rice
c Fish, yoghurt, olive oil

4 Which statement about eating breakfast is true?
a You don't need to eat breakfast. Not eating breakfast will help you to cut down on calories.
b Breakfast is one of the most important meals of the day, helping you to concentrate during the morning.
c You should only eat breakfast if you did not have a large meal the evening before.

CD 1 Track 14

You'll Be Lucky to Live to 60 Here. But It's Not the Third World ... It's Glasgow's East End

by David Smith

Glasgow's West End may be booming with trendy restaurants but, across the city, Shettleston, in the East End, is possibly the alcohol and fast-food capital of Britain.

Men in Shettleston die younger than anywhere else in the country. At 63, life expectancy is 14 years less than the national average and comparable with Iraq and some countries in the Third World. It is also nearly 18 months shorter than a decade ago – Britain's first reduction in lifespan since the Second World War. And now health experts are profoundly concerned about what the future holds for Shettleston's children whose diet often consists of crisps, burgers, chips and sugary drinks.

'There are lots of people eating fast food,' said Hayridden Keles, manager of the Tandoori Hut. 'I see the same faces every day. It's a lazy generation who can't be bothered to cook and feed their children properly. I've been here 10 years and it's getting worse.' One of the men who has to pick up the pieces is Dr Gerry Spence, a local GP. 'People know what's wrong with their diets. They have got the messages: they should eat five pieces of fruit or vegetables daily. But a lot of

4 life expectancy *Lebenserwartung*
5 comparable *vergleichbar*
7 lifespan *Lebensdauer*
8 profoundly *zutiefst*
concerned *besorgt*
13 can't be bothered *keine Lust haben*
14 pick up the pieces *die Scherben aufsammeln*

17 be on benefits *Unterstützung bekommen*
rely on *sich auf etw verlassen*
convenience food *Fertiggericht(e)*
18 ability *Möglichkeit*
21 flourish *florieren*
victim *Opfer*
circumstance *Umstand*
22 sort sth out *etw in Ordnung bringen*
24 be called to account *zur Rechenschaft gezogen werden*
25 pin one's hopes on sth *seine ganze Hoffnung auf etw setzen*
28 it's not rocket science *es ist keine hohe Wissenschaft*
28 daft *doof*
29 afford sth *sich etw leisten*
32 undertaker *Leichenbestatter*
35 take sth in your stride *sich keine Gedanken um etw machen*

people are on benefits, living from week to week and relying on convenience foods. Give people jobs and the ability to be masters of their own destinies and they will make healthy decisions about their lives. You bring employment into here and I guarantee that children will be fed more healthily and the place will flourish. You can't blame the people when they are victims of circumstances. It's not really a medical problem, it's something for the politicians to sort out. I hope the drop in life expectancy is a turning point and the politicians are called to account. They should hang their heads in shame.'

Frank McAveety, a local politician, has pinned his hopes on schools to end ignorance about drinking, smoking and unhealthy eating. But Bob Holman, who spent 16 years living in east Glasgow working with young people, said: 'This is not rocket science. Parents are not daft and they do know fat and crisps are bad for children but they can't afford the alternative. The Government has to give them the means. Initiatives are not going to change anything unless you've got the cash in your pocket. If you buy a salad at Sainsbury's, it's still very expensive.'

Another in the front line is Mary McGregor, a local undertaker's assistant. 'Recently there have been young people who suffered sudden, unexplained deaths,' she said. 'But east-enders are east-enders, they take everything in their stride. Maybe that's part of the problem. They just accept it.' (446 words)

The Observer, 14 March 2004

WORKING WITH THE TEXT

2 Match the four people mentioned in the text with the views they express.

Dr Gerry Spence | Frank McAveety | Bob Holman | Mary McGregor

a Local people do not question the way things are.
b More health education would solve the problem.
c Jobs are the solution.
d People don't have enough money to buy healthy food.

L ▸ Lesen schwieriger Texte: Suche nach Einzelinformationen (p. 108)

3 Say whether the statements about the article are true, false or unclear. Correct the false statements.

1. The East End of Glasgow has more restaurants than the city's West End.
2. Men in Shettleston live 14 years longer than men in some Third World countries.
3. Men in Shettleston live for a decade less than they did 18 months ago.
4. Health experts are very worried about the health of children in the area.
5. The Tandoori Hut has the same customers every day.
6. Dr Gerry Spence says that people do not understand how to eat a healthy diet.
7. Frank McAveety thinks that schools should provide better health education.
8. Bob Holman thinks that parents are not intelligent enough to feed their children properly.

4 a Which solutions to poor diet are suggested in the text and what arguments are given to support them?

b Discuss what YOU think the solution to poor diet is.

WORKING WITH WORDS

5 **Rewrite these slightly adapted sentences from the text using the phrases in the box and your own words.**

results in an important change | be ashamed of themselves | with first-hand experience | not difficult to understand | getting social security | will happen in years to come

1. Health experts are concerned about what the future holds. (line 8)
2. A lot of people are on benefits. (lines 16–17)
3. I hope the drop in life expectancy is a turning point. (lines 22–23)
4. They should hang their heads in shame. (line 24)
5. This is not rocket science. (lines 27–28)
6. Another in the front line is Mary McGregor, a local undertaker's assistant. (line 32)

LOOKING AT LANGUAGE

6 a **What are the adjectives or adverbs that come from the words in the text?**

G ▸ Adjectives and adverbs (p. 135)

Adjective	trendy	…	lazy	daily	healthy	…
Adverb	…	profoundly	…	…	…	recently

b **Use the correct forms (adjective or adverb) of the words in the box to complete the following article. Some of the words can be used more than once.**

current | daily | healthy | lazy | normal | organic | proper | trendy

Young people's eating habits are …[1] news. But should we be as concerned about …[2] diet among British teenagers as the media …[3] suggests? We spoke to four young people from the King Charles Sixth Form College in Stoke Newington to find out what they eat.

Sarah: "I try to eat as …[4] as possible. I eat three pieces of fruit and two fresh vegetables …[5]. But lots of my friends still eat …[6] and don't really think about their diets."

Tom: "To be honest, I don't really think about what I eat. I eat lots of crisps and chocolate and fast food. But I do eat a …[7] breakfast though."

Brian: "My mum doesn't let me eat anything other than …[8] food. She's against any food in the supermarket which is …[9] packaged and I can't remember the last time I had a burger or a pizza."

Fiona: "We don't have much money at home, so we have to eat what we can afford. Fruit and veg which is produced …[10] is too expensive. That means we just eat the …[11] stuff from the supermarket. But we still manage to eat a …[12] diet."

3 disease *Erkrankung*
4 obese *fettleibig*
5 be at play *mit hineinspielen*
10 deep-fry *frittieren*
13 pie *Pastete*
18 brisk *rege*
ongoing *im Gange*

INFO

The Scottish Diet

In recent years, health studies have identified Scotland as 'the sick man of Europe'. Practically, this means that Scots are more likely to suffer from diet-related illnesses such as heart disease than people living elsewhere in Europe. They are also more likely to be obese and die younger.

Of course, a number of factors are at play here. Ready-made convenience foods which are high in unhealthy fats and salt are eaten with as much delight by Scots as by people elsewhere. And Scotland has high rates of smoking and alcohol consumption. But these other factors aside, a traditional love of fatty foods continues to contribute to unhealthy eating habits in Scotland. A major problem lies in one of the country's most popular cooking methods – deep-frying. This is the method by which French fries, for example, are cooked everywhere. The problem in Scotland is that deep-frying does not end there – pretty much everything you can think of can be and is deep-fried. Go to a chip shop for fish and chips and the fish is also deep-fried. It's the same with sausage, pies – or even pizza! Some Scottish chip shops even offer things like deep-fried Mars Bars.

What with so much deep-frying going on it's not hard to understand why large numbers of people in Scotland are unhealthy and obese. In 2005 around 20% of Scottish 12-year-olds were obese. This represented a 3% increase since 2000. No wonder then that there is a brisk ongoing public debate in Scotland over diet, health and young people.

INTERPRETING A CARTOON

L ► Interpretation von Bildern und Karikaturen (p. 119)

7 Look at the cartoon and follow the steps below.

1 Work with a partner and take turns to describe the cartoon.
2 Compare the cartoon with the information in the info box above.
3 Now work in a small group. What do you think the doctor actually meant when he recommended a varied diet? Give examples.

L ► Gruppengespräche und Diskussionen führen (p. 122)

WRITING A LEAFLET

HANDS-ON TASK

8 Work in groups. You are going to write a leaflet advising young people what to eat in order to have a varied, healthy diet.

L ► Einen Text sinnvoll gliedern (p. 118)

1 Decide what information about food should be included in the leaflet.
2 Decide what tone the leaflet should be written in. Remember that young people are put under pressure to buy unhealthy foods by advertising: they possibly do not find the subject of healthy eating very interesting or cool. Your leaflet will have to appeal directly to them.
3 Write your leaflet. When you are finished put it up on the classroom wall together with the leaflets written by other groups. Read the other leaflets. Which is the best?

TEXT 3 A Short History of Scotland

WARM-UP

1 **Use the timeline and illustrations to help you put the following short history of Scotland (a–h) in the right order.**

a After the First World War, Scottish industries start to decline and Scotland loses its place as a major centre of industrial production.

b At the same time that industrialisation is taking place, agriculture changes. Traditional farming practices end and are replaced by more modern methods.

c By the end of the 19th century, Scotland is a centre of industry. Most of the iron and steel, and even ships, in the world are built here.

d Due to changes in agriculture, hundreds of thousands of people are no longer needed on the land. In what becomes known as the 'Highland Clearances', many are forced to leave their small, traditional farms. They go to work either in the new factories in the Scottish lowlands near Glasgow and Falkirk, or emigrate to America and Canada.

e Industrial decline continues after WW2. By the 1970s, even new, 'light' industries, such as car manufacturing, are in trouble. Many factories close and entire towns are left without work for the people who live there. Many people leave the towns they have spent their lives in to look for work elsewhere.

f Scotland is a country where most people work on the land. There is little industry except farming.

g Scotland slowly starts to industrialise. Factories are opened and the country becomes a centre of iron and cotton production.

h Scotland's economy is reborn. High-tech industries, such as the manufacture of computer chips, and the service sector are booming.

2 **What do you know about the economic history of the area you live in? In what ways is it similar to that of Scotland?**

2 decline *zurückgehen*
13 due to sth *aufgrund von etw*
agriculture *Landwirtschaft*
16 clearance *Räumung*
24 entire *ganz*
35 be reborn *wieder aufleben*

CD 1 Track 15

34 mutual *gemeinsam*
37 (to) roam sth *durch etw. ziehen*

Letter from America

by The Proclaimers

When you go will you send back
A letter from America?
Take a look up the railtrack
From Miami to Canada.

Broke off from my work the other day
I spent the evening thinking about
All the blood that flowed away
Across the ocean to the second chance
I wonder how it got on when it reached
the promised land?

When you go will you send back
A letter from America?
Take a look up the railtrack
From Miami to Canada.

I've looked at the ocean
Tried hard to imagine
The way you felt the day you sailed
From Wester Ross to Nova Scotia
We should have held you
We should have told you
But you know our sense of timing
We always wait too long

When you go will you send back
A letter from America?
Take a look up the railtrack
From Miami to Canada.

Lochaber no more
Sutherland no more
Lewis no more
Skye no more

I wonder my blood
Will you ever return
To help us kick the life back
To a dying mutual friend
Do we not love her?
I think we all clearly love her.
Do we have to roam the world
To prove how much it hurts?

When you go will you send back
A letter from America?
Take a look up the railtrack
From Miami to Canada.

Bathgate no more
Linwood no more
Methil no more
Irvine no more

WORKING WITH THE TEXT

3 **a** **Read the place names on the map on the opposite page. Now listen to the song. Which places are mentioned?**

b **Which of the places mentioned are likely to have been cleared of people during the 'Highland Clearances'? Which places were probably centres of industrial production? Look at the map and the timeline again to find the answers.**

4 **Read the song lyrics again and choose the most plausible endings to the statements.**

L ▸ Lesen schwieriger Texte: Detailverständnis (p. 108)

1 The railtrack mentioned in the first verse suggests:
a modern transport and the ease with which people could travel
b the great distance between people who left Scotland and those who stayed behind

2 The 'promised land' mentioned in the first verse probably refers to:
a pieces of land that were promised to people when they went to America
b a new country full of opportunity and promise for the people that went there

3 The singer tries 'hard to imagine' how it must have felt to leave Scotland in the second verse. This is probably because:
a he has never left the country
b he finds it hard to sense the mixture of feelings at such historical distance

5 **Read between the lines.**

1 In what way does the song suggest a sense of loss to you?
2 The song was a hit in the UK towards the end of the last period of Scottish industrial decline. Find the period in the Warm-up section on page 47 and say in what ways the song mirrors the history of Scotland. Which parallels does the song draw between different periods in Scottish history?

6 **Explain the imagery suggested by 'the blood that flowed away' (line 7) and 'kick the life back / To a dying mutual friend' (lines 32–33).**

WORKING WITH WORDS

7 **a** **Use *break* and *get* to complete the sentences. Take care to put the verbs in the correct form.**

1 Mike … on well with Jonathon. They are best friends.
2 Clare is … on well at school at the moment and always gets good exam results.
3 Would you like some of my chocolate? Hold on and I'll … off a piece for you.
4 James … off from his homework early to watch the football on TV last night.
5 Susan is … off her relationship with her boyfriend at the moment so she's a bit unhappy.
6 I have to … on with my homework now because it has to be finished by this afternoon.

b **In which sentences above do the phrasal verbs have the same meaning as in the song (lines 5 and 9)?**

WORKING WITH THE DICTIONARY

L ▸ Umgang mit unbekannten Vokabeln (p. 109)

8 **Use your dictionary to find the various meanings of these phrasal verbs. How would you translate these into German?**

a break down
b break up
c break with
d get ahead
e get around
f get along

9 **Now use your dictionary to complete the phrasal verbs with *take*.**

1 Our plane took *off/up* 20 minutes late but we still arrived on time.
2 We're going to have some dictation now. Take *down/over* what I say.
3 Craig is a very aggressive football player. He would rather take *off/out* other players than kick the ball.
4 Tourism in Scotland has really taken *off/up* in the last ten years.
5 I took *over/up* tennis after I decided that I needed to do more sport.
6 Go and take *out/up* your anger on someone else. Don't shout at me.
7 Take *off/out* your dirty shoes before you come into the house!
8 Kelly loves going to the library. She takes *out/over* at least three books a week.
9 Not many people have taken *out/up* mobile internet services even though they are quite cheap now.
10 Take *off/over* putting up the tent while I get the sleeping bags from the car.
11 Paul lost his job after a big company took *over/up* the company he works for.
12 Take *down/up* that picture of me! I don't want old, ugly photos of myself on the wall.

TRANSLATION

L ▸ Übersetzung (p. 123)

10 **Translate the following slightly adapted sentences from the info box on the opposite page. Then say in what way the English sentences differ from the German.**

1 Scotland has been part of Great Britain since 1707.
2 The 1707 Act of Union eventually led to Scotland being ruled by the national parliament in London.
3 But in several respects Scotland kept its own identity, maintaining, for example, its own education and legal systems.
4 Despite continuing rivalries, many Scottish people came to see themselves as being more or less British, a fact illustrated by the hundreds of thousands of Scots who have fought and died in British wars since the beginning of the 18th century.
5 Scotland's relations with its larger neighbour England were often unsettled; this continues to be the case.

MEDIATION

L ▸ Mediation (p. 122)

11 **Now read the info box on the opposite page and summarise the following points in German:**

a the union between Scotland and England
b the national identity of the Scottish people
c the future of relations between England and Scotland

INFO

Scotland and the United Kingdom

The Scottish Parliament

Scotland has been part of Great Britain since 1707. An act of parliament of that year – the Act of Union – created a political union between Scotland and England and brought the former under the rule of the English king. This ended a centuries-long history of struggle and warfare between the two countries. It did not, however, end the rivalry which, in one form or another, continues to shape relations between Scotland and England.

The 1707 Act of Union eventually led to Scotland being ruled by the national parliament in London, which irritated, and continues to irritate, many people north of the Scottish border. But in several respects Scotland kept its own identity, maintaining, for example, its own education and legal systems and, later, its own national football team. However, despite continuing rivalries, many Scottish people came to see themselves as being more or less British, a fact illustrated by the hundreds of thousands of Scots who have fought and died in British wars since the beginning of the 18th century.

Nevertheless, in the course of the second half of the 20th century, the view within Scotland that the country should have some degree of independence from the rest of the United Kingdom (which by that time comprised Scotland, England, Wales and Northern Ireland) became increasingly widespread. There was a general feeling that the parliament in London did not act in the interests of Scotland; that Scotland got a bad deal when it came to government spending. While some people wanted more political power devolved to Scotland within the framework of the UK, others wanted outright independence from the rest of Britain. The Scottish independence movement has, to date, failed in its aim of creating a separate Scottish state. However, since 1999, Scotland has had its own parliament based in Edinburgh which has the power to pass laws relating to certain areas of domestic policy, such as education, the environment and health.

While some people believe that the Scottish parliament will satisfy the desire for greater political independence, others see it as one step further down the road to the eventual break-up of the United Kingdom. Historically then, Scotland's relations with its larger neighbour England were often unsettled. This continues to be the case.

2 act *Gesetz*
7 struggle *Auseinandersetzung*
8 warfare *Krieg*
11 irritate *ärgern*
19 comprise *umfassen*
23 devolve sth to sb *jdm etw übertragen*
framework *Rahmen*
outright *total*
24 fail *scheitern*
27 domestic policy *Innenpolitik*
31 unsettled *unbeständig*

GIVING A PRESENTATION

12 You are going to write a short history of the area you live in similar to that on page 47 which should also include some pictures and a timeline. You will present the short history to a group of foreign students who are visiting your school.

1 Work with a partner and decide how you are going to find historical information about the area. You will be able to do this, for example, on the Internet or in your local library.
2 Decide which facts to include in your short history and write sentences about them.
3 Find and print out pictures and photographs which you can use to illustrate your short history. Design a timeline which you can use to illustrate it.
4 Now present your short history using the illustrations and timeline to make sure that the students fully understand it. Be prepared to answer questions at the end of your presentation.

HANDS-ON TASK

L ▸ Suche nach Informationen im Internet (p. 112)
L ▸ Die Arbeitsergebnisse präsentieren (p. 119)

TEXT 4 American Regions and Cities

A

B

C

WARM-UP

1 a **Match the names of the structures and their descriptions to the photographs.**

D

E

The Seattle Space Needle
The Gateway Arch
The Brooklyn Bridge
Mount Rushmore
The Sears Tower

1 This was built between 1869 and 1883 and the main part of it has a span of 1,596 ft.
2 This futuristic structure was built in 1962. It is topped by an observation deck and a revolving restaurant.
3 This became a famous American landmark after an artist carved the heads of four great presidents on it.
4 This was finished in 1965. Visitors can ride to the top in special tram cars.
5 At a height of 1,450 ft, this is the tallest of its kind in the US.

b **Test your knowledge. Which cities are these structures in or near?**

c **Now look at Table 1 below. What do you know about cities listed in the table?**

Table 1

City	State	Estimated population (2005)	Population according to census (1990)	Population change (1990–2005)
Austin	Texas	690,252	465,622	+224,630
Sacramento	California	456,441	369,365	+87,076
Boston	Massachusetts	559,034	574,283	–15,249
Milwaukee	Wisconsin	578,887	628,088	–49,201
Memphis	Tennessee	672,277	610,337	+61,940
Chicago	Illinois	2,842,518	2,783,726	+58,792
New York City	New York	8,143,197	7,322,564	–820,633
Denver	Colorado	557,917	467,610	+90,361
Berlin	Berlin	3,404,037	3,420,183	–16,146
Leipzig	Saxony	506,578	557,341	–50,763
Freiburg	Baden-Württemberg	217,547	178,672	+38,875

estimate *schätzen*
census *Volkszählung*

Table 2

	Average temperature – Jan °C	Average temperature – Jul °C	Daily hours of sunshine – Jan	Daily hours of sunshine – Jul
Austin	9	29	5	10
Sacramento	7	24	5	14
Boston	–1	23	5	9
Milwaukee	–6	22	5	10
Memphis	4	28	5	11
Chicago	–5	23	4	10
New York City	0	25	5	9
Denver	0	23	7	11
Berlin	–1	19	2	7
Leipzig	–1	19	1	7
Freiburg	1	19	2	8

WORKING WITH THE TABLES

2 **Look at the map on the inside back cover. Which of the American cities mentioned in Table 1 are on the East coast, or in the West, the South or the Midwest?**

3 **Look at the tables and map again and answer these questions.**

1 Which of the following distances are greater?
a Austin – Sacramento / Chicago – New York City
b Milwaukee – Memphis / Boston – Denver
2 Which of the American cities lies furthest to the south?
3 Which German city most resembles Milwaukee with regard to the estimated population in 2005?
4 Which city has experienced the lowest proportional population increase since 1990?
5 Which two cities have the highest variation in temperature over the year?
6 Which city has the lowest variation in temperature over the year?
7 Which city has experienced the highest proportional population increase since 1990?
8 Which of the American cities lies furthest to the north?
9 Which American city most resembles Berlin with regard to the latter's recent population decline?
10 Which city has experienced the highest proportional population decline since 1990?
11 Which city has experienced the lowest proportional population decline since 1990?
12 Which German city most resembles Chicago with regard to the latter's population growth?
13 Which American city most resembles Leipzig in terms of its climate?
14 Which German city most resembles New York City and Boston with regard to the daily hours of sunshine in July?
15 Which city differs the most from Denver with regard to the daily hours of sunshine in January?
16 In which city do the daily hours of sunshine in January differ the most from the daily hours of sunshine in July?

SPEAKING

L ▸ Interpretation von Grafiken, Diagrammen und Tabellen (p. 121)

4 **Talk about the charts. Use language like this.**

Austins … Milwaukees … Berlin's … Freiburgs …	population is … climate is …	almost … nearly … more or less … about …	double that of … the same as … similar to that of … growing at about the same rate as …

L ▸ Gruppengespräche und Diskussionen führen (p. 122)

5 **Work in small groups and answer the following questions.**

1 Based on what you already know about the United States, which cities' climates surprised you the most? Which surprised you the least?

2 Which city's climate is most similar to that of the town or city that you live in?

WORKING WITH WORDS

6 **Rewrite the sentences using the American English words in the box. Be careful: there are two words too many.**

crisps | fries | gas | line | mail | pants | path | sidewalk | sweater | vacation

1 Jenny is off to Florida on holiday this week.
2 Look at the queue in front of the museum! Let's go to the cathedral instead.
3 We've got to drive quite far today so I'll just stop and buy some petrol.
4 Julie has just gone out to post a letter to her mother.
5 It's cold today. I need to buy a new jumper.
6 Have you seen my new trousers? They're dirty already.
7 You can't ride your bike here! The pavement's too narrow.
8 Can I have tomato sauce with my chips, please?

LISTENING

CD 1 Track 16

L ▸ Das Hörverständnis üben (p. 111)

7 **Copy out the climate tables. Then listen to the geography lesson and complete the tables.**

New York City	Jan	Jul	Year
Temperature (°F)	…	…	…

San Francisco	Jan	Jul	Year
Temperature (°F)	…	…	…

WRITING

L ▸ Suche nach Informationen im Internet (p. 112)

L ▸ Einen Text sinnvoll gliedern (p. 118)

8 **Work in a group. Choose three German cities not mentioned in this unit and write a report comparing their climates and populations. Make tables similar to those at the beginning of the unit to illustrate your report. The following language will help you.**

Introduction	*In this report I will be looking at / discussing …*
	But what are the real facts? If we look at …
Main part	*The most interesting finding is …*
	Readers may be surprised to learn that …
Conclusion	*In short, …*
	To give a general overview, …

TEXT 5 Out and About in the American Midwest

WARM-UP

1 a Work with a partner. Collect words describing the place where you live in a mind map. Report to the class, explaining why you have chosen those words.

b Now read the text. Which of the words you have found could the author use to describe Des Moines?

L ▶ Mind Mapping (p. 114)

L ▶ Lesen schwieriger Texte: Grobverständnis (p. 108)

CD 1 Track 17

I Come From Des Moines. Somebody Had To.

When you come from Des Moines you either accept the fact without question and settle down with a local girl named Bobbi and get a job at the Firestone factory and live there for ever and ever, or you spend your adolescence moaning at length about what a dump it is and how you can't wait to get out, and then you settle down with a local girl named Bobbi and get a job at the Firestone factory and live there for ever and ever.

Hardly anyone ever leaves. This is because Des Moines is the most powerful hypnotic known to man. People who have nothing to do with Des Moines drive in off the interstate, looking for gas or hamburgers, and stay forever.

When I was growing up I used to think that the best thing about coming from Des Moines was that it meant you didn't come from anywhere else in Iowa. By Iowa standards, Des Moines is a Mecca of cosmopolitanism, a dynamic hub of wealth and education, where people wear three-piece suits and dark socks, often simultaneously. During the annual state high school basketball tournament, when the hayseeds from out in the state would flood into the city for a week, we used to accost them downtown and snidely offer to show them how to ride an escalator or negotiate a revolving door. This wasn't so far from reality. My friend Stan, when he was about sixteen, had to go and stay with his cousin in some remote, dusty hamlet called Dog Water or Dunceville or some such improbable spot – the kind of place where if a dog gets run over by a truck everybody goes out to have a look at it. By the second week, delirious with boredom, Stan insisted that he and his cousin drive the fifty miles into the main town in the county, Hooterville, and find something to do. They went bowling at an alley with warped lanes and chipped balls and afterwards had a chocolate soda and looked at a *Playboy* in a drugstore, and on the way home the cousin sighed with immense satisfaction and said, 'Gee thanks, Stan. That was the best time I ever had in my whole life!' It's true.

I had to drive to Minneapolis once, and I went on a back road just to see the countryside. I remember one long stretch where I could see a couple of miles down the highway and there was a brown dot beside the road. As I got closer I could see it was a man sitting on a box showing inordinate interest in my approach. He watched me zip past and in the rear-view mirror I could see him still watching me going on down the road until at last I disappeared into a heat haze. The whole thing must have taken about five minutes. I wouldn't be surprised if even now he thinks of me from time to time. (494 words)

Abridged and slightly adapted excerpt from: Bill Bryson, *The Lost Continent*, Blackswan, 1999

3 adolescence *Jugend*
moan about sth *über etw jammern*
4 dump *Kaff*
5 settle down *sesshaft werden*
9 interstate *etwa: Autobahn (in den USA)*
12 hub *Knotenpunkt*
14 tournament *Turnier*
15 hayseed *Landpomeranze*
16 accost *ansprechen*
snide *abfällig*
17 negotiate *bewältigen*
revolving door *Drehtür*
19 remote *abgelegen*
hamlet *kleines Dorf*
21 delirious *im Delirium*
insist *darauf bestehen*
23 (bowling) alley *Kegelbahn*
warped *verzogen*
24 lane *Bahn*
chipped *abgestoßen*
soda *Limonade*
25 sigh *seufzen*
31 inordinate *außerordentlich*
approach *Herankommen*
32 zip *sausen*
rear-view mirror *Rückspiegel*
33 haze *Dunstschleier*

L ► Lesen schwieriger Texte: Detailverständnis (p. 108)

WORKING WITH THE TEXT

2 **Which of the photographs is probably Des Moines? Which is likely to be a photograph of the region that surrounds the city? Give reasons.**

3 **Match the sentence halves to make statements about the text. Be careful: one sentence beginning and one sentence ending cannot be matched. Use your own words to turn these two sentence halves into complete sentences.**

1 The author suggests that most …
2 A lot of people who live in Des Moines …
3 The author thought when he was younger that …
4 Des Moines is one of the largest, most …
5 The author seems to think that people who come …
6 Stan's cousin lived in a place …
7 The attention given to the author's car by the man on the road …

a from rural areas outside Des Moines are rather simple.
b interesting towns in the state of Iowa.
c suggests that he led an uneventful life.
d where nothing much ever happened.
e because normally nothing very exciting happened where he lived.
f people born in Des Moines stay there even though they don't like it.
g work at one large factory in the city.

4 a **Find sections in the text which you think may have been exaggerated for effect and explain what this effect might be.**

b **Identify three sections which may have been exaggerated to make the point that nothing very exciting ever happens in the places mentioned.**

WORKING WITH WORDS

5 a **Find seven words in the text which can be matched with the pictures below.**

b **Five of the words you have found can be ranked in order of size. Put them in order starting with the largest first.**

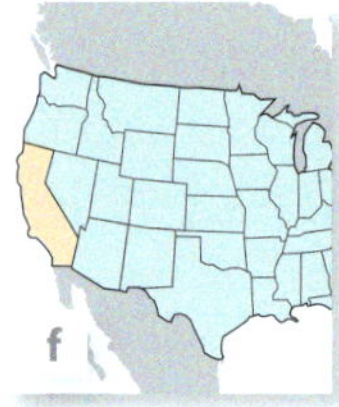

READING

L ► Lesen schwieriger Texte: Grobverständnis (p. 108)

6 **Read the following excerpt from *On the Road*, a novel by Jack Kerouac written in 1951. Do you think the book is most likely to be about:**

1 a young man who grows up in rural Nebraska but wants to leave and live in the big city?
2 a young man who grows up in New York but wants to see the 'real America' of the West?

CD 1 Track 18

We stopped along the road for a bite to eat. The cowboy went off to have a spare tire patched, and Eddie and I sat down in a kind of homemade diner, I heard a great laugh, the greatest laugh in the world, and here came this rawhide old-timer Nebraska farmer with a bunch of other boys into the diner; you could hear his raspy cries clear across the plains, across the whole gray world of them that day. Everybody else laughed with him. He didn't have a care in the world and had the hugest regard for everybody. I said to myself, Wham, listen to that man laugh. That's the West, here I am in the West. He came booming into the diner, calling Maw's name, and she made the sweetest cherry pie in Nebraska, and I had some with a mountainous scoop of ice cream on top. 'Maw, rustle me up some grub afore I have to start eatin myself raw or some damn silly idee like that.' And he threw himself on a stool and went hyaw hyaw hyaw. 'And throw some beans in it.' It was the spirit of the West sitting right next to me. I wished I knew his whole raw life and what the hell he'd been doing all these years besides laughing and yelling like that. Whooee, I told my soul, and the cowboy came back and off we went to Grand Island. (241 words)

1 bite to eat *Happen zu essen*
2 spare tire *Ersatzreifen*
to patch *flicken*
homemade diner *einfache Imbissstube*
3 rawhide *raubeinig*
4 bunch *Gruppe*
5 raspy *rau*
plain *Ebene*
7 regard *Respekt*
8 to boom *dröhnen*
9 cherry pie *Kirschkuchen*
10 scoop *Kugel*
to rustle sth up *etw fertigmachen*
11 raw *roh*
15 to yell *schreien*

WORKING WITH THE TEXT

7 Answer these questions on the text.

L ▸ Lesen schwieriger Texte: Detailverständnis (p. 108)

1. Why did the author and his companions take a break from their journey?
2. What impression do you have of the place they went to eat?
3. Describe the mood of the farmer who came into the diner.
4. What sort of food did the author eat?
5. Did the farmer order the same thing to eat?
6. Describe the mood of the author when he encountered the farmer.

8 Read between the lines. Find sections in the text which show that the narrator is excited and pleased to be in the diner.

WRITING

9 Write about the possible reasons for Bryson and Kerouac's contrasting views of the rural Midwest. Use sentences such as the following:

L ▸ Einen Aufsatz schreiben (p. 117)

Kerouac feels that …, while Bryson feels that …
While Bryson sees the Midwest as …, Kerouac takes the view that …
From Kerouac's perspective …
The reason for this could be that … / This is possibly because …

LOOKING AT LANGUAGE

10 What are the comparatives and superlatives of these adjectives and adverbs?

bad | beautiful | boring | close | dull | dynamic | exciting | fantastic | far | fascinating | good | great | interesting | near | silly | tedious | uneventful | uneventful | uninteresting

G ▸ Comparison of adjectives (p. 135)

11 Think of two places you have visited. Work with a partner and tell him/her about the two places, making comparisons between them, eg.:

*Glasgow is **as** big **as** Cologne. But it is **not as** nice **as** Cologne.*
*Leipzig is smaller **than** Warsaw.*

TEXT 6 On the Road in the US

WARM-UP

1 a **Tell your partner about a journey that you would like to make. Describe how and why you would like to make the journey and what you would like to see.**

b **Now read the following text about a journey across the USA.**

CD 1 Track 19

On the Road

I suddenly realized I was in California. Warm, palmy air – air you can kiss – and palms. Along the storied Sacramento River on a superhighway; into the hills again; up, down; and suddenly the vast expanse of bay (it was just before dawn) with the sleepy lights of Frisco festooned across. Over the Oakland Bay Bridge I slept soundly for the first time since Denver; so that I was rudely jolted in the bus station at Market and Fourth into the memory of the fact that I was three thousand two hundred miles from my aunt's house in Paterson, New Jersey. I wandered out like a haggard ghost, and there she was, Frisco – long, bleak streets with trolley wires all shrouded in fog and whiteness. I stumbled around a few blocks. Weird bums (Mission and Third) asked me for dimes in the dawn. I heard music somewhere. 'Boy, am I going to dig all this later! But now I've got to find Remi Boncoeur.'

Mill City, where Remi lived, was a collection of shacks in a valley, housing-project shacks built for Navy Yard workers during the war; it was in a canyon, and a deep one, treed profusely on all slopes. There were special stores and barber shops and tailor shops for the people of the project. It was, so they say, the only community in America where whites and Negroes lived together voluntarily; and that was so, and so wild and joyous a place I've never seen since.

(...)

It was Sunday. A great heat wave descended; it was a beautiful day, the sun turned red at three. I started up the mountain and got to the top at four. All those lovely California cottonwoods and eucalypti brooded on all sides. Near the peak there were no more trees, just rocks and grass. Cattle were grazing on the top of the coast. There was the Pacific, a few more foothills away, blue and vast and with a great wall of white advancing from the legendary potato patch where Frisco fogs are born. Another hour and it would come streaming through the Golden Gate to shroud the romantic city in white.

Jack Kerouac

I spun round till I was dizzy. And before me was the great raw bulge and bulk of my American continent; somewhere far across, gloomy, crazy New York was throwing up its cloud of dust and brown steam. There is something brown and holy about the East; and California is white like washlines and emptyheaded – at least that's what I thought then. (422 words)

2 storied *sagenumwoben*
3 expanse *Fläche, Weite*
4 festoon *hier: aufhängen*
5 sound *fest*
rude *unsanft*
jolt *aufrütteln*
8 haggard *ausgezehrt*
bleak *trostlos*
9 trolley *Straßenbahn*
shroud *einhüllen*
stumble *stolpern*
10 bum *Penner/in*
Mission and Third *Mission Street/Third Street*
dime *(US) Zehncentstück*
dawn *Morgendämmerung*
11 dig *hier: (umgs.) auskosten*
13 shack *Baracke*
15 treed *bewaldet*
profuse *üppig*
slope *Abhang*
20 descend *sich herabsenken*
22 cottonwood *Pappel*
brood *brüten*
peak *Gipfel*
24 foothill *Gebirgsausläufer*
25 advance *herankommen*
patch *Landstück*
28 spin *herumwirbeln*
dizzy *schwindlig*
29 bulge *Wölbung*
bulk *Masse*
30 gloomy *düster*

WORKING WITH THE TEXT

2 **The text is an excerpt from Jack Kerouac's novel *On the Road* written in 1951 in which he describes his journey through the USA (see also Text 5 on page 57). Which of the following words best describe the writer's feelings about San Francisco and California? Explain your reasons for the answers you give.**

bored | cynical | enthusiastic | excited | fascinated | sceptical

3 **Find parts of the text which mention the things shown in the photographs.**

L ▸ Lesen schwieriger Texte: Suche nach Einzelinformationen (p. 108)

4 **Match the sentence beginnings (1–7) to the sentence endings (a–g) to make statements about the text. Be careful: one sentence beginning and one sentence ending cannot be matched. Use your own words to turn these two sentence halves into complete sentences.**

L ▸ Lesen schwieriger Texte: Detailverständnis (p. 108)

1 As the text opens the writer is …
2 The writer is asleep as he enters the city …
3 When he arrives in San Francisco …
4 His friend lives in a new part of the city …
5 The writer goes to Mill City …
6 In the second part of the text the writer …
7 It takes the writer an hour to reach the top …

a sets off in the mid-afternoon to walk up a hill.
b and is woken up only by the bus stopping.
c the fog coming in from the sea to cover the city.
d of the hill from which he can see out over the Pacific Ocean.
e which, though it is a poor area, is very lively.
f travelling by bus through California in the direction of San Francisco.
g the writer's first task is to find his friend.

5 **Read between the lines.**

1 What evidence is there in the text that the writer's journey has been a long, tiring one?
2 What is unusual about Mill City?
3 Which part of the text suggests that the writer will change his mind about California in the future?

6 **a** **Which of the following words best characterises the style of the text?**

a) argumentative b) descriptive c) political

b **Find evidence in the third paragraph which support your answer to Part a. Use the following language.**

I think the text …
The text has many examples of …
This paragraph is characterised by …

WORKING WITH WORDS

7 **Complete the sentences by choosing the correct preposition.**

1 Drive *along/through* the Rhine between Boppard and Koblenz. The road at the side of the river is much nicer than the motorway.
2 I walked *over/under* the Brooklyn Bridge to Brooklyn when I was in New York.
3 San Francisco is about 4700 kilometers *from/to* New York.
4 Sarah and her friend bought an old car and drove *across/over* America last summer.
5 When you stand *on/under* the Golden Gate Bridge and look down, it's hard to believe how high it is.
6 Brian was born *from/in* Boston but has lived most of his life in Houston.
7 Let's go *in/into* the city centre tonight and get something to eat.
8 We didn't really stop in New York. We just went *through/under* the city on our way to Washington DC.

INFO

San Francisco

These days, San Francisco is seen as being one of the most relaxed and liberal cities in the United States. The city has a long history of attracting visitors – but of a different kind from the modern-day tourists who travel there now.

The population of the city grew most dramatically during the Second World War as people moved there to work in the naval shipyards that serviced the Pacific war fleet. In the years after the war and throughout the 1950s, people continued to visit and settle in the city in large numbers. Many of them belonged to what became known as the 'Beat Generation'. These were young people who wanted America to be a more relaxed, less conservative kind of society. Many of them were artists, musicians and writers, such as Jack Kerouac, who grew up on the American East coast, which they thought of as old-fashioned, and who saw California and San Francisco as places full of promise and new possibilities.

In the late 1960s, San Francisco once again attracted new visitors who, though they had something in common with the Beat Generation of the 1950s, had their own ideas and style. These were the hippies. The highpoint of hippie culture in the city came in 1967 – the 'summer of love'. Young people from across the States made the trip to the West coast to experience and contribute to the 'counter-culture' ('free love', anti-war protests, drugs and an alternative lifestyle) which had taken root there.

5 naval *Marine-*
service *warten*
fleet *Flotte*
17 contribute to *beitragen zu*

8 **Read the info box. What evidence can you find in the text on page 58 for points mentioned in the info box?**

LOOKING AT LANGUAGE

9 **Complete the sentences by putting the adverbs in the correct place.**

G ▶ Word order – positions of adverbs (p. 135)

1 Neil wants to go because he's bored. (into town / now)
2 We have to go if we want to get to your mum's on time. (quickly)
3 When we were on holiday we went to cafes for a drink. (often / in the afternoon)
4 San Francisco is a lovely city and the sun shines. (usually / every day)
5 I've seen a picture of that tall building. (somewhere / before)
6 Sara sent me a text message saying she wanted to meet me but she's late. (by the river / in ten minutes)
7 People living in this area play music. (always / loudly / in their homes)
8 We went to visit Jack and his wife. (yesterday / in Mill City)

WORKING WITH A SONG

San Francisco

(Be Sure to Wear Some Flowers in Your Hair)
Scott McKenzie

If you're going to San Francisco
Be sure to wear some flowers in your hair
If you're going to San Francisco
You're gonna meet some gentle people there

For those who come to San Francisco
Summertime will be a love-in there
In the streets of San Francisco
Gentle people with flowers in their hair

All across the nation such a strange vibration
People in motion
There's a whole generation with a new explanation
People in motion people in motion

For those who come to San Francisco
Be sure to wear some flowers in your hair
If you come to San Francisco
Summertime will be a love-in there

CD 1 Track 20

[4] gentle *sanft, gutmütig*
[6] love-in *Liebesrausch*

10 **Listen to the song. Which statement do you think is true?**

The song was released …
a recently to encourage tourists to come to San Francisco.
b around 1950 to describe the Beat Generation in San Francisco.
c in 1967 and came to represent the hippie movement in San Francisco.

11 **Answer the following questions on the song.**

1 What do you think is signified by the 'flowers' in the song?
2 Explain the phrase 'strange vibration'.
3 Say who you think the 'generation' are and what the 'new explanation' is.
4 Explain two possible meanings of 'people in motion'.
5 In what way do the lyrics of the song tie in with the information box?

TOPIC 3

The Media Today

TEXT 1 Virtual Friends?

WARM-UP

1 **Before you read the text, look at the cartoon strip and say what is happening.**

CD 2 Track 2

The MySpace Age

A In little more than a couple of years MySpace.com has gone from zero to being a top five website. It's simplicity itself, enabling anyone to build their own home page, listing likes, dislikes, favourite bands, top books, best movies, general interests, relationship status, and then hook up with other like-minded folk.

B "The appeal of MySpace lies in the crucial part of the adolescent socialisation process which we all go through … finding your identity," says Jo Twist, from the Institute for Public Policy Research. The ideas are not new, says Dr Twist, but what is characterising the trend now is the "ease with which people can upload and share their own 'digital assets' – motifs that say something about who they are."

C And teenagers on MySpace can share these 'digital assets' with large numbers of other people – many users have upwards of 200 online 'friends'. Some have their doubts about the phenomenon. Any psychologist will tell you that close friendships with more than half a dozen people are not possible, says Mark Vernon, author of *The Philosophy of Friendship*.

D MySpace friendships are more akin to "audience reach … like a TV show" than traditional 'social reach'. "Friendship takes time to develop. The person who says they have hundreds of friends wants our compassion not our envy. The heart of friendship is wanting to know someone and be known by them. This is not the same as knowing about someone which is what you get if you never meet your online pal face to face."

E But anyway, perhaps the biggest headache anyone with a couple of hundred mates needs to deal with is how to manage their Christmas card list. (280 words)

Source: bbc.co.uk

3 likes (pl.) *Vorlieben*
4 relationship *Beziehung*
hook up with sb *sich mit jdm zusammentun*
like-minded *gleich gesinnt*
5 appeal *Reiz*
crucial *entscheidend*
adolescent *jugendlich*
8 ease *Leichtigkeit*
9 asset *Wert*
11 upwards of *mehr als*
15 akin to sth *einer Sache ähnlich*
reach *hier: Sphäre, Bereich*
17 want *brauchen*
compassion *Mitleid*
envy *Neid*
20 pal *Kumpel*

WORKING WITH THE TEXT

2 **Match the subheadings to the most appropriate paragraphs (A–E) in the text. Give reasons.**

L ▸ Lesen schwieriger Texte: Grobverständnis (p. 108)

1. Do you really know your friends?
2. Lots of friends at MySpace – the big disadvantage
3. The reason for MySpace's success among young people
4. The rapid growth of MySpace
5. So many friends – it can't be true.

3 **Answer the questions about the text using your own words as far as possible.**

L ▸ Fragen zum Text beantworten (p. 114)

1. What does MySpace allow users to do?
2. In what way does MySpace appeal to teenagers according to the text?
3. What makes some people doubtful about users having a lot of friends on MySpace?
4. What distinction does Mark Vernon make between the way people know their friends and the way they know other MySpace users?

4 **Now read the following comments posted by readers of the article 'The MySpace Age'. Which contributor to the discussion thread thinks that MySpace might be of wider social benefit and in what way?**

I don't agree that you can't 'know' someone if you never meet face to face. If you spend time with them instant messaging and on the telephone I feel like you can know them just as well as a 'real life' friend. I have friends online who I have never met that may know me better than my 'real' friends. ***Laura, Brighton***

Human contact and relationships are sorely stretched in this day and age. If everyone were friends on MySpace, it might help repair some of the damage done due to cultural isolation and misinterpretation.
Oliver, Kennesaw, USA

MySpace is just an outlet for self-obsessed teenagers. And that's fine. Better on MySpace than in real life. Plus you look a hell of a lot cooler on MySpace.
Adrian Abbott, Toulouse, France

In my view, MySpace is great. People need to lighten up about it. I use MySpace to talk to old friends and make new ones. But that doesn't mean I don't go out and make friends in real life.
Matt, London

People who spend a lot of time on MySpace should get a life. Real life – and real friendships – happen in the real world and not online. I think one of the big problems with MySpace is that it tricks people into believing they have lots of friends while really they are becoming more and more isolated, spending increasing amounts of time alone in front of their PCs. ***Ben, Leicestershire***

(228 words)
Source: bbc.co.uk

WRITING

5 a **Read the forum messages again. Who do you agree with and why? Make notes.**

L ▸ Eine Stellungnahme schreiben (p. 115)

b **Write your own contribution to the discussion thread saying whether you agree or disagree and why.**

WORKING WITH WORDS

6 a **Find words in these sentences from the text which can be replaced by the words in the box so that the sentences still have the same meaning.**

decisive | egocentric | jealousy | sympathy | problem

1 Perhaps the biggest headache anyone with a couple of hundred mates needs to deal with is how to manage their Christmas card list.
2 MySpace is just an outlet for self-obsessed teenagers.
3 The person who says they have hundreds of friends wants our compassion not our envy.
4 The appeal of MySpace lies in the crucial part of the adolescent socialisation process which we all go through … finding your identity.

b **Now rewrite the sentences using the words in the box and your own words.**

WORKING WITH A DICTIONARY

7 a **Use your dictionary to match the words in the box to the correct vowel sounds.**

al**o**ne | app**ea**l | **a**sset | **au**dience | **au**thor | c**ou**ple | cr**u**cial | d**ou**bt | d**o**zen | **ea**se | en**a**ble | end**u**re | fr**ie**nd | h**ea**dache | h**oo**d | id**ea** | incr**ea**sing | l**igh**ten | r**ea**l | rep**air** | sh**are** | s**ore**ly | st**a**tus | w**a**nt

1 ɪ	**4** ɒ	**7** iː	**10** eə	**13** ʊ
2 e	**5** ʌ	**8** eɪ	**11** æ	**14** aʊ
3 aɪ	**6** ɔː	**9** əʊ	**12** ʊə	**15** uː

b **Now match the words in the box below with the words in phonetic symbols. Two words from a–j cannot be matched. What are these words?**

card | chance | chat | child | chill | choose | chord | crucial

a tʃuːz	**c** kɑːd	**e** tʃɪl	**g** kɔːd	**i** tʃɑːns
b tʃæt	**d** kæt	**f** kəʊd	**h** tʃaɪld	**j** 'kruːʃl

READING

8 **Read the rules about how to behave in Internet forums and compare them with the discussion thread on the opposite page.**

Netiquette – or Being Nice on the Internet

When you contribute to Internet forums, you should:

- not use CAPITAL LETTERS – this is thought of as 'shouting' and is difficult to read.
- not use Capital Letters for the first letter of each word – again, this is difficult to read.
- be polite to other forum users.
- not insult other forum users.
- follow standard grammar and spelling rules and not use slang.
- stay 'on topic' – this means that you should not write about subjects which the forum is not interested in.

People who have a MySpace are a lot of SAD IDIOTS. Its obvious they dont have any real friends. **Kim**

Kim u should SHUT UP! You have no rite to say stuff like that. MySpace is great. U r the LOOSER if you can't c that! **Ejay**

Can We Be Nice To Each Other Please? Stop Shouting You Lot. **Ross**

YOU ARE ALL SAD PEOPLE if you think that this subject is important. What about other stuff like the war in iraq. We Should Talk About That. **Benno**

Yes Benno. But this forum is about MySpace, so if you want to talk about Iraq go somewhere else. **Calvin**

INFO

Online Advertising

Websites like MySpace are free to use, but they are still commercial ventures designed to make money for their owners. They do this by selling advertising space. All of these banner adverts are paid for by companies who want their message to reach millions of young people online.

Online advertising is big business these days. At first, advertisers were afraid to invest their money in online advertisements. However, since the beginning of 2003, sales of online ads have been steadily growing. In 2006, around 10% of all money spent by companies on advertising was spent on the Internet.

Advertisers like online advertising because it offers them the chance to measure how many people respond to their advertisements. With newspaper or television advertising it is very difficult to do this. But with online advertising the number of 'clicks' an advert receives can be counted and it is sometimes even possible to see if someone buys something as a result of seeing an advertisement on the Internet.

Experts are predicting a bright future for websites like MySpace. In 2005, Rupert Murdoch, who owns a large number of newspapers, television stations and film companies around the world, bought the company that owns MySpace for $580 million. He did so because he believed that MySpace would make a lot of money through advertising.

1 venture *Unternehmen*
9 measure *messen*
10 respond *reagieren*

CARRYING OUT A CLASS SURVEY

9 Work with a partner and complete the following task.

1. Brainstorm with your partner all of the things that the Internet can be used for and make a written list.
2. Now use your list to write a questionnaire to find out how someone uses the Internet. Start your questions with 'How often do you …' and then give the following options: frequently; sometimes; occasionally; rarely.
3. Work with a new partner and ask them about how they use the Internet. Take a note of their answers. Answer your partner's questions.
4. Present what you found out about your partner to the rest of the class.

HANDS-ON TASK

L ▸ Die Arbeitsergebnisse präsentieren (p. 119)

TEXT 2 The TV Business

WARM-UP

1 a Work with a partner and match the photographs to the different types of programme (a–f).

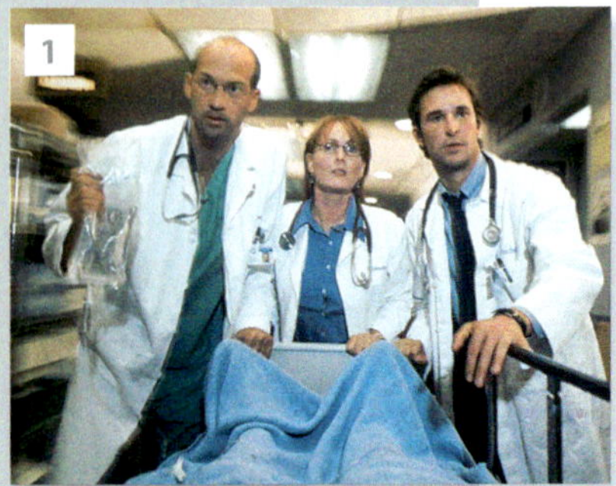

a chat show
b game show
c drama
d sitcom
e reality TV
f news

b What other types of TV programme can you think of?

c Now discuss with your partner which types of TV programme you enjoy and watch most often. Explain why.

L ▸ Gruppengespräche und Diskussionen führen (p. 122)

CD 2 Track 3

1 touch up *ausbessern*
2 icicle *Eiszapfen*
snowdrift *Schneewehe*
3 double for *(im Film) darstellen*
4 set *Szenenbild*
9 lot *Gelände*
bulk *Großteil*
10 prime time *Hauptsendezeit*
11 grip *Kontrolle*
12 conglomerate *Konzern*

TV is Big Business

A The California sun is burning hot, but the TV studio workers are touching up icicles and snowdrifts. This is the set of *ER*, a medical drama, and the far corner of the Warner Brothers studio is doubling for Chicago. Across from this is the entrance of the White House. This set is Washington, DC, home to *The West Wing*, a drama about an American president. Round the corner, they are dressing the interior set for *Friends*, another hugely successful TV show, set in New York.

B These are just three of America's most popular TV shows, set in three different corners of the country and exported around the globe. But they are all shot by one studio, on one lot, in the shadow of the Hollywood Hills. The bulk of the stuff that fills prime-time television in America is filmed between two valleys in Los Angeles and is in the grip of a handful of production companies belonging to large media conglomerates.

C Over the past decade the country's television industry has enjoyed a boom that has brought millions of dollars to this West Coast city. The men in black T-shirts picking at salads in the smarter Beverly Hills restaurants – writers, producers, TV executives, actors and agents – have been the beneficiaries of the most sustained boom anyone in the business can recall. Movies may still have the edge for glamour, but as a business television dwarfs feature films, even in America: with a total turnover of $100 billion, it is around six times bigger.

D Despite the formidable array of new gadgets – electronic games, computers, portable MP3-players, mobile telephones – that is now rivalling the television set for attention, the flickering image of the 75-year-old box still captivates people. The average American spends four hours a day watching television and keeps the set turned on longer than that. Watching TV was the single most popular way to spend an evening, Americans said in a recent Gallup poll: three times more so than seeing their friends. And according to research by MTV, a music-video channel, even the widespread use of the Internet has not eaten significantly into TV time.

E 'In most cases,' says Betsy Frank, head of research and planning at MTV Networks, 'what TV viewers do less of, now that they are spending more time on the Internet, is sleeping, talking and personal hygiene.' (390 words)

Adapted from *The Economist*, 13 April 2002

15 pick at sth *in etw herumstochern*
16 beneficiary *Nutznießer*
17 sustained *anhaltend*
recall *sich erinnern an*
have the edge *einen Vorsprung haben*
18 dwarf *in den Schatten stellen*
20 formidable *gewaltig*
array *Ansammlung*
gadget *Gerät*
22 flicker *flimmern*
captivate *faszinieren*
25 poll *Umfrage*
27 eat into *verringern*

WORKING WITH THE TEXT

2 **Match the headlines to the most appropriate paragraphs (A–E). Write headlines for the two remaining paragraphs.**

L ▸ Lesen schwieriger Texte: Grobverständnis (p. 108)

1. How much TV Americans watch
2. The TV business is big business
3. Chicago goes to Hollywood

3 **What does the text say or imply about the following?**

L ▸ Lesen schwieriger Texte: Suche nach Einzelinformationen (p. 108)

1. the production of popular TV programmes in America
2. changes in the TV business in America in the last ten years
3. differences between television and films
4. the relationship between TV and other, newer media devices
5. the TV-watching habits of Americans
6. the ways in which Americans save time in order to watch TV and use the Internet

4 **What do you think?**

1. In your own experience, do Germans use TV and the Internet in a similar way to Americans?
2. Do you see the way that people use TV and the Internet as problematic?
3. What do you think of American TV shows?
4. Why is TV still more attractive to most people than the Internet?

TRANSLATION

5 **Translate the third paragraph of the text into German. Watch out for structures that are different in German.**

L ▸ Übersetzung (p. 123)

WORKING WITH WORDS

L ▸ Mind Mapping (p. 114)

6 **In groups, collect the TV vocabulary from the text and the warm-up section in a mind map.**

7 **Use words you have found in Exercise 6 to complete the sentences. One of the words can be used twice.**

1. The … for *Frasier* may look like an apartment in Seattle. But the programme is filmed in a … in Hollywood.
2. Europeans have the wrong idea about American TV. Only the best American TV … are on here.
3. Can we turn over to the other … ? The news is on now.
4. I don't like … TV. I prefer more interesting TV late at night.
5. We can't watch the football at Pete's house tonight. His TV … isn't working.
6. George Clooney used to be an … in *ER*, didn't he?
7. … don't write TV shows. But they co-ordinate their production.

LOOKING AT LANGUAGE

G ▸ Participle constructions (p. 137)

8 **Rewrite these sentences, replacing the parts in italics with participle clauses.**

1. *Now that most people have Internet access,* television is no longer so dominant.
2. *After George Clooney left ER,* he went on to act in films.
3. I just checked my email quickly, *since I'd left the computer online anyway.*
4. *Since you like TV so much,* you won't mind watching it with me tonight.
5. *Now that we have watched the news,* I would like to turn over to the sport.
6. *After he had switched to his favourite TV channel,* Stephen settled down on the sofa.
7. *When she had checked that the TV was switched off,* she went to bed.
8. She went for a bath, *since she had discovered there was nothing interesting on TV.*

13 conversely *umgekehrt*

INFO

How Much Television Do Europeans Watch?

Despite the arrival of the Internet, Europeans are still managing to spend large amounts of time in front of their television sets. There are, of course, differences in the number of hours people in different countries spend watching TV. British people put in the most time on the sofa: on average they spend 28 hours a week watching 'the box'. Interestingly, this is the same as the American average. After them come the Italians, who watch TV for 27 hours a week on average. The French and Germans follow with 23 hours. Then come the Dutch and Danes with 20 hours. Next up it's the Belgians who spend a weekly average of 19 hours channel-surfing. The nationalities which spend the least time developing 'square eyes' are the Finns, Norwegians and Swedes who all watch on average 18 hours of TV a week.

At a glance, these figures may be surprising. After all, one might expect people living in Northern Europe, where the weather is colder and daylight in shorter supply, to be more inclined to 'just see what's on television'. Not so. Conversely, southern Europeans, such as the Italians, surprisingly don't seem to take advantage of their warmer weather by turning off the television and 'doing something more interesting instead'.

There must, of course, be other reasons which explain the amounts of time different nationalities spend watching TV. However, these remain a matter of speculation.

9 **Read the info box. With a partner, turn the information about the number of hours people in different countries spend watching television into a bar chart.**

L ▸ Grafiken, Diagramme und Tabellen (p. 121)

WRITING

10 **Discuss other reasons which might explain the amount of time different nationalities spend in front of the television.**

L ▸ Eine Stellungnahme schreiben (p. 115)

LISTENING

11 **You are going to listen to a radio report about television's past, present and future. With a partner, decide which order you think the following points will be mentioned in. Then listen and check your answers.**

CD 2 Track 4

L ▸ Das Hörverständnis üben (p. 111)

a Cable and satellite services were introduced.
b Digital TV was introduced. Some digital channels let viewers decide when they watched programmes.
c Video cassette recorders gave people the chance to record programmes and watch them when they wanted.
d In the future, TV stations may have to end traditional scheduling and give viewers access to programmes whenever they want to watch them.
e The Internet is changing people's attitude towards when they watch things.
f When television was still quite new and exciting, people had no problem being told when their favourite programmes were on.

12 **Listen again. Which text best summarises what the radio report says?**

1 The introduction of new television technologies has slowly changed the way that people watch TV. However, the Internet will certainly not have an impact on TV.
2 Video cassette recorders introduced the idea that people could choose when to watch their favourite programmes. The Internet continues this trend and may result in the end of traditional TV scheduling.
3 The end of television is approaching very quickly. The Internet has already taken over and the older medium has absolutely no future.

MEDIATION

13 **Your friend listens to the radio report but does not understand it. Summarise it for him/her in German.**

L ▸ Mediation (p. 122)

ROLE-PLAYING A MEETING

14 **Work in a group and prepare a meeting between teachers and parents on the effect that viewing too much television can have on young people.**

HANDS-ON TASK

L ▸ Die Arbeitsergebnisse präsentieren (p. 119)
L ▸ Gruppengespräche und Diskussionen führen (p. 122)
L ▸ Suche nach Informationen im Internet (p. 112)

1 Brainstorm in your group the negative effects that too much television can have on teenagers.
2 On the Internet research some of the technical solutions which are currently available for reducing the amount of television that young people can watch (eg. TV allowance, V-chip, pedal power TV).

TEXT 3 snd me a txt (Send Me a Text Message)

WARM-UP

1 a **Complete the questionnaire and add some further things you use text messaging for. Then discuss your answers with a partner.**

How frequently do you use text messaging for the following things: often, sometimes, occasionally or never?

- to make arrangements to meet a friend
- to cancel a meeting you have arranged with a friend
- to communicate with your parents
- to argue with someone
- to apologise for something you have said
- to flirt with someone you like
- to ask for a date with a potential boyfriend/girlfriend
- to get information (about train times, for example)
- to split up with a boyfriend/ girlfriend
- to communicate with your teacher

b **Do you think it is wrong to use text messaging for any of these things? Say which and why.**

CD 2 Track 5

Text Messages "Part of Young People's Secret Language"

The craze among young people for arranging dates and dumping their partners via mobile phone text messages is typical of different groups in society using "secret" languages to evade the attention of others, a psychologist says.

The research organisation MORI has just completed a survey into how young people use text messages. Brian Forbes from MORI told us, "Young people in the 15–24 age group are most likely to use text messages for flirting, with 19% having sent a text message to ask for a date and 44% apologising for an argument."
A shameless 13% even admit to having dumped their partners by sending a text message, says Forbes.

Psychologist Dr Guy Fielding, who specialises in communication, said, "This use by teenagers of text messages seems to be part of an alternative channel of communication with its own secret language".
Dr Fielding said text messaging is the ideal way for shy teenagers to chat up members of the opposite sex.

He said: "Written communication is much more controllable than speaking to someone face to face, because you have time to think about your message and edit it before you send it. And you can also think about what has been said to you, you don't have to respond to texts immediately.

"You can also say things that you wouldn't be brave enough to say face to face – it's easier to say difficult things when you are not looking at each other. Sending text messages is a way of communicating in private while in a public place.

"Text message senders have short abbreviations which they know the meaning of and others have no idea about – they are a signal that you are a member of an "in-group" and exclude others such as parents, adults and other authority figures."

1 craze *Mode*
dump sb *(umgs.) mit jdm Schluss machen*
3 evade *sich einer Sache entziehen*
13 chat up *jdn anbaggern*
17 edit *bearbeiten*
19 brave *mutig*
22 abbreviation *Abkürzung*

Some teachers are concerned that the text messaging craze is leading to a decline in standards of written English. Sarah Collins, spokesperson for WordUp!, an English teachers' organisation, told us, "The way that young people write an SMS is creeping into their written work at school. This is a problem because some people forget how to write properly."

And some young people are themselves worried about the effect of using text messages. Clara Norman, a 15-year-old pupil at a north London comprehensive school, commented, "Lots of my friends speak directly to each other less now. They don't even speak on the phone. When you are arguing with someone, it's easier to tell them to get lost with a text which is bad for your friendship. If you have to speak to someone it's much harder to say something like that and you can sort your arguments out better." (448 words)

Source: www.ananova.com

29 creep *sich einschleichen*
34 argue with *sich streiten mit*
35 get lost *(umgs.) abhauen*

WORKING WITH THE TEXT

2 Read the text and decide who is most likely to have said the following things.

L ► Lesen schwieriger Texte: Heraussuchen von Einzelinformationen (p. 108)

1

Dr Guy Fielding

2

Clara Norman

3

Brian Forbes

4

Sarah Collins

a "Apart from anything else, text messages can cause problems with spelling in normal writing."
b "Text messages offer young people a means of keeping in touch with each other in a way that excludes adults."
c "One of my mates doesn't even answer her phone anymore. If you call her, she just sends you a text which says 'txt me'."
d "While we found that a lot of young people use text messages to apologise for an argument, far fewer use them to carry out arguments."

3 Match the sentence halves to make statements about the text. There is one sentence half in each list which cannot be matched. Complete these two sentences in your own words.

L ► Lesen schwieriger Texte: Detailverständnis (p. 108)

1 Young people use a language …
2 According to the MORI survey, almost half of …
3 Some young people even use text messages to …
4 Text messaging is a good way for shy young people …
5 Young people who send texts often shorten words …
6 Some teachers are worried that the way texts are written …
7 Using text messages to argue with friends can …

a in order to be members of an exclusive group which adults are not part of.
b it's not as easy to say something which will be bad for your friendship.
c which is not understood by adults when they write text messages.
d to communicate because they can take time to think about what they want to say next.
e lead young people to be less careful about what they say.
f split up with their boyfriends or girlfriends.
g is leading to young people being unable to write properly.

WRITING

L ▶ Eine Stellungnahme schreiben (p. 115)

4 a List what the text says about text messaging under the three headings. Can you think of other things for each of the headings?

what you can do with text messages	arguments for text messaging	arguments against text messaging

b Do you disagree with any of the arguments for or against text messaging? Write a comment.

ANALYSING A CARTOON

L ▶ Interpretation von Bildern und Karikaturen (p. 119)

5 a Describe the cartoon.

b What are the teenagers actually saying to each other?

c What is the cartoonist suggesting about the effect of text messages on young people?

d Do you agree with the points that the text and cartoon make about young people's use of text messaging? Explain your reasons.

WORKING WITH WORDS

6 a Match the words and phrases in the box to words and phrases in the sentences from the text with the same meaning.

courageous | drop | fashion | finished | in person | reply | SMS | straightaway | worried

1 The research organisation MORI has just completed a survey into how young people use text messages.
2 You don't have to respond to texts immediately.
3 You can say things that you wouldn't be brave enough to say face to face.
4 Some teachers are concerned that the text messaging craze is leading to a decline in standards of written English.

b Now rewrite the sentences using the words and phrases in the box and your own words. Try to vary the sentence structure wherever possible.

7 a Read the info box on the opposite page. Then work with a partner and decide what the following abbreviations stand for.

1 c m	**4** ur	**7** r u	**10** b4
2 c u	**5** u r	**8** gr8	**11** cul8er
3 thx	**6** atm	**9** hw	**12** asap

b Now write a text message of 100 characters in length to your partner using as many abbreviations as possible. Can your partner translate the message into standard English?

INFO

Abbreviations in Text Messages

Many people have expressed concern about the new language that has emerged as a result of text messaging and the impact that it is having on young people's ability to write English. But what exactly is this language and how is it formed?

The first point to be made is that 'SMS speak' is not a fixed language but one which is constantly changing. In short, the people who use it are also its creators and they constantly innovate ways of expressing what they want to say. There are, however, some general rules to follow. These can be summarised as follows:

- Phrases are often reduced to the first letter of each word in the phrase. So, for example, 'on the other hand' becomes **otoh.**
- Similarly, longer words can be abbreviated using two or three letters – usually consonants – from the words. For example, 'girlfriend' could be written as **gf.**
- Finally, words are reduced, whenever possible, to their phonetic components. Here, for example, 'tomorrow' could be **2moro.**

Anyone who has had to write even quite a short text message on their mobile phone will know that these abbreviations save time, space and money. However, while it is useful to know them, it must be remembered that the abbreviations are hardly ever appropriate in anything other than text messages.

1 emerge *aufkommen*
2 impact *Auswirkung*
6 innovate *erneuern*
12 component *Bestandteil*
17 appropriate *angemessen*

LOOKING AT LANGUAGE

8 Choose the best modal verbs to complete the sentences.

G ▸ Modal auxiliary verbs (p. 129)

1. If you have a 50 SMS per month tariff, you *can/must* pay extra if you send over 50 texts in a month.
2. You *should/may* turn your mobile off at night otherwise someone might wake you by calling.
3. You *mustn't / don't have to* call Ben. I've already explained everything to him.
4. *Should/must* I call later if you're busy just now?
5. I *can/should* try to call earlier in the evening but you're often speaking to someone else on the phone then.
6. *Should/can* I borrow your mobile? I need to make a call.
7. You *needn't/mustn't* call me so late at night. I'll get into trouble with my dad.
8. If I'm not careful with how I use my mobile, I *can/must* have a big phone bill at the end of the month.
9. *Can/must* you call me later? I'll have time to talk in about an hour.
10. We *mustn't / don't have to* use mobile phones in the library. It's not allowed.

GROUP PROJECT

HANDS-ON TASK

9 a **Work in a small group and decide when and where you think it is reasonable to be allowed to use mobile phones in school.**

b **In your group draw up a set of guidelines for the use of mobile phones in your school which you think is reasonable.**

c **Compare your guidelines with those written by other groups.**

L ▸ Gruppengespräche und Diskussionen führen (p. 122)

TEXT 4 Criticising the Media

WARM-UP

1 Work with a partner. Which heading would you group the following under: a) popular culture or b) high culture?

- **a** Big Brother
- **b** Beethoven's Symphony No. 5
- **c** Disneyland Paris
- **d** jazz music
- **e** a manga comic
- **f** country and western music
- **g** Westminster Abbey
- **h** a painting by Picasso

Now read the article about the media and culture by Robert Crumb, a famous American cartoonist who is well-known for his critical views.

CD 2 Track 6

The Meat and the Butcher

Almost all of our mass culture is a quick snack aimed at providing fast and easy pleasure. If it has any real nutritional value, that's just a side effect. At the Cannes Film Festival I saw thousands of people gawking at movie stars. The worshipful behaviour of the crowd was deeply disgusting to behold. You'd have thought that Brad Pitt really was the Greek hero Achilles come to Earth.

Brad did a good warrior act in the movie *Troy*, but he's just an actor. He is just the 'meat'. He might be well paid, but it's the butcher behind the scenes who is really raking it in!

The way the world works, it's much smarter to be the butcher, but no one tells you this. Glamour and glory aside, there are vast amounts of money to be made in the film industry and in the music business. The film industry is a filthy, rotten business, and I don't want anything more to do with it. I don't want to be the 'meat'. But who am I kidding. I *am* the meat. I let the butchers go at me, chop me in little pieces and put me on the counter. I didn't know what I was doing when I first got myself into this situation. Fame also brought media attention. The media is a big hungry beast. I've known a few who've died from too much of it.

The people who work in the media business are part of a conspiracy against the average man to get his money. They are not concerned with what effect their product might have. They are always looking for the lowest common denominator, the broadest possible market. They don't care what that might be. If Jesus movies are filling cinemas, that's what they'll make. If ultra-violence appeals to a certain segment of the population, the butchers are happy to provide it.

Before industrial civilisation, local and regional communities made their own culture. This culture was based on traditions that went far back in time. But part of the con of mass culture is to make you forget history; disconnect you from tradition and the past. Tradition keeps culture on an authentic human level, the homespun as opposed to the mass-produced. But then industrial civilisation figured out how to manufacture popular culture and sell it back to people. The problem is that the longer this buying and selling goes on, the more hollow the culture becomes. It loses fertility, like worn-out farmland. (417 words)

Abridged from: *The R. Crumb Handbook*, London 2005

2 nutritional value *Nährwert*
3 gawk *gaffen*
4 worshipful *vergötternd*
disgusting *widerlich*
behold *sehen*
6 warrior *Krieger*
8 rake it in *abkassieren*
9 smart *clever*
11 filthy *schmutzig*
rotten *verdorben*
13 kid sb *jdm etwas vormachen*
chop *(zer)hacken*
14 counter *Ladentisch*
15 fame *Ruhm*
17 conspiracy *Verschwörung*
19 lowest common denominator *kleinster gemeinsamer Nenner*
25 con *Schwindel*
27 homespun *selbst gestrickt*
as opposed to *im Gegensatz zu*
29 hollow *hohl*
30 fertility *Fruchtbarkeit*

WORKING WITH THE TEXT

2 **Which of these statements best summarises Robert Crumb's view of the media and entertainment industry? Give reasons.**

L ▸ Lesen schwieriger Texte: Grobverständnis (p. 108)

1 The media and entertainment industries have got their bad sides but they give people what they want to watch and there's nothing wrong with that.
2 The media and entertainment industries are dirty businesses which care much more about making money than about what they entertain people with.
3 If the media and entertainment businesses only make low quality products, normal people are to blame because that's all they ask for.

3 a **Complete the statements about the text (1–6) with sentences a–f.**

L ▸ Lesen schwieriger Texte: Detailverständnis (p. 108)

1 Crumb has decided to have no further involvement in the film industry. (...)
2 (...) They are not interested in what this market might be.
3 (...) However, the really large sums of money are made by people who never appear in films.
4 The main aim of the media business is to provide people with easily enjoyable culture. (...)
5 (...) Now it is mass-produced and people buy it without creating it.
6 (...) The people involved in it are not interested in what effect their products have.

a Anything of value in what it produces is only there by accident.
b In the past, culture was something that people produced themselves.
c He thinks it is a dirty business.
d The main concern of the media industry is to make money.
e The people who work in the media industry aim to please the biggest market possible.
f Actors are paid a lot for their work.

b **Now write up the complete statements in the order in which those points appear in the text.**

4 a **Explain what is meant by 'meat' and 'butcher' in the text.**

b **Find other images in the text and explain what they mean.**

TRANSLATION

5 **Translate the last paragraph of the text into German.**

L ▸ Übersetzung (p. 123)

SUMMARY

6 **Summarise in English the contrast between traditional and industrial culture as described in the text.**

L ▸ Einen Text zusammenfassen (p. 116)

DISCUSSION

7 **Work in groups and discuss whether you agree with Robert Crumb's view of the media and entertainment industry. Is it too cynical and extreme? State your reasons for your ideas.**

L ▸ Gruppengespräche und Diskussionen führen (p. 122)

WORKING WITH WORDS

8 a **Match the words in the box to the words below to form common expressions.**

attention | culture | mass | nutritional | segment | well

1 mass …
2 … value
3 … paid
4 media …
5 certain …
6 …-produced

b **Use the expressions to complete the sentences. Two of the expressions are not used.**

1 … is not all bad and Hollywood sometimes produces some good films.
2 The problem with fast food is that it often has little … .
3 Some stars, like Pete Doherty, receive a little bit more … than is healthy.
4 While a lot of people listen to pop music, a … of music lovers prefer classical music.

c **Now write sentences about the text on page 74 using the remaining two expressions.**

INFO

The Debate about Mass Culture

Robert Crumb makes the case very strongly that 'mass culture' is a bad thing. However, his ideas are not new. Commentators, thinkers and policy makers have been arguing for decades about 'mass culture' and its value – or lack of it.

In the second half of the 20th century, the tone of this debate was set by writers such as Richard Hoggart. In his 1957 book *The Uses of Literacy*, Hoggart complained that 'authentic' culture was disappearing and being replaced by a 'plastic' mass culture. Whereas in the past people had made their own culture out of such things as folk songs and stories, now everything was served up to them ready-made by new media like television and film. The audience for mass culture no longer had a role in producing it, but merely sat back and passively consumed it.

Other thinkers took this argument further. According to them, the problem was not just that people now consumed culture passively. Mass culture also told them what to think. Many Europeans understood mass culture to be an American creation and feared that the American world view and lifestyle were being sold to Europe by means of films and television programmes. Therefore, Europeans were being taught to think like Americans.

In the 1980s other thinkers started to reject this view. They argued that to see audiences as being merely passive was condescending. Rather, they thought, people who con-sumed mass culture made their own active choices about what to consume, rejecting the bad bits and enjoying the good bits.

What has been placed in opposition to mass culture in all of these debates is 'high culture'. Indeed, the 'high culture versus mass culture' debate has been very heated in Britain in the last few years. Here, the supposedly high culture of classical music, 'good books' and fine art is seen as being under threat from a rapidly advancing 'low culture'.

Given that these debates have been going on for so long, they will probably never be resolved. However, as popular cultural content continues to proliferate via the Internet and digital TV, the one thing that is certain is that the debate will continue.

7 literacy *die Fähigkeit, lesen und schreiben zu können*
18 reject *ablehnen*
19 condescending *herablassend*
27 resolve *entscheiden*
proliferate *wachsen*

LOOKING AT LANGUAGE

9 **Use the gerund or infinitive form of the verbs in brackets to complete the sentences. Identify which sentences both can be used in.**

G ▸ Gerund and infinitive (p. 133)

1. He enjoys … (buy) theatre tickets rather than spending his money on going to watch bands.
2. I plan … (watch) less television and read more books instead.
3. Jim began … (dislike) Brat Pitt as an actor after he saw him in *Troy*.
4. I expect Brian will choose … (go) and see that new action film with Bruce Willis this weekend.
5. Sarah decided … (stay) at home on Saturday night because there was nothing interesting on at the cinema.
6. Trevor stopped … (go) to the video shop for his films when he discovered he could download them from the Internet.
7. What? You don't like … (go) to the cinema? What do you do in your spare time then?
8. I usually avoid … (spend) money on CDs as I can download music for free.
9. Clara hates … (watch) action movies. She says they're mindless.
10. Belinda loves … (listen) to music in bed at night because it helps her go to sleep.

WRITING A FILM REVIEW

HANDS-ON TASK

10 **Work with a partner to complete the following task.**

L ▸ Einen Text sinnvoll gliedern (p. 118)

1. Films made in Hollywood sometimes tell you something new about the world as well as entertaining you. Talk with your partner to find out which Hollywood film you have both seen and felt was instructive as well as entertaining.
2. Discuss the film to decide which elements of it were instructive. What did the film tell you that you did not know before?
3. Working on your own now, write a review of the film for the cinema section of the school magazine stressing the ways in which it is both instructive and entertaining.
   Try to use the following language:

   … is a film by … starring …
   I found … both entertaining and instructive because …
   My first point is that …
   … is great in the main role because …
   On the other hand …
   What I found especially interesting was …
   In conclusion, …
   … is one of the best films I've seen, as …
   I certainly would not hesitate to recommend …

   Decide which scene should be used in a photograph beside the article to illustrate the theme of the film.
4. You and your partner should now swap reviews. Read your partner's review and make notes on it suggesting improvements and corrections. You should pay special attention to the structure of the text, the sentence structure and whether your partner uses a wide enough variety of words and connecting phrases.
5. Read your partner's suggestions as to how your review could be improved.

TEXT 5 Reporting the Royals – the Quality and Popular Press in Britain

WARM-UP

1 a Which are the serious 'quality' newspapers in Germany? Which are the more sensational 'popular' newspapers? Which papers do you like best? Why?

b In which sort of paper are you likely to find more of the following?

a national news
b international news
c longer articles analysing serious issues
d celebrity news
e human interest stories
f sports news
g business and economic news
h reports about art, films and music

c Who is the woman in the photograph? Why is she famous?

WORKING WITH THE TEXT

L ▸ Lesen schwieriger Texte: Suche nach Einzelinformationen (p. 108)

CD 2 Track 7

2 a Look at the two articles and decide which comes from the quality newspaper *The Guardian* and which from *The Sun*, a popular newspaper. How can you tell?

b Now read the articles quickly. What role do the following play: a) Clarence House, b) Matt Lauer, c) Paddy Harverson?

1 works for the princes and speaks to the media on their behalf
2 the London home of Prince Charles, father of William and Harry
3 works for NBC television in the US

Harry 'Will Never Stop Wondering' about Diana's Death

Princes talk openly about the crash 10 years ago

Clarence House plays down US TV interview

Stephen Bates

Clarence House attempted to ward off a potential bout of renewed speculation about the death of Princess Diana last night following comments by Prince Harry in an American television interview that he would "never stop wondering" about the crash that killed his mother nearly 10 years ago.

The remarks came in an interview with the prince and his older brother William to be broadcast by NBC in America.

The interviewer, Matt Lauer, had been warned that discussing the accident was off limits. But he was rewarded by some of the most open remarks the princes have ever made about the effect their mother's death has had on them.

In extracts released yesterday, Harry says, "You know, when people think about it, they think about her death. They think about how wrong it was. They think about whatever happened in that tunnel, you know, no one will ever know."

Asked whether he had stopped wondering, the prince replied: "I'll never stop wondering about that."

Clarence House officials stressed that the remarks meant that the prince would never stop wondering whether the crash in Paris could have been prevented and he was not speculating about the crash itself.

Pointing to the princes' positive reaction to the exhaustive police inquiry, a spokesman said: "Of course Prince Harry and Prince William will always be thinking a lot about what happened that night and whether the accident could have been avoided. But they have never doubted their mother's death was an accident."

"When the Stevens report [into the accident] came out last December they said they hoped its conclusive findings would put an end to the speculation."

Elsewhere in the interview, the princes spoke of their desire to be normal, about their image in America, their friends and what they would have done if they had not been princes.

(320 words)

Adapted from *The Guardian*, 13 June 2007

1 attempt *versuchen*
ward off *abwenden*
2 bout *Runde*
15 off limits *tabu*
20 extract *Auszug*
34 prevent *verhindern*
37 exhaustive *umfassend*
38 inquiry *Untersuchung*
47 conclusive *eindeutig*
50 desire *Sehnsucht*

We Will Never Stop Wondering What Happened

TORMENT OVER DIANA CRASH

BY DUNCAN LARCOMBE AND EMILY SMITH

Princes William and Harry have finally spoken out about their mother Diana's death – and admitted they will NEVER stop wondering what happened.

The brothers speak candidly about the August 1997 accident which killed the Princess to a US television interviewer.

And Harry says: "Whatever happened in that tunnel – no one will ever know."

Harry, 22, and William spoke to reporter Matt Lauer at Clarence House. Both agreed to "go public" in tribute to their late mother as the tenth anniversary of her tragic death approached. Speaking about Diana's car crash in Paris, Harry says: "Whatever happened in that tunnel, you know, no one will ever know. And I'm sure people will always think about that the whole time."

Asked by Lauer whether **HE** has stopped wondering, Harry replies: "I'll never stop wondering about that."

William, 24, also reveals his ongoing torment over his mother's death.

He says: "There's not a day goes by I don't think, you know, that I don't think about it once in the day."

The emotional interview – conducted by American TV station NBC – will be aired on Monday with the full support of Clarence House.

Sources within the Royal household insist the boys took the brave decision to speak due to their frustration over the constant flow of conspiracy theories surrounding their mum's death.

The princes' spokesman Paddy Harverson said last night: "They have never doubted that their mother's death was an accident."

KINGS OF FLIRTING

Matt Lauer told how the princes flirted with a pretty music reporter before the interview.

NBC's Lauer said: "She was an attractive blonde in a short skirt. I finally said 'are you guys done flirting with her yet?' They were disappointed going from her to me."

Adapted from *The Sun*, 13 June 2007

torment *Qual*
5 candid *offen*
15 in tribute to *zu Ehren von*
16 anniversary *Jahrestag*
33 air *ausstrahlen*
50 be done with sth *mit etw fertig sein*

L ▸ Lesen schwieriger Texte: Suche nach Einzelinformationen (p. 108)

3 Choose the correct sentence endings to make statements about what the texts say.

1 Clarence House is trying to …
  a encourage people to think about how Princess Diana died.
  b stop people thinking again about how the princess died.

2 The TV interviewer was told …
  a not to ask questions about Diana's accident.
  b to ask questions about the accident.

3 Clarence House said that the princes would never stop wondering whether …
  a their mother's accident could have been prevented.
  b the car crash that killed their mother was actually an accident.

4 The interviewer spoke to the princes …
  a at NBC in America.
  b in London.

5 Clarence House is …
  a in favour of the interview appearing on television.
  b opposed to the interview appearing on television.

L ▸ Lesen schwieriger Texte: Detailverständnis (p. 108)

4 a Work with a partner and decide in which order the different elements of the story (a–e) appear in each of the two reports. Are some elements not mentioned by one or other of the reports?

a what the interviewer Matt Lauer said about the interview
b aspects of the princes' lives other than the death of their mother
c official comment from the royal family in the form of statements made by Clarence House
d comments about official investigations made into Diana's accident
e what the princes actually said during the interview

b What does the order of these elements and the attention given to them show about the different priorities of the two newspapers?

c Make further comparisons between the approaches of the two newspapers to the story. Consider the effect of aspects such as:

- headlines and sub-headlines
- 'emotional' language
- adjectives
- type style – **bold** letters, CAPITAL letters, *italics*

HIGHLAND CLEARANCE . . . Dargo is off

Killie want Dargo back

KILMARNOCK are weighing up a shock second time around swoop for Inverness striker Craig Dargo — if they lose prize asset Stevie Naismith.
SunSport can reveal Killie boss Jim Jefferies is ready to move, despite Bosman star Dargo leaving Rugby Park under a cloud two years ago.
Since … has

WORKING WITH WORDS

5 Explain these expressions from the text on page 79 using your own words.

1 speak candidly (line 5)
2 go public (line 14)
3 ongoing torment (lines 26/27)
4 brave decision (line 36)

WRITING

6 Rewrite one of the two short texts below in the style of 'popular' newspaper articles, paying particular attention to the aspects mentioned in Exercise 4c.

1 Miroslav Klose suffered an injury in a game against Manchester United on Saturday. The high point of the match was a goal scored by Wayne Rooney in the second half.

2 Three men were arrested by police in Milton Keynes on Friday after they were involved in a fight in a pub. A lawyer for one of the three said that the incident was not their fault – another man had started the fight.

DISCUSSION

7 Read the info box below. With a partner, discuss these questions.

1 How important is it for the public to know about the private lives of members of the royal family?
2 Who do you think benefits more from their interrelationship: the media or the royal family?

L► Gruppengespräche und Diskussionen führen (p. 122)

INFO

The Royal Family and the Popular Press

Since the beginning of the 1980s, 'quality' and 'popular' newspapers in Britain have been criticised for treating the British royals with a lack of respect and for reporting in detail aspects of their private lives. It was with Diana's appearance on the royal scene that this tendency among newspapers started.

In 1981, when the forthcoming marriage of Prince Charles to Diana was announced, members of the press were fascinated. In the months leading up to the royal wedding, reporters and photographers constantly pursued the future princess. They did this as they might have pursued a pop or film star and not a future royal. Despite criticism, this new style of royal reporting continued. In the early years of Charles and Diana's marriage, the press followed the couple's activities with enormous interest. Later, as it became clear that the marriage was not a happy one, newspapers carried stories about a series of 'scandals' involving Diana. Such stories may previously have been considered 'off limits' – now they were 'fair game'. This type of reporting continued through Diana's separation and divorce from Charles and up until the point of her death.

The royal family has, from time to time, complained bitterly about the way that its members have been profiled by the newspapers. Some of the loudest complaints came from Diana herself. However, some commentators in Britain felt that Diana was in a two-way relationship with the papers. They reported embarrassing stories she might have preferred to remain private. But they could also be used to spread her side of the story regarding her failed marriage to Charles. In short, Diana seemed to become quite skilled in using newspapers and the rest of the media for her own purposes.

The tendency for British newspapers to report royal scandal in such detail may have appeared at the same time as Diana herself. But it did not disappear along with her. For instance, the royal family was much criticised for its handling of her death in the media. One of the greatest challenges facing British royalty, then, is how best to handle its public image in the media.

3 appearance *Erscheinen*
5 forthcoming *bevorstehend*
7 pursue *verfolgen*
13 fair game *erlaubt*
16 profile *berichten über*
18 embarrassing *peinlich*
19 remain *bleiben*

INTERNET PROJECT

HANDS-ON TASK

8 Work in a small group and do the following tasks.

1 Find the websites of a range of British 'quality' and 'popular' newspapers.
2 Identify some news stories covered by both types of newspaper. Compare the coverage of the stories, paying attention to the language they use.
3 Compare the content of the stories. What information do all the reports give? Do any of the reports miss out any of the points mentioned in other newspapers?
4 Which report gives the strongest emotional picture? Which report gives the most information? Find examples from the text.
6 Decide which is the best newspaper story. Give reasons.

L► Suche nach Informationen im Internet (p. 112)

TEXT 6 Reporting a War

WARM-UP

L ▶ Interpretation von Bildern und Karikaturen (p. 119)

1 Describe the cartoon.

2 a What does the statement "the first casualty of war is truth" mean?

b Does the cartoonist agree or disagree with this idea? State the reasons for your opinion.

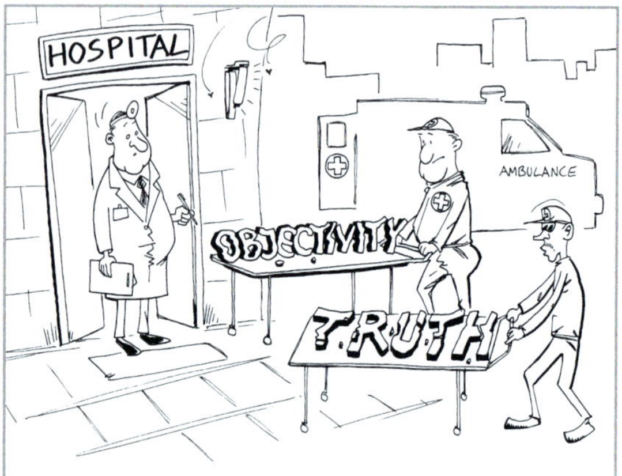

Some more war news casualties

L ▶ Einen Text zusammenfassen (p. 116)

3 Read the information box and summarise in your own words the difference between how the Iraq war and previous wars were reported.

INFO

Reporting the War in Iraq

Journalists have always reported on wars. In the past, they were sometimes given access to battlefields, but often they had to write their reports based on censored information which was given to them by the military authorities, without seeing what was going on with their own eyes.

However, this was not the case during the war in Iraq in 2003. During this war the US along with Britain invaded Iraq because it claimed that the Iraqis possessed dangerous 'weapons of mass destruction'. The war itself was over quickly – the invasion began on 20 March and the Americans declared their victory on 15 April. However, fighting and instability continued in the country up until the time of writing in 2007. During this conflict the American military authorities allowed around 800 journalists (20% of them from non-American media organisations) to live and travel with the military units which were doing the fighting. These 'embedded' journalists were allowed to report on what they saw more or less uncensored.

There was a lot of criticism of embedded journalists – or 'embeds' – during the war. Many people believed that the journalists censored themselves and did not report openly on what was happening. Alternatively, others believed that the media reported on the Iraq War in a more open and accurate way than ever before.

12 embed *einbetten*

L ▶ Lesen schwieriger Texte: Grobverständnis (p. 108)

4 Read these questions and skim the texts on the following page to find the answers.

Which journalist …

a … is more questioning of the war in Iraq?
b … saw actual fighting?
c … gives more of a soldier's perspective of the war?
d … gives more of a civilian's perspective of the war?

Reporting from the Front Line

Gavin Hewitt and Ryan Dilley both covered the war in Iraq for the BBC.

CD 2 Track 9

Gavin Hewitt – Kuwait to Baghdad

There was one particular day when the reality of war really came home to me. The 3rd Infantry Division, the unit I was with, was pushing in from the west. Suddenly, we were under fire from artillery. This was one moment where there was indecision as to where to go. For what seemed like an eternity we were just sitting on the highway and I saw real fear in the eyes of American soldiers. Then we moved. We all crouched behind a wall. Another shell came in. After it hit, you could hear the shrapnel and little bits falling everywhere. It was very frightening.

At the outset there were critics of "embedding" correspondents with US troops, and I myself was concerned that this would inhibit what we were going to be able to say. But just before we crossed into Iraq we were told we would never be prevented from saying what we felt, even if it was critical. The only problem was that we could not say precisely where we were or what future plans were. Beyond that I had freedom as a journalist to report in precisely the way that I wanted.

When we were editing in the evening, sometimes the soldiers would become curious and would gather around the vehicle to watch what we were doing, but no one ever said to me "you can't say that" or "that's unfair".

The Pentagon, I believe, promised from the start that this would be unlike any kind of reporting of a war before. They were right.

4 push in *eindringen*
9 eternity *Ewigkeit*
12 crouch *(sich) niederkauern*
13 shell *Granate*
14 shrapnel *Bombensplitter*
17 at the outset *am Anfang*
20 inhibit *hemmen, einschränken*
32 curious *neugierig*

Ryan Dilley – Kuwait City, Umm Qasr and Basra

As a war correspondent, I feel like something of a fraud. While others, the so-called "embeds", witnessed the fighting at first-hand, I visited the battlegrounds days after the firing had ceased.

While others roughed it, I for the most part enjoyed room service and clean sheets.

But I saw enough to know that I had seen very little of what conflict has to offer. And I understand only little of what I did observe.

I saw utter terror in the eyes of Kuwaitis when the sirens warned of an incoming Iraqi missile, but witnessed a carnival atmosphere when locals rushed to see the one projectile that did hit their city.

I saw callous and calculated acts of destruction perpetrated by both sides, but balanced by acts of great generosity and kindness.

I have seen a boy enraged because he was denied a chocolate bar, while another youth – shot through the middle and dying – behaved with utter composure, politeness and dignity.

I have seen a palace the splendour of which was made all the more sickening by the poverty, filth and want around it. I have seen people with great intelligence and potential, trapped in a situation surely created by fools.

What I am really not sure about is whether I have seen a liberation or an invasion. (474 words)

Source: bbc.co.uk

2 fraud *Betrüger/in*
3 witness *(mit)erleben*
6 cease *aufhören*
7 rough it *primitiv leben*
9 sheet *Betttuch, Laken*
14 utter *völlig*
20 callous *gefühllos*
21 perpetrate *verüben*
22 generosity *Großzügigkeit*
24 enraged *wütend*
28 composure *Fassung*
dignity *Würde*
29 splendour *Pracht*
31 filth *Schmutz*
32 want *Not*
34 trap *einschließen*

WORKING WITH THE TEXT

L ▶ Lesen schwieriger Texte: Suche nach Einzelinformationen (p. 108)

5 Which of these statements are true and which are false? Correct the false statements.

1. According to Gavin Hewitt, the soldiers with him were never afraid.
2. At the beginning of the war Hewitt was worried that he would have difficulties reporting in the way he wanted.
3. Journalists were prevented from reporting the position of troops and where they were going next.
4. The soldiers were never interested in the work of the journalists.
5. At the beginning of the war, the Pentagon said that this war would be reported in a new way.
6. Ryan Dilley does not feel like a real war correspondent.
7. Ryan Dilley's experience gave him a full understanding of war.
8. At times, the Kuwaitis were very frightened of Iraqi missiles.

L ▶ Eine Stellungnahme schreiben (p. 115)

L ▶ Aus dem Text zitieren (p. 115)

6 Read the texts again and compare their style. For example, which text is more reflective in its tone and which is more positive? Why? Find sections of the texts to justify your answers. Also, say which style of text you prefer and why. Try to use the following phrases:

It seems to me that …
The first text is a bit more …
For example, it says in the first text that …
However, the second text takes a more … approach.
The second text suggests, for instance, that …
I like the approach of the first text better because …
I feel that the style of the second text is better because …

MEDIATION

L ▶ Mediation (p. 122)

7 a In German, explain the difference between a war correspondent and an 'embedded' journalist.

b Work with a partner and take turns to describe in German the contrasts Ryan Dilley witnessed in Iraq. Do not translate word for word but try to summarise the text using your own words.

DISCUSSION

L ▶ Gruppengespräche und Diskussionen führen (p. 122)

8 Look again at the cartoon on page 82. After reading the texts, do you think that 'truth was the first casualty of war' in Iraq?

WORKING WITH WORDS

9 Find words and expressions in the text which mean the opposite of these words and expressions.

a decisiveness (lines 1–16/Hewitt)
b a short time (lines 1–16/Hewitt)
c justified (lines 30–39/Hewitt)
d started (lines 1–13/Dilley)
e allowed (lines 24–35/Dilley)

10 Find words and expressions in the text which mean the same as the following words and expressions.

a became clear (lines 1–16/Hewitt)
b restrict (lines 17–29/Hewitt)
c stopped (lines 17–29/Hewitt)
d inquisitive (lines 30–39/Hewitt)
e cold-hearted (lines 14–23/Dilley)

11 Explain the following expressions in the text in your own words.

a be under fire (line 6/Hewitt)
b crouched (line 12/Hewitt)
c precisely (line 29/Hewitt)
d roughed it (line 7/Dilley)
e carnival atmosphere (line 17/Dilley)

LOOKING AT LANGUAGE

12 Use the conditional types 1, 2 or 3 to complete these sentences.

G ▶ Conditionals (p. 133)

1 If there … (be) more about war on the TV news tonight, I … (turn) it straight off.
2 If the American government … (keep) the media more under control during the Vietnam war, it … (not have) as many problems with public opinion.
3 There … (be) no need for wars if people … (learn) to solve conflicts by talking.
4 If the US army … (not embed) journalists during the Iraq war, we … (have) less information about the conflict.
5 Trevor … (go) on the anti-war demonstration on Saturday if you … (go) too.
6 I … (meet) Sally last night if that programme on television about embedded journalists … (not be) so interesting.
7 If Pete … (be offered) the opportunity, he … (love) to work as a journalist.
8 If I … (watch) one more television report about Iraq, I … (go) mad!

WRITING

13 Do you agree that embedded journalists are more likely to report accurately what is going on in a war? Write a letter to the editor of a newspaper expressing your views on this issue. Use the following as a framework for your letter:

L ▶ Eine Stellungnahme schreiben (p. 115)

Dear Sir or Madam,

I am writing to express my support of / disapproval of …
In my view/opinion …
One positive/negative aspect of this is that …
I feel that journalists should …
It is a journalist's job to …
It is not a journalist's role to …
Journalists should not …
Rather, they should …

Yours faithfully,

(your name)

TOPIC 4

The State We're In – USA and UK

TEXT 1 Young People and Politics

WARM-UP

1 **Do you think politicians could do more to communicate with young people and encourage their interest and trust in politics? Make a list of the things that politicians could do to make politics more relevant to you.**

CD 2 Track 10

'A Real Chance to Improve British Politics' – Votes at 16 Campaign

A real chance to improve British politics exists and it is up to politicians and the Government to grab it. That is the message of the Votes at 16 Campaign.

The campaign, a coalition of charities, pressure groups, political parties and groups representing young people, wants to see the voting age lowered for all public elections and lobbies politicians and provokes debate among young people.

Bishop Roger Sainsbury, Chair of the National Youth Agency, said:

"Young people have so much to contribute to British politics, but they often do not feel they are viewed as real citizens. As a result, they become disconnected and the quality of public decision-making suffers.

"The National Youth Agency believes that a massive step towards reconnecting young people with politics will be taken by lowering the voting age. That is why we back this campaign."

Jade Farrington, a 16-year-old school student from Staffordshire, said:

"If you lower the voting age to 16, you tell young people that our views are valid and you force more politicians to listen to us and bear us in mind when deciding their policies. I believe that, over time, young people will regain some of their faith in politicians and elections and will show this by voting. That is why I support Votes at 16."

Liberal Democrat Youth Affairs Spokesperson, Matthew Green MP, said:

"Young people are passionately interested in politics and political issues but they see politicians as being out of touch and unresponsive to their needs. Allowing 16- and 17-year-olds to vote will encourage politicians to listen to young people and address the issues which concern them."

Mandy Telford, President of the National Union of Students, said:

"It is wrong to say that 16- and 17-year-olds do not understand the issues. Citizenship education in schools from the age of 5 to 16 is helping to create political literacy among young people. Lowering the voting age would encourage young people to make use of this knowledge and get them into the habit of voting."

Lord Lucas, a Conservative peer who is putting his weight behind a Private Members' Bill on lowering the voting age through the House of Lords at the moment, said:

2 grab *ergreifen*
4 charity *Wohlfahrtsorganisation*
14 back *unterstützen*
17 valid *berechtigt*
18 regain *wiedererlangen*
31 unresponsive *unempfänglich*
28 citizenship education *Staatsbürgerkunde*
32 peer *Mitglied des Hochadels*
put one's weight behind sth *sich für etw stark machen*
33 bill *Gesetzentwurf*

"We give young people the burdens of the world to carry at 16, we let them choose to leave school, get married or join the armed forces, we let them leave home. That responsibility gives them a right to a say in how things are run."

(416 words)

Source: www.votesat16.org.uk

35 burden *Last*

WORKING WITH THE TEXT

2 Complete the tasks using your own words as far as possible.

L ▸ Lesen schwieriger Texte: Detailverständnis (p. 108)

1 Describe the groups which make up the Votes at 16 Campaign.
2 List a) the negative effects of not allowing people under 18 to vote, and b) the positive effects that lowering the voting age to sixteen will have.
3 Find proof in the text that 16-year-olds are mature enough to vote.

3 a Match the statements to the names in the box by referring back to what the people were quoted in the text as saying. There is one statement too few. Write a statement for this person.

L ▸ Lesen schwieriger Texte: Suche nach Einzelinformationen (p. 108)

Bishop Roger Sainsbury | Jade Farrington | Lord Lucas | Mandy Telford | Matthew Green MP

1 At 16 people already have many responsibilities. Why not the responsibility of the vote as well?
2 Sixteen-year-olds do have enough understanding to vote.
3 Votes for sixteen-year-olds will make politicians take notice of us.
4 The fact that people can't vote at 16 affects the quality of the decisions made by politicians.

b Now summarise what each of the people quoted in the text said in as few words as possible.

L ▸ Interpretation von Bildern und Karikaturen (p. 119)

"At last, a politician we can trust!"

ANALYSING A CARTOON

4 Describe the cartoon. What do you think the cartoonist is saying about politics and politicians?

WORKING WITH WORDS

5 Find words or expressions from the text which match these definitions.

1 organisations which aim to help people (lines 1–7)
2 organisations which aim to create discussion around certain issues and encourage politicians to think about them (lines 1–7)
3 people with full political rights (lines 8–14)
4 worthwhile and of value (lines 15–25)
5 plan of action by the government (lines 15–25)
6 person who represents a group of people and speaks for them (lines 15–25)

6 Explain the phrases from the text in your own words.

1 out of touch (line 23)
2 citizenship education (line 28)
3 political literacy (line 29)
4 putting his weight behind (line 32)
5 the burdens of the world (line 35)

7 a **Match the verbs in the box to the nouns they are used with in the text.**

address | grab | provoke | regain | take

a faith **b** an issue **c** a chance **d** debate **e** a step

b **Now use the phrases from Exercise 7a in the correct form to complete the following text.**

What young people think of politics – and you!

One-day conference

An open invitation to MPs to come to meet your future voters on Friday 14 March at 2pm in the Collingwood Hall, Westminster

If young people are to … …¹ in politics, politicians have to … …² to make sure that politics are relevant to young people. Our aim is to … …³ between politicians and the young – and to get you to … the …⁴ which are important them.

Come along and … this …⁵ to meet your future voters face-to-face.

c **Say who the text above is written for and what its aims are.**

TALKING ABOUT GRAPHS

L ▸ Interpretation von Grafiken, Diagrammen und Tabellen (p. 121)

8 a **Work with a partner and take turns to describe the trends in voting among young people illustrated by the line graph.**

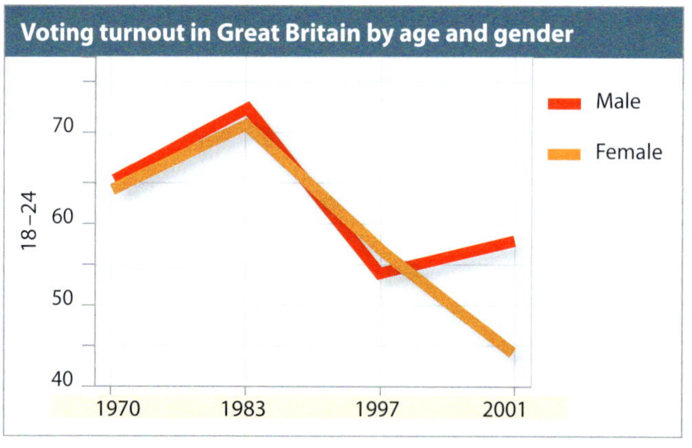

Source: British Election Study, National Centre for Social Research, University of Essex

b **Compare the information in the text on page 86/87 with the information shown by the graph. Does the graph support or contradict the idea behind the Votes at 16 campaign? In what way?**

L ▸ Suche nach Informationen im Internet (p. 112)

c **What happened to voter turnout among young people in the 2005 British general election? Use the Internet to find out.**

MEDIATION

L ▸ Mediation (p. 122)

9 **Read the info box on the opposite page and explain in German what the text says about a) 5-year-old British children, b) 16-year-old British teenagers, c) 18-year-old British teenagers.**

INFO

Citizenship Education

As mentioned in the text, the age of 16 is the threshold[1] at which people are regarded, in many respects, as adults in Britain. This is the age at which you are allowed to move away from your parents, get married, leave school, buy cigarettes and become a full-time employee. If you want to buy alcohol, you have to wait until you are 18. This is also the case if you want to express a political view through voting.

Despite the fact that one is not allowed to vote until the age of 18 in Britain, schools in England and Wales are required by law to begin citizenship education with children as young as 5 and it plays a role in their education until they are at least 16.

Citizenship education aims to promote three key concepts among children. The first is social and moral responsibility "both in and beyond the classroom, towards those in authority and towards each other". Then comes community involvement where pupils learn "about becoming helpfully involved in the life and concerns of their neighbourhood and communities".

Finally, the intention is that children become politically literate, "learning about the institutions, problems and practices of our democracy and how to make themselves effective in the life of the nation, locally, regionally and nationally through skills and values as well as knowledge".

Contains material from the Department for Children, Schools and Families

[1] threshold *Schwelle*

TRANSLATION

10 **Translate the last two paragraphs of the info box into German. Watch out for gerunds and participles.**

L ▶ Übersetzung (p. 123)
G ▶ Gerunds (p. 133), Participle constructions (p. 137)

DISCUSSION

11 **Compare the situation for young people in Britain and in Germany regarding a) the ages at which you are allowed to do various things, b) citizenship education.**

L ▶ Gruppengespräche und Diskussionen führen (p. 122)

WRITING A POLITICAL MANIFESTO

12 **In groups, write a 'political manifesto' for young people, presenting ideas which you think represent the views of teenagers to politicians.**

HANDS-ON TASK

L ▶ Gruppengespräche und Diskussionen führen (p. 122)
L ▶ Die Arbeitsergebnisse präsentieren (p. 119)

1. Discuss which areas of politics you think should be included in the manifesto. Regarding which issues are politicians out of touch with the needs and wishes of young people?
2. Once you have decided which ideas to include, write your manifesto. Use the following phrases to help you:

   We firmly believe that …
   It is our strong belief that …
   We call upon politicians to …
   The time has come for …
   If politicians are to reconnect with young people, they will have to …

3. Now present your manifesto to the rest of the class.

TEXT 2 The Most Powerful Leader in the World

WARM-UP

1

2

3

4

5

1

How much do you know about the president of the United States?

1 Match the names of the presidents (a–e) with the photos (1–5).

a George Washington c John F Kennedy e George W Bush
b Abraham Lincoln d George H W Bush

2 Which of the following has never been president of the United States?

a Franklin D. Roosevelt b Dick Cheney c Jimmy Carter

3 Historically the president has always come from one of the two main political parties in the US. What are they?

a Democrats and Republicans
b Labour and Conservative
c Democratic Republicans and Republican Democrats

4 When in Washington, the president lives in:

a the Pentagon b Camp David c the White House

5 Which president once said to a crowd in Berlin, "Ich bin ein Berliner"?

a Bill Clinton b John F Kennedy c Ronald Reagan

6 Who was the first black president of the United States?

a Jessie Jackson
b Martin Luther King
c There has never been a black president of the United States.

7 How long is the term in office of a US president?

a 4 years b 5 years c 6 years

8 How many terms in office can a US president serve?

a one b two c three

2 a Work with a partner and make a list of the personal qualities and other requirements that you think are needed to become president of the United States.

ambitious, has to know what he/she wants, has to have good connections ...

b Now read the text on the opposite page quickly. Were any of the he points on your list mentioned in it?

L ▸ Lesen schwieriger Texte: Grobverständnis (p. 108)

How to Become President of the United States

American kids grow up hearing that anyone can become president, but so far fewer than 50 people have done it (and they've all been white men). You need drive, charisma, money and backing – not to mention experience, diplomacy, connections, cunning and a commanding knowledge of foreign and domestic issues.

STEP 1
Be at least 35 years old and a citizen born in the United States, Guam, Puerto Rico or the U.S. Virgin Islands (or to American parents abroad). You also need to have been a U.S. resident for at least 14 years.

STEP 2
Hold a law degree. Out of 43 presidents, 25 have been lawyers. It also helps to have government service on your résumé – 17 governors, 15 senators and 19 members of the House of Representatives have become president.

STEP 3
Start raising money – lots of it. You've got a long way to go. The Bush-Cheney ticket, for example, spent $186 million campaigning in 2000.

STEP 4
Gather a bright, devoted and tireless campaign staff, including strategists, spokespeople and speechwriters.

STEP 5
Campaign like crazy before and during your party's primaries and caucuses. They begin in January of each election year.

STEP 6
Name your running mate. When you look at potential candidates for vice president, take into consideration the voting block he or she is supported by and can help deliver (the South, the labor vote, women, senior citizens, military veterans). If your experience is weak in certain areas, your running mate can strengthen it with his or her own background. The bottom line is – pick someone who would be a good president should you die or otherwise leave office.

STEP 7
Win the majority of delegates who will vote at your party's national convention. If you don't have more than half in your camp going into the convention, work on the unpledged delegates. These include high-ranking party members, governors and congressional representatives.

STEP 8
Celebrate your convention victory, and campaign like crazy all over the country until elections in November.

STEP 9
Win a majority of the electoral college, which isn't the same thing as the popular vote*. There are 538 electoral votes, and you need 270 of them to become president.

STEP 10
Practice reciting the oath for the inauguration ceremony on January 20: "I do solemnly swear (or affirm) that I will faithfully execute the office of President of the United States, and will to the best of my ability preserve, protect and defend the Constitution of the United States."

(418 words)

Source: www.ehow.com

*The voters who take part in the November election do not directly elect the new president. Instead their votes determine the make-up of the electoral college, a body consisting of 538 electors. It is this electoral college that goes on to vote for the new president 41 days later and their votes represent the wishes of the ordinary people (the popular vote).

CD 2 Track 11

3 backing *Unterstützung*
4 cunning *Schläue*
commanding *hier: umfassend*
domestic *inner/e/s, inländisch*
14 degree *Universitätsabschluss*
17 résumé *Lebenslauf*
22 raise *hier: sammeln*
24 ticket *Wahlliste*
25 campaign *Wahlkampf machen*
27 bright *klug, intelligent*
devoted *begeistert*
29 spokespeople *Sprecher (Pl.)*
32 primary *Vorwahl*
33 caucus *Parteikonferenz zur Wahlvorbereitung*
36 running mate *Vizekandidat*
39 voting block *Wählerstamm*
40 deliver *hier: mitbringen*
41 labor vote *die Arbeiterstimmen*
45 the bottom line *das Entscheidende*
51 national convention *Nominierungsparteitag*
54 unpledged *(noch) nicht verpflichtet*
55 high-ranking *hochrangig*
63 electoral college *Wahlmännergremium*
65 popular vote *Gesamtzahl der abgegebenen Stimmen bundesweit*
electoral vote *Stimmen der Wahlmänner*
69 recite *aufsagen*
oath *Eid*
70 inauguration ceremony *Amtseinführungszeremonie*
71 solemn *hier: aufrichtig*
swear *schwören*
affirm *bekräftigen*
72 execute an office *ein Amt ausüben*

WORKING WITH THE TEXT

L ▶ Lesen schwieriger Texte: Detailverständnis (p. 108)

3 **Put the stages of how to become president in the order mentioned in the text.**

a Work on ensuring support at the national gathering of your party which will finally choose who will be the presidential candidate.
b Build up your campaign before the first important gatherings of your party.
c Build up support among ordinary voters who will choose electors to represent them at the presidential election.
d Ensure that your campaign has the right people around it.
e Announce who will campaign alongside you for the office of vice-president.
f Make sure that you have enough money to run your campaign.

4 **Read between the lines.**

1 Why might it be helpful to have been a lawyer or have held a political post before becoming president?
2 What do you think the large amounts of money are spent on during presidential campaigns?

MEDIATION

L ▶ Mediation (p. 122)

5 **With a partner, take turns to summarise in German steps 1–10 for a friend who does not understand English.**

WORKING WITH WORDS

6 **Find the English expressions in the text for these German words.**

1 Regierung
2 Wahlkampf
3 Wahl
4 Kandidaten
5 Stimme
6 Mehrheit
7 Sieg
8 Verfassung

7 a **Match the words on the left with those on the right to make two-word expressions used in the text. Read the text again to check your answers.**

1 domestic	**a** mate
2 campaign	**b** convention
3 running	**c** vote
4 voting	**d** issues
5 national	**e** ceremony
6 popular	**f** staff
7 inauguration	**g** block

b **Now match the two-word phrases to the definitions.**

1 the candidate for the vice-presidency
2 a gathering of a political party involving people from all over the country
3 the election among the general population
4 the event at which the president is sworn into office
5 the subjects which are of importance at home in the US
6 a section of the electorate
7 the team of people who help a presidential candidate

DISCUSSION

8 **Work in a small group and discuss the differences between the two election campaigns shown in the photos.**

L ▶ Gruppengespräche und Diskussionen führen (p. 122)

INFO-BOX

The American System of Government

The United States is governed not only by the president and his administration – the executive branch of government – but also by Congress; the legislative branch. This consists of the House of Representatives and the Senate. The members of both these Houses of Congress are elected at state level and represent the interests of the people who live in their states.

The president is elected separately from Congress. This can lead to the situation where the majority in Congress comes from a different party than the president. If this is the case, the president must work hard to convince Congress to pass the laws he wants to introduce. Congress can make its own laws which the president can veto if he does not agree with them. However, Congress can ignore a presidential veto if two-thirds of its members agree with this. When the president and the congressional majority belong to different parties, it is clear that political compromise is extremely important, otherwise government could come to a standstill.

Finally comes the judicial branch which is headed by the Supreme Court. Its task is to interpret laws, re-interpret them as circumstances in the country change and to decide whether laws are in line with the constitution. In the 1960s the Supreme Court famously decided that the laws which segregated black people from white American society were unconstitutional, creating the legal framework for the success of the civil rights movement.

The president exercises some control over the Supreme Court in that he appoints its judges. However, the appointment of Supreme Court judges is subject to approval by the Senate which once again holds in check the power of the president.

8 pass a law *ein Gesetz verabschieden*
9 veto *sein Veto einlegen gegen*
17 segregate *trennen*
20 exercise *ausüben*
appoint *ernennen*
21 be subject to sth *einer Sache unterliegen*
approval *Genehmigung*
22 hold in check *unter Kontrolle halten*

GIVING A PRESENTATION

9 **In small groups, use the information about how a president is selected and elected in this unit to prepare a presentation about this process. Then give your presentation to the class.**

HANDS-ON TASK

L ▶ Die Arbeitsergebnisse präsentieren (p. 119)

TEXT 3 The British Electoral System

WARM-UP

1 Work with a partner and match the definitions (a–d) to the words written in *italics* in sentences 1–9.

a the places where people go to vote
b the day on which an election is held
c the person in charge of an election at a local constituency level
d Members of parliament – the candidates elected to represent people locally

1 It is now clear which party has the majority of *MPs* in parliament.
2 It's the day of the general election. *Polling day* is always a Thursday in Britain.
3 *Polling stations* close at 9 pm on election day.
4 The Queen invites the leader of the party with the majority of seats in parliament to form a government.
5 The votes are counted in all the constituencies across the country.
6 The *returning officer* in each constituency announces the results of the election there.
7 The Prime Minister calls the general election and sets a date for it.
8 After some days the Prime Minister announces which MPs will get jobs in the government.
9 Political parties campaign to have their candidates elected to parliament.

2 Now put the sentences in the right order to make a flow chart of the British general election process.

CD 2 Track 12

How the British Elect Their Governments

The British electoral system is based on "First-Past-The-Post" (FPTP) rather than on "proportional representation" (PR). The candidate who wins the highest number of votes within a constituency wins that election. FPTP is as clear and as brutal as that. This is in contrast to PR under which other parties that get fewer votes can also receive a share in political power.

Take these election results as an example. The main candidates are from the three most prominent national parties. The result is as follows:

Brian Stevens (Labour):	22,000 votes
Clara Norton (Tory):	17,000 votes
John Cuthbert (Liberal Democrats):	13,000 votes

In this example, the winner is Brian Stevens with a majority over Clara Norton of 5,000 votes. He gets a job in Westminster as the MP although the majority of people voted against him. Clara Norton and John Cuthbert have to look for other jobs or try again to get elected at a future election!
As the example shows, FPTP throws "democratic elections" into question. After all, the party with the simple majority of seats in the House of Commons forms

[2] proportional representation *Verhältniswahlrecht*
[3] constituency *Wahlkreis*

the Government. If most of the electorate across a high proportion of constituencies do not actually vote for the person who becomes their MP, can this be said to be democratic? Are these voters actually democratically represented in Westminster?

In Britain the situation where the majority vote against the eventual winner of an election is common. The same is true at the national level. In fact, no government since 1935 has had a majority of public support as expressed through total votes cast.

The results of the 1997 general election graphically illustrate the situation. The victorious Labour Party gained 43.2% of the total votes cast and won 63.6% of seats at Westminster. The combined number of votes for the Tory and Liberal Democrats represented 47.5% of the total votes (nearly 4% more than Labour) yet between them they got 32.1% of the seats available at Westminster. The figures clearly demonstrate why some people think that FPTP is 'undemocratic'.

However, FPTP has created within Great Britain a political system that is essentially stable, as politics is dominated by just two parties. The political instability created by the proportional representation systems of Italy and Israel, where governments are very unstable, is avoided using FPTP. Minority governments have occurred in the UK using FPTP, but the lifespan of those governments was limited. In recent years, governments have been strong as a result of the clear mandate given to them using the FPTP system. (421 words)

Source: www.historylearningsite.co.uk

22 electorate *Wählerschaft*
27 eventual *letztendlich*
32 cast one's vote *seine Stimme abgeben*
35 victorious *siegreich*
41 essentially *im Wesentlichen*
44 occur *vorkommen*

WORKING WITH THE TEXT

3 Which statement best summarises what the text says?

L ▸ Lesen schwieriger Texte: Grobverständnis (p. 108)

1 The British system is the fairest, most democratic way of electing a government in the world.
2 It is questionable how democratic and representative the British system is but it generally leads to political stability.
3 The British electoral system leads to stability but should be reformed because it does not allow voters to be fairly represented in parliament.

4 Read between the lines.

L ▸ Lesen schwieriger Texte: Detailverständnis (p. 108)

1 Is it likely that candidates from smaller political parties in Britain stand a strong chance of being elected to parliament?
2 Why might politicians in Italy or Israel argue that their political systems are more democratic and representative despite the instability they cause?
3 List the arguments for and against the British system of FPTP in the text. Can you think of any further arguments?

MEDIATION

5 Explain FPTP and its advantages and disadvantages in German for the politics section of a website for teenagers.

L ▸ Mediation (p. 122)

GAPPED SUMMARY

6 **Complete the following short summary of the text with suitable words from the text. One of the words can be used more than once.**

> Under …[1] the candidate with the …[2] number of votes in a constituency goes on to become …[3], whereas under …[4] parties which do not win the majority of constituencies can also have a share in political power. In Britain the …[5] with the greatest number of MPs in the House of Commons forms the …[6]. Some people question whether under FPTP the …[7] of people are …[8] represented. These feelings are understandable – since 1935 no British government has received a majority of all the …[9] cast. But the system has created political stability and governments which do not have the …[10] of MPs in …[11] generally do not stay in power long.

DISCUSSION

L ▸ Gruppengespräche und Diskussionen führen (p. 122)

7 **Work in a group and discuss which features of the British electoral system are different from that in Germany.**

6 legislation *Gesetzgebung*
12 noble *adlig*
13 hereditary *erblich*
16 peerage *Adelsstand*
retain *bewahren*
19 scrap *abschaffen*

INFO

The House of Lords

Parliamentary elections in Britain are held to select the MPs who will sit in the House of Commons (the lower house of Parliament). However, there is a further source of political power at Westminster, the members of which are not elected. This is the House of Lords (the upper house of Parliament).

The Lords play an important role in the making of new laws in Britain. Most pieces of legislation proposed by the government are considered not only by the Commons but also by the Lords. The latter have the power to stop legislation becoming law if they disapprove of it, though these powers are limited in areas such as legislation about public finance.

The House of Lords has, in contrast to the lower house's 646 MPs, 731 members and draws its membership from several sources. Traditionally, the bulk of members were of noble birth and took their seat in the Lords automatically. They are referred to as Hereditary Peers. Then there are Life Peers – members of the Lords who are appointed by the government. Finally, a small percentage of the Lords' membership is made up of senior churchmen and judges. There is ongoing debate in Britain as to whether hereditary peerages should be retained. The general tendency of reform of the House of Lords is towards replacing these with life peerages.

The considerable political power of the Lords leads many in Britain to suggest that the upper house should be scrapped altogether. They see it as having no legitimate right to exist and to exercise power because it is unelected. However, few people would argue that there is no need for a second chamber at Westminster. The second chamber plays an important role in increasing the amount of consideration given to legislation. As a result it prevents the House of Commons from becoming too powerful. The solution generally proposed is that the Lords should be replaced with an elected second chamber.

While there is uncertainty, then, about the future of the House of Lords, it is very likely that the existing upper house will be retained, though in a somewhat more democratic form.

WORKING WITH WORDS

8 **The following word pairs are often mixed up. Complete the sentences by choosing the correct words. Take care to put them in their correct form.**

1 *current – actual*

a Chris Sackmore is … a Liberal Democrat MP. He used to be a Labour MP.

b I thought I was going to get a majority of only a few hundred in the election but my … majority was almost 3,000!

c So the … situation is that the government have a commons majority of 143 MPs. But after the general election tomorrow that could all change.

2 *eventual – possible*

a Certainly, the new government will … look at reforming the electoral system. But that will not be for some time and we will continue with first-past-the-post for the foreseeable future.

b It is … the case that the government has not spent enough on education and we will look at changing this.

c I am against electoral reform. The … outcome of it would, almost definitely, be political instability.

3 *become – get*

a Steve Norman … 18,000 votes in the general election.

b If I … MP for this constituency, I promise to spend more time here – and less at Westminster – than our last MP!

c He's just had a meeting with the Prime Minister. He … a warning for voting against the government last week.

LISTENING

9 a **Copy the table into your exercise book then listen to the election night news programme and complete the table. Listen again to check your answers.**

CD 2 Track 13

b **Which party do you think has most cause to complain about first-past-the-post after this election and why?**

L ▸ Das Hörverständnis üben (p. 111)

Results of the 2005 General Election

Party	Seats	Gains	Losses	Seats %	Votes %	Votes
Labour	…	0	…	…	35.3	…
Conservative	…	…	…	30.7	…	8,772,598
Liberal Democrats	62	…	…	…	…	5,981,874

c **Now work with a partner and take turns to explain to each other the statistics in the table.**

L ▸ Interpretation von Grafiken, Diagrammen und Tabellen (p. 121)

WRITING

10 **Do you think the British electoral system is democratic or undemocratic? Write a letter to the Prime Minister expressing your views on the subject. Use the following language to help you:**

L ▸ Einen Text sinnvoll gliedern (p. 118)

Dear Mr / Mrs / Ms …,
I am writing to …
In my view …
I also feel that …
In conclusion, I would like to point out that …
Yours sincerely,

TEXT 4 Putting Politics Online

WARM-UP

1 **Voters can communicate to governments what they think in a number of ways. Work in a small group and make as long a list of these as possible. Use the photographs to help you get started.**

L ▶ Lesen schwieriger Texte: Grobverständnis (p. 108)

2 **Read the text quickly and choose the best headline for it.**

a **Government Planned to Abandon E-petitions**

b **Despite Problems, Government Remained Positive About E-petitions**

c **Despite Government Efforts, Public Were Uninterested in E-petitions**

CD 2 Track 14

In the past, Britons who wanted to make a point to government normally had only one way of doing it – a long walk along Downing Street to hand in their earnestly gathered petition. Either that, or wait for polling day. Then came e-petitions – and with them a very different means of lobbying. In its first few months, No. 10's e-petition website racked up more than 3,700 petitions on subjects ranging from health service cutbacks to road pricing.

Previously, the Government had never been obliged to disclose details of the petitions it received. But what began as an exercise in openness became something with the ability to cause some serious embarrassment. For example, a large number of petitions called for action against Tony Blair over Iraq, and then there was the "just go now" petition submitted by a political blogger.

Ministers were forced to defend plans for the introduction of road-pricing schemes after a petition calling for the idea to be scrapped topped the one million-signature

1 make a point *ein Anliegen vorbringen*
3 earnest *gewissenhaft*
polling day *Wahltag*
5 rack sth up *auf etw kommen*
6 cutback *Kürzung*
7 oblige *verpflichten*
disclose *bekannt geben*
9 embarrassment *Peinlichkeit*
11 submit *einreichen*

mark. The Association of British Drivers claimed that the petition represented only a small proportion of the motorists opposed to road charging.

Douglas Alexander, the Transport Secretary, stood by his plans for road pricing, but he stressed that the scale of the response showed the need for more debate.

The road-pricing petition was by far the most popular on the site in its first months. Scrapping inheritance tax had 46,000 signatures and repealing the Hunting Act was backed by 23,000. There was even a petition with 2,874 signatures which demanded that the pop group Spandau Ballet's "Gold" became the new national anthem.

At one point in 2007, there were more than 2,800 active petitions, which could run up to a year, 290 of which had been closed and more than 600 of which had been rejected. The petitions graphically illustrated the vast range of concerns troubling British citizens.

The government remained sanguine about e-petitions. A spokesman said, "e-petitions are an important innovation. They allow members of the public to express views directly to Downing Street and in turn enable Downing Street to more easily communicate with petitioners."

However, not everyone saw it that way. This was illustrated by a petition that called for an end to petitions. It was backed by seven people. (378 words)

Adapted from *The Independent*, 12 February 2007

15 be opposed to sth *gegen etw sein*
17 response *Reaktion*
19 inheritance *Erbschaft*
repeal *aufheben*
22 national anthem *Nationalhymne*
26 trouble *beunruhigen*
27 sanguine *zuversichtlich*

WORKING WITH THE TEXT

3 Which of the statements about the text are true, false or unclear? Correct the false statements.

L ▶ Lesen schwieriger Texte: Suche nach Einzelinformationen (p. 108)

1. In the past, petitions were collected on paper and taken to the Prime Minister.
2. After the introduction of e-petitions the government received more petitions than ever before.
3. Before e-petitions, the British Government always had to make public details of the petitions it received.
4. None of the e-petitions were problematic for the government.
5. Douglas Alexander decided not to abandon road pricing after the petition.
6. The anti-road-pricing petition was only slightly more popular than other petitions on the site.
7. Once accepted, a petition could remain on the site for a year.
8. The government continued to be positive and optimistic about e-petitions.

4 Write a summary in English of what the text says.

L ▶ Einen Text zusammenfassen (p. 116)

5 Read between the lines.

L ▶ Lesen schwieriger Texte: Detailverständnis (p. 108)

1. Explain the British government's probable aim when it launched e-petitions.
2. Classify the e-petitions mentioned in the text as serious or non-serious. Give reasons.
3. Find evidence in the text that suggests that not everyone who supports a particular petition signs it.
4. Describe the government's reactions to e-petitions.
5. Think of possible reasons why petitions might be rejected.

DISCUSSION

L ▸ Gruppengespräche und Diskussionen führen (p. 122)

6 **Which of these views do you agree with more and why?**

Using the Internet to communicate with voters is a positive development and will increase in the future, probably replacing more traditional communication between governments and the people they serve.

Using the Internet to communicate with voters is just an attempt by governments to be trendy. It probably does not have a long-term future because the traditional means of communication are better.

INFO

Public Access to Political Decision-Makers in the UK

In Britain, there is a common saying which runs along the lines that "the only time a politician is interested in speaking to normal people is at election time." According to this view, after an election is over, MPs disappear back to Westminster only to be seen again before the next election. In the meantime, ordinary people just have to sit back and wait – or raise a petition.

This, however, is not the case. MPs in Britain perform two important functions. Obviously, they work in the Houses of Parliament considering and contributing to government legislation. On Fridays, however, business is usually concluded at lunch-time in order to allow MPs to perform their other important role – making themselves available to the people who live in their constituencies.

Most MPs, then, make their way back to their constituencies on Friday afternoons so that they can be approached by their constituents at their Saturday 'surgeries'. These are open-door sessions to which constituents can bring their questions and problems. This is the primary means by which ordinary voters in the UK can get direct access to their MP and, therefore, to the political establishment. Of course, people can also write to their MP asking for assistance – letters can be addressed either to an MP's office in Westminster or his/her constituency office.

12 surgery *Sprechstunde*

People use this open access to MPs to put political questions to them. Alternatively, MPs are often approached by people seeking help with problems. MPs are more or less obliged to help constituents who are experiencing difficulties connected with state services such as public health, education or housing.

If somebody believes that they have received a poor quality of service from their MP – or if they wish to complain about unfair or poor services from central government without going to their MP – they can take their case to the Parliamentary Ombudsman. This is an organisation which can carry out independent investigations into complaints about government and/or MPs made by the public.

WORKING WITH THE DICTIONARY

L ▸ Umgang mit unbekannten Vokabeln (p. 109)

7 a **Use your dictionary to look up the meanings of any of the words (a–i) which you do not understand. Then match them to the underlined words in the sentences on the opposite page.**

a abandon **b** require **c** way **d** submit **e** positive **f** illustrate **g** defend **h** size **i** generate

b **Now use your dictionary to find synonyms for as many of the remaining words in the sentences as possible. Rewrite the sentences using the words a–i and your own synonyms.**

1 Voting in elections is the most powerful means of communicating with politicians.
2 The Iraq war racked up more complaints against Tony Blair than any other issue.
3 In Britain you are not obliged to vote in elections.
4 The pressure group Give Africa a Chance have handed in a four million-signature petition to the government. It called for debt repayments to be scrapped.
5 Tony Blair stood by his involvement in the Iraq war.
6 Not even the scale of the demonstrations against the war made him change his mind.
7 But the demonstrations show how unpopular the war was.
8 Even after the US and Britain won the war, many people were not sanguine about the future in Iraq.

WRITING

8 a **Use the information on pages 98–100 to make a mind map of all the different ways in which people can get in contact with politicians.**

b **Write a composition outlining the different methods for contacting politicians in Britain, as well as the advantages and disadvantages of each of these methods.**

L ▸ Mind Mapping (p. 114)
L ▸ Einen Aufsatz schreiben (p. 117)

HOLDING A CLASSROOM DEBATE

HANDS-ON TASK

L ▸ Gruppengespräche und Diskussionen führen (p. 122)

9 **Work with a partner to complete the following tasks.**

1 Read the example petitions.

http://petitions.pm.gov.uk/list/open?cat=439

We, the undersigned, believe that the Iraq war should be ended and call upon the British government to withdraw British troops from Iraq immediately. **More details**
Submitted by Pete Holt – **Deadline to sign up by:** 26 December 2008 – **Signatures:** 674,233

We, the undersigned, believe that there are not enough cycle paths in British cities and call upon the British government to take action to increase facilities for cyclists with immediate effect. **More details**
Submitted by Laura Thubron – **Deadline to sign up by:** 11 July 2007 – **Signatures:** 72,476

2 Talk with your partner to find out which political issues you both agree on. Choose one issue and write a petition to the government about it. Use the following language:

We, the undersigned, believe that …	is inadequate … is in need of reform … should be increased/decreased … should be brought to an end …	and call upon the government to …	increase … decrease … take action … act …	immediately. with immediate effect. as soon as is possible.

3 Now debate the petitions with the whole class. Each short debate should end with a vote to establish what the class thinks about the petitions.

TEXT 5 Politics and Personal Responsibility

WARM-UP

L ▸ Gruppengespräche und Diskussionen führen (p. 122)

1 a Work in a small group and read the list of things that some people do to live 'ethically'. Choose the three items from the list you think are most important and say why. If you think none of the items are important, explain why not.

a Buying things second-hand rather than new so that products have a longer life
b Recycling glass, paper and plastics
c Eating organic food
d Travelling by bicycle whenever possible
e Buying 'fair trade' products
f Not travelling by plane whenever possible

b Who do you think should be responsible when it comes to 'ethical' issues like these – the government or individuals?

c How many other things that help to save the environment could you take responsibility for? Make a list.

WORKING WITH THE TEXT

L ▸ Lesen schwieriger Texte: Grobverständnis (p. 108)

2 Read the text and match the headings 1–5 to the correct paragraphs (A–E).

1 Taking the challenge
2 It's a strange and sad world
3 Some important questions
4 What was the plan?
5 And what do I do?

CD 2 Track 15

A Life Stripped Bare

A We are all struck at some point in our lives by the need to answer some of life's Big Questions: Who am I? What am I doing with my life? Is this it? Am I a good person? And what is it, I have wondered, that stops me from getting up out of my chair and doing something that might actually prove to be a positive force – however insignificant – on the world?

B The paradox of our Western lifestyle, of course, is not that we are unaware of the negative impact it has on ourselves, our neighbours and the environment, but that we choose to journey on anyway, blinded by a convenient fog of apathy. I can't get through a day, it seems, without reading newspaper stories about mercury-filled salmon, deodorants being linked to cancer, and increasing levels of social exclusion and inequality. I gasp at the facts about our wasteful and self-obsessed lives. Here are some of those facts. Globally, US$33 billion is spent on make-up and perfume annually. Just US$29 billion a year would be required to end hunger and provide clean water to all. The US has more private vehicles on the road than people licensed to drive them. Half the world's population survive on the equivalent of two dollars a day – less than I spend on a coffee on the way to work.

C But I prefer to take my daughter out for a walk round the park rather than dwell too long on all that nasty, negative stuff. Besides, what can I do about it all, anyway? That's why we vote, isn't it?

bare *nackt*
1 be struck by sth *jdn überkommen*
7 impact *Auswirkung*
8 convenient *bequem*
10 mercury *Quecksilber*
salmon *Lachs*
11 gasp *den Atem verschlagen*
wasteful *verschwenderisch*
self-obsessed *egozentrisch*
19 dwell on sth *sich den Kopf über etw zerbrechen*
nasty *scheußlich*

D It was against this backdrop that I was set a challenge by the *Guardian*, where I work as a journalist. Could I take a step back from my daily habits and consumer choices, and try to understand their true impact? Could I, over the course of a few months, start to lead a more 'ethical' life, in which I reduced, to use a popular expression, my 'footprint on the earth', as well as being a more positive force both to myself and those around me? Could I join the small but growing proportion of society striving to live more thoughtfully and less wastefully; those who, according to the Ethical Consumerism Report 2004, pushed sales of organic food well over the billion pound mark, up from £390 million in 1999, and who in 2003 spent £24.7 billion on a wide range of ethical purchases, from free-range eggs to A-rated energy efficient appliances?

E This wasn't to be an exercise in dropping out and taking up life as a hermit on a small farm in the Scottish Highlands. I wouldn't have a manifesto as such pinned to my fridge for constant reference; the idea was simply to see where the journey would lead me. (467 words)

Adapted from: Leo Hickman, *A Life Stripped Bare*, 2005

21 backdrop *Hintergrund*
challenge *Herausforderung*
27 strive *nach etw streben*
28 consumerism *Konsumverhalten*
30 purchase *Kauf*
free-range *frei laufend*
31 appliance *Gerät*
32 hermit *Einsiedler/in*

3 Read the text and complete the tasks.

L ▸ Lesen schwieriger Texte: Detailverständnis (p. 108)

1 List in your own words the general factors which motivated the author to try to live 'ethically'.
2 Explain the paradox in our lifestyle identified by the author.
3 Interpret the facts that the author uses to illustrate the wastefulness of our lives.
4 Analyse the significance of the figures provided by the author about sales of organic food between 1999 and 2003.
5 Describe in your own words the approach taken by the author to his new life and the approaches he rejected.

4 Read between the lines.

1 What stopped the author from changing his lifestyle before he took the 'ethical' challenge?
2 What do you think 'ethical consumerism' is?

5 What do you think?

L ▸ Gruppengespräche und Diskussionen führen (p. 122)
L ▸ Eine Stellungnahme schreiben (p. 115)

If you want to make the world a better place, you have to tell politicians what you think. You have to shout it loud. There's no point in just buying organic tomatoes and hoping that this will make a difference.

Nonsense! Protesting about the way the world is just doesn't work. Nobody listens. You have to use your power as a consumer to make a real difference. Ethical consumerism really makes a difference. Talking and hot air don't.

WORKING WITH WORDS

6 a Match 1–6 with a–f to make expressions from the text. Read the text again to check your answers.

1	positive	**a**	habits
2	negative	**b**	choices
3	social	**c**	force
4	social	**d**	inequality
5	daily	**e**	impact
6	consumer	**f**	exclusion

b Use the expressions to complete the sentences. Two of them are not used.

1 We need to change our … and do something every day which is good for the environment.
2 … can be a big problem among immigrants who cannot participate fully in society.
3 These days we have so many more … . There's so much to buy in the shops!
4 In the past people did not know about the … of smoking on their health.

c Now write sentences using the remaining two expressions.

consumption *Konsum*
7 straightforward *einfach*
20 (to) verify *nachweisen*

FAIRTRADE
Guarantees a **better deal** for Third World Producers

Look for this mark on Fairtrade products
www.fairtrade.org.uk

INFO

Ethical Consumption

In recent years, there has been a growing awareness in the developed, western world of the impact that our shopping habits have, both on the environment and on the people who make the things we buy. Ethical consumption is an increasingly popular way of addressing these problems. The basic idea behind it is that buying goods which are environmentally friendly and produced by people who are paid fairly for making them will have a real impact, reducing environmental damage and poverty.

This may seem straightforward enough but it can be quite difficult in practice. Consumers who decide to shop ethically have to inform themselves about the products they buy. For example, they have to know where and how goods and foodstuffs were produced. This information is not always provided in full on product packaging.

Then there are one or two dilemmas that have to be sorted out. For example, should you buy that organic watermelon grown in Zimbabwe? It's good that it's organic but then it has to be transported almost halfway around the world, which in itself has a negative impact on the environment. On the other hand, if you don't buy it on the basis that it's better to buy organic food produced locally, organic farmers in Zimbabwe may go out of business.

Fortunately for consumers who want to shop ethically there are now some standards in place which should guide their choices and make ethical consumption a little easier. For example, the FAIRTRADE Mark, which appears on the packaging of a growing range of products, verifies that the people who produced the goods in question received fair payment for them plus a premium payment for community development projects. Then, of course, there are the labels which verify that foodstuffs have been grown and processed organically.

Ethical consumption is growing quite rapidly and is no longer confined to small health food or organic shops. Indeed, such is the popularity of the idea that large, mainstream food retailers in Britain and the US are actively promoting Fairtrade certified and organic labelled products. Whether or not you have thought about ethical consumption yet, it's coming to a supermarket near you.

TRANSLATION AND MEDIATION

8 **a Translate the first paragraph of the info box on page 104 into German. Watch out for gerunds and participles.**

b Explain in German what ethical consumption is and what has to be considered when deciding to 'shop ethically'.

L ▶ Übersetzung (p. 123)
G ▶ Gerunds (p. 133), Participle constructions (p. 137)
L ▶ Mediation (p. 122)

LISTENING

9 **a The text's author's attempt to live ethically was only supposed to last a year. Which statement do you think is most likely to have summed up his feelings at the end of the year?**

1 "I couldn't wait to give up all that ethical living stuff when the year was over."
2 "Of course, I have learned a lot from this and will try hard to think about my consumer choices in the future. But there are some things that I just can't give up permanently, such as flying."
3 "I'm committed to living ethically now and will never do anything harmful to the world again."

b Now listen to what he had to say at the end of the year to check if you were correct.

CD 2 Track 16

L ▶ Das Hörverständnis üben (p. 111)

GIVING A PRESENTATION AND HOLDING A CLASSROOM DEBATE

10 **Work in small groups to complete the following tasks.**

HANDS-ON TASK

1 You are going to take part in a debate about whether ethical consumption can make a difference in the world. Your teacher will tell your group whether you are going to argue 'for' or 'against'.

2 Split the following points into two lists: arguments for the effectiveness of ethical consumption and arguments against. Add your own ideas.
a it makes politicians realise how important environmental and ethical issues are to people
b there are too many examples in the past of 'ethical' products which turned out to be not ethical at all – how do we know things are really ethical just because it says on the pack they are?
c it makes us think about what we buy, leading us to buy less
d it means that people think less about politics which is what really changes things
e it makes you feel good about yourself
f it creates markets for products which are produced in an ethical way
g it is undemocratic because ethical products are generally more expensive which means that people with less money cannot take part in 'making a difference' through ethical consumption
h it forces companies to make their products in a more environmentally friendly way

3 Prepare a short presentation of your arguments.

4 Give your presentation and carry out the debate. Finally, hold a vote in the class to find out what the majority of people think.

L ▶ Die Arbeitsergebnisse präsentieren (p. 119)
L ▶ Gruppengespräche und Diskussionen führen (p. 122)

ROLE CARDS

(Topic 1, Text 3, Exercise 11)

Parent

You trust your son/daughter but do not want him/her to wear a hoodie to school. You have seen a lot of reports on television which say that hoodie-wearing teenagers often commit petty crimes. Though you do not think your son/daughter would do such a thing, you are worried about what teachers at the school will say about him/her. You want him/her to do well at school and do not want anything to create a negative impression among teachers. You are also worried that, by wearing a hoodie, he/she will make friends with teenagers who you do not trust.
You know your child is not a troublemaker, but …

Useful language

Look, there's something I want to talk to you about.
I don't want to tell you what to wear to school, but …
Can we talk this over calmly like adults?
Come on. Let's not fall out about this.
There's no need to talk to me like that.
We're just a bit worried that …
I know that you're really very sensible but …
It's just that …
Listen, how about this for an idea?
Couldn't you / Why don't you …?

Son/daughter

You want to wear your hoodie to school because you really like it and the way it makes you look. Anyway, many of your school friends wear their hoodies and you do not see why you should look different. You are angry that your parents think that, by wearing a hoodie, you will get a bad reputation. You try hard with your school work and stay away from teenagers who cause trouble. You want your parents to let you be an individual and choose your own clothes for school. But how?

Useful language

What's up? / What's the matter?
I can't believe you think this is a problem.
Look, it's none of your business, is it?
I wear my hoodie because I like it. Nothing else.
My hoodie doesn't make me a troublemaker.
I try really hard at school. You should be proud of me.
It's not my fault if some kids who wear hoodies get into trouble.
Wasn't it just the same with other clothes when you were at school?
You're not letting me make my own mind up.
I don't want you to get annoyed, but this is my decision.

LERNSTRATEGIEN

Übersicht über die Lernstrategien

REZEPTION

Lesen schwieriger Texte

Texte werden zu unterschiedlichen Zwecken gelesen. Manchmal braucht man nur zu wissen, worum es geht, dann reicht in der Regel ein aufmerksames Überfliegen des Textes. Oft müssen gezielt Informationen herausgesucht werden, dann kommt es darauf an, die richtigen Schlüsselwörter zu finden. Will man sich gründlich mit einem Text auseinandersetzen, um z. B. Fragen zu beantworten oder einen Aufsatz dazu zu schreiben, ist gründliches, möglicherweile zweimaliges Lesen erforderlich.

Grobverständnis: Sich einen schnellen Überblick über einen Text verschaffen

Manchmal werden Sie im Buch aufgefordert, einen Text schnell zu lesen, um das Thema grob zu erfassen.

1. Schritt: Suchen Sie nach Anhaltspunkten, die Ihnen Aufschluss über den Textinhalt geben: Titel und Zwischenüberschriften, fett gedruckte Wörter, Bilder und Bildunterschriften.

2. Schritt: Sind Sie noch unsicher, lesen Sie die ersten und letzten Sätze jedes Absatzes. Bleiben Sie nicht an Einzelwörtern, schwierigen Zitaten usw. hängen.

Suche nach Einzelinformationen im Text

Bei vielen Textverständnisfragen oder Aufgaben vom Typ *True or false* geht es darum, schnell die gesuchte Information im Text zu finden und nicht jedesmal den ganzen Text neu zu lesen.

1. Schritt: Suchen Sie den Text nach Schlüsselbegriffen für die gesuchten Informationen ab. Geht es etwa um die Meinung des Autors zu einem bestimmten Thema, halten Sie nach Wörtern wie *think, believe, opinion* usw. Ausschau. Geht es um Informationen zu einem Thema, rufen Sie sich ein paar Schlüsselbegriffe in Erinnerung, nach denen Sie Ausschau halten. Manchmal hilft es, sich den gesuchten Begriff als gedrucktes Wort vor dem geistigen Auge vorzustellen.

2. Schritt: Gehen Sie falls nötig mit dem Finger die Zeilen entlang, während Sie suchen. Wenn Sie sich wie oben beschrieben vorbereitet haben, springen Ihnen die gesuchten Begriffe sofort ins Auge.

Detailverständnis: Gründliches Lesen

Lesen Sie nicht einfach drauflos. Ein paar einfache Schritte helfen Ihnen, den Text besser zu verstehen, ohne sich in Details zu verlieren.

1. Schritt: Der erste Schritt sollte darin bestehen, sich ein grobes Verständnis vom Textinhalt zu verschaffen (siehe oben). So werden Sie unklare Stellen besser in den Gesamtzusammenhang einordnen können. Es ist hilfreich, sich die wichtigsten Stichwörter kurz zu notieren. Zu dem Text *How to become President of the United States* auf S. 91 etwa könnten Sie nach kurzem Überfliegen aufschreiben: *The text seems to be about the procedure of presidential elections in the US. It gives an overview over the stages of the election. The tone seems to be slightly humorous.*

2. Schritt: Machen Sie sich die Struktur des Textes bewusst. Wo ist die Einleitung? Welcher Teil enthält die Hauptinformationen, und wie sind sie aufgebaut (Zwischenüberschriften, Absätze usw.)? Achten Sie auf Strukturwörter wie *only, but while, that's why, while, however* usw., mit denen der Verfasser seine Argumentation gliedert.

3. Schritt: Lesen Sie den Text nun aufmerksam. Notieren Sie sich Schlüsselstellen (z. B. im Text auf S. 91: *The Bush-Cheney ticket spent $186 million campaigning in 2000; primaries and caucuses; running mate; win the majority of delegates who will vote at your party's national convention; win a majority of the electoral college*). Schlagen Sie Wörter beim ersten Lesen nur nach, wenn die Bedeutung des ganzen Satzes an ihnen hängt. Oft lässt sich die wesentliche Bedeutung durch den Kontext erschließen.

4. Schritt: Notieren Sie sich den Textinhalt in strukturierter Form, etwa einer Mind Map oder einer Liste (Themen, pro/kontra). Fügen Sie auch Formulierungen hinzu, die Ihnen später helfen, sich in eigenen Worten über den Textinhalt zu äußern. Schlagen Sie jetzt das notwendige Vokabular nach.

▸ Note Making, S. 113
▸ Mind Mapping, S. 114

Umgang mit unbekannten Vokabeln

Fragen Sie sich bei neuen Vokabeln immer, ob sie für das Verständnis des Zusammenhangs unbedingt notwendig sind. Nachschlagen kostet Zeit und hilft oft nicht beim Verständnis des wirklich Wichtigen.

Erschließen der Bedeutung aus dem Kontext

- Ein Wort, das unbekannt scheint, kann z. B. mit einem anderen, Ihnen bekannten Wort verwandt sein (Ableitungen wie *aggressor* von *aggressive*). Oder das Wort hat einen bekannten Wortstamm und einen angehängten Wortteil, mit dessen Hilfe Sie die Bedeutung erkennen können (*formal* – ***in****formal, clockwise* – ***anti****clockwise, change* – *change****able****, stupid* – *stupid****ity***). Manche Wörter haben Ähnlichkeiten mit einem deutschen Wort (vgl. etwa *initial* und „Initialen", *potential* und „potenziell").

- Sind Sie sich immer noch nicht sicher, kann der Satzzusammenhang Aufschluss geben. Machen Sie sich zunächst die Wortart bewusst: Suchen Sie nach einem Substantiv? Wofür steht das gesuchte Substantiv wahrscheinlich – für ein Gebäude? Eine Person? Handelt es sich um ein Adjektiv, das die Situation näher beschreibt oder jemanden charakterisiert?
  Schauen Sie sich den folgenden Absatz an und versuchen Sie die Bedeutung der fett gedruckten Wörter aus dem Zusammenhang zu erschließen:
  Business is bad at the moment and we don't expect it to ***rally*** *for at least a year. All the signals are very* ***inauspicious****, I'm afraid.*

Umgang mit dem einsprachigen Wörterbuch

Machen Sie sich mit Ihrem Wörterbuch vertraut, so dass Sie die Symbole, Abkürzungen und die Lautschrift verstehen und die Hilfen, die vorne und hinten im Wörterbuch oder auf Zusatzseiten angeboten werden, nutzen können. Auf der folgenden Seite sehen Sie ein Beispiel eines typischen Wörtbucheintrags.

Wörterbucheintrag

uncountable = unzählbares Nomen

North American English = Aussprachevariante

Wortart

Erste Bedeutung

Verweis auf einen anderen Eintrag

Zweite Bedeutung

countable = zählbares Nomen

idiom = Redewendung

Synonym

verb/noun + *'to' infinitive* = zusammengesetzter Ausdruck, in dem das Verb von *to* + Infinitiv gefolgt wird

verb/noun = zusammengesetzter Ausdruck aus Verb und Nomen

> **alarm** /əˈlɑːm; *NAmE* əˈlɑːrm/ *noun, verb*
> ▪ *noun* **1** [U] fear and anxiety that sb feels when sth dangerous or unpleasant might happen: *'What have you done? Ellie cried in alarm.* ◇ *I felt a growing sense of alarm when he did not return that night.* ◇ *The doctor said there was no cause for alarm.* ⇨ note at FEAR **2** [C, usually sing.] a loud noise or a signal that warns people of danger or of a problem: *She decided to* ***sound the alarm*** (= warn people that the situation was dangerous). ◇ *I hammered on all the doors to* ***raise the alarm***. – see also FALSE ALARM **3** [C] a device that warns people of a particular danger: *a* ***burglar/fire/smoke alarm.*** ◇ *The cat* ***set off the alarm*** (= made it start ringing). ◇ *A car* ***alarm went off*** *in the middle of the night* (= started ringing). **4** = ALARM CLOCK: *The* ***alarm went off*** *at 7 o'clock.* IDM **a'larm bells ring / start ringing** if you say that **alarm bells are ringing**, you mean that people are starting to feel worried and suspicious
> ▪ *verb* **1** to make sb anxious or afraid SYN WORRY: [VN] *The captain knew there was an engine fault but didn't want to alarm the passengers.* [also VN **to** inf] ⇨ note at FRIGHTEN **2** [VN] to fit sth such as a door with a device that warns people when sb is trying to enter illegally

- Notieren Sie sich alle Wörter, deren Bedeutung Sie suchen, und schlagen Sie dann alle hintereinander nach.
- Lesen Sie nicht den gesamten Eintrag, sondern beschränken Sie sich auf die Verwendung Ihres Stichworts in der gesuchten Wortart (z. B. Sie suchen *alarm* als Verb, also ignorieren Sie den ersten Teil des oben stehenden Eintrags). Den entsprechenden Abschnitt mit allen zusammengesetzten Ausdrücken und den Beispielsätzen, die Ihnen helfen zu unterscheiden, in welchen Zusammenhängen welche Bedeutung zutrifft, müssen Sie dann allerdings gründlich lesen.
- Schauen Sie sich auch die Einträge in der unmittelbaren Umgebung Ihres Stichworts an, um eine Vorstellung von dem Wortfeld zu bekommen.
- Notieren Sie sich die passende Bedeutung, damit Sie sie nicht wieder vergessen.

Lernen neuer Vokabeln

Es gibt verschiedene Möglichkeiten, Vokabeln zu lernen – suchen Sie sich die, die Ihnen am besten liegt. Eines gilt jedoch für alle Methoden: Wörter prägen sich am besten ein, wenn man nicht nur das Stichwort aufschreibt, sondern auch noch dazugehörige Ausdrücke, Synonyme, Gegenteile, verwandte Wörter und Verwendungsbeispiele, evtl. auch Aussprachehinweise. Besonders wichtig sind zusammengesetzte Ausdrücke. Dazu gehören auch *phrasal verbs* (*set about, put off* usw.). Der Eintrag für das Stichwort *pay* könnte z. B. so aussehen:

pay (noun)	–	Bezahlung, Gehalt, Lohn
payslip	–	Gehaltsabrechnung
pay day	–	Zahltag
pay-off	–	Abfindung
pay (verb)	–	zahlen
pay for sth	–	etw bezahlen
pay off	–	auszahlen
pay as you go (phone)	–	Prepaid(-Handy)

Natürlich brauchen Sie nicht gleich komplette Wörterbucheinträge aufzuschreiben. Überlegen Sie sich jedoch, welche Ableitungen Ihnen zu dem neuen Wort schon bekannt sein könnten oder in welchem zusammengesetzten Ausdruck es Ihnen begegnet ist. Lassen Sie Platz für spätere Hinzufügungen, so dass die Einträge nach und nach „wachsen".

Karteikarten: Sie benötigen Karteikarten und einen Karteikasten mit mehreren Abteilungen. Schreiben Sie das englische Wort mit den dazugehörigen Ergänzungen auf eine Seite einer Karteikarte und die deutschen Bedeutungen auf die Rückseite. Sobald Sie ein Wort wissen, wandert es von der ersten in die zweite Abteilung des Karteikastens. Die Wörter in der zweiten Abteilung schauen Sie sich in größeren Abständen nochmal an, um diejenigen, die Sie wissen, dann in die dritte Abteilung fürs Langzeitgedächtnis abzulegen. Was Sie nicht wissen, kommt zurück in die erste Abteilung, die Sie sich möglichst oft anschauen sollten.

Vokabelheft: Wenn Sie es im Unterricht neue Vokabeln mitschreiben wollen, bietet sich ein Vokabelheft an. Benutzen Sie ein zweispaltiges Heft, damit Sie eine Spalte leicht bedecken können. Gestalten Sie das Lernen weniger schematisch, indem Sie die Seiten, die Sie lernen wollen, zufällig auswählen und ab und zu mal Deutsch–Englisch statt Englisch–Deutsch lernen.

Wortfamilien: Fertigen Sie Listen mit Wortfamilien an, um sich zusammen mit einem neuen Wort auch noch seine Ableitungen einzuprägen (*approve – approval – disapprove – disapproval – approving*).

Wortfelder: Die beste Methode, Wortfelder, also zusammenhängende Wortgruppen zu einem Thema zu lernen, sind Mind Maps, also grafisch angelegte Wortnetze. Diese Methode ist gut geeignet, um den Themenwortschatz für eine Klassenarbeit zu lernen. Um den Schlüsselbegriff herum werden einzelne Oberbegriffe für die wichtigsten Aspekte des Themas herum angeordnet. Um jeden Oberbegriff werden nun die dazugehörigen Vokabeln herumgeschrieben. Zum genauen Vorgehen siehe unten S. 114.

▸ Mind Mapping, S. 114

Vokabeltrainer: Wer gerne am Computer lernt, findet problemlos einen geeigneten Vokabeltrainer im Handel. Solche Software enthält meistens vielerlei Übungen, die das Vokabellernen unterhaltsam und spielerisch gestalten. Achten Sie darauf, dass es sich um eine Software handelt, die auf Ihre Schulart abgestimmt ist. Es gibt auch zahlreiche kostenlose Online-Vokabeltrainer im Internet.

Das Hörverständnis üben

Um gesprochenes Englisch zu verstehen, z. B. in Unterhaltungen, Telefongesprächen, Vorstellungsgesprächen, im Fernsehen u. a., sollten Sie sich gut auf die jeweilige Situation vorbereiten. Oft beeinträchtigen der Akzent, Hintergrundgeräusche und andere Störungen das Verständnis so, dass man sich auf das Wichtigste konzentrieren muss. Eignen Sie sich die unten beschriebene Methode an, wenn Sie die Hörverständnisaufgaben in *Crossover* bearbeiten. Damit lassen sich Barrieren bei schwierigen Hörtexten leicht abbauen.

Vor dem Hören

- Lesen Sie die gesamte Aufgabenstellung sorgfältig durch. Nutzen Sie alle Hilfen, die Ihnen zur Verfügung stehen – Abbildungen, Überschriften usw.
- Schreiben Sie wenn möglich **Schlüsselbegriffe** auf und rufen Sie sich, wenn genug Zeit ist, kurz wichtige Wortfelder zum Thema in Erinnerung.

Während des Hörens

- Hören Sie sich den gesamten Hörtext zunächst in Ruhe an, um zu verstehen, worum es geht. Machen Sie in dieser Phase keine Notizen.
- Achten Sie bei einem zweiten Hören nur auf die für die Aufgabe wichtigen Informationen. Konzentrieren Sie sich nicht auf einzelne Wörter und Ausdrücke, die Sie nicht verstehen.
- Achten Sie auf Ausdrücke, die den logischen Gedankengang verdeutlichen, z. B. *however, in my view, in conclusion* usw. Sie helfen Ihnen, den roten Faden nicht zu verlieren.
- Notieren Sie Informationen nur **stichpunktartig**, nie in ganzen Sätzen. Dabei kann ein Raster sehr hilfreich sein. In diesem Beispiel handelt es sich um den Wandel der Geschlechterrollen in unserer Gesellschaft:

	changed role	reasons	consequences
men			
women			

- Verwenden Sie Zeichen, Abkürzungen und Wortverkürzungen, um beim Notieren Zeit zu sparen:

Zeichen		Abkürzungen		Wortverkürzungen	
=	*the same as*	e.g.	*for example*	govt	*government*
≠	*not the same as*	km	*kilometres*	impt!	*important*
+	*and*	w., w/o	*with, without*	kids	*children*

Nach dem Hören

- Formulieren Sie Ihre Stichpunkte so schnell wie möglich aus – vielleicht können Sie später Ihre Aufzeichnungen nicht mehr lesen oder ihre Wortverkürzungen nicht mehr verstehen.
- Versuchen Sie, alle Fragen zu beantworten. Wenn Sie einige Informationen nicht verstanden haben, stellen Sie eine begründete Vermutung an.

Suche nach Informationen im Internet

Das Internet bietet riesige Ressourcen für die Recherche, z. B. für Aufsätze oder Präsentationen, aber es ist wichtig zu wissen, wo und wie man am besten sucht.

1. Schritt: Notieren Sie, wonach Sie genau suchen, und halten Sie passende Suchbegriffe fest. Ohne eine solche Vorgabe, die so spezifisch wie möglich sein sollte, gerät man vom Suchen leicht ins Surfen.

2. Schritt: Überlegen Sie sich, wo Sie mit der Suche beginnen sollten. Es ist sinnvoll, sich mit der Zeit einen Grundstock an englischsprachigen Ressourcen zusammenzustellen, z. B. *online encyclopedias* (etwa www.encyclopedia.com), *online dictionaries* (z. B. www.leo.org), *facts and figures about different countries* (etwa https://www.cia.gov/cia/publications/factbook/), *news sites* (z. B. www.bbc.co.uk), *science and technology sites* (etwa www.howstuffworks.com).

3. Schritt: Suchen Sie sich die beste Suchmaschine und geben Sie möglichst spezifische Suchbegriffe ein. Machen Sie sich mit allen Suchfunktionen vertraut. Schränken Sie die Sprache der angezeigten Ergebnisseiten auf Englisch ein.

4. Schritt: Achten Sie darauf, nur verlässliche Quellen zu benutzen. Im Durchschnitt ist das Internet nicht sehr zuverlässig, da jeder Nutzer beliebige Informationen einstellen kann. Prüfen Sie immer, wer für die jeweiligen Inhalte verantwortlich ist, und verlassen Sie sich nicht auf die nächstbeste Information.

5. Schritt: Bevor Sie einzelne Artikel Satz für Satz lesen, überfliegen Sie sie. Sind nur einzelne Abschnitte für Ihr Thema relevant, suchen Sie sich diese heraus und ignorieren Sie die übrigen Teile.

► Grobverständnis, S. 108

6. Schritt: Anstatt ganze Textabschnitte in Ihr Dokument herüberzukopieren, machen Sie sich gezielt Notizen. Speichern Sie die Seite unter Ihren Favoriten, wenn Sie später noch einmal darauf zurückkommen oder Materialien bzw. Zitate von der Seite verwenden möchten.

► Note Making, S. 113

PRODUKTION

Note Making

Es ist sinnvoll, sich beim Lesen und Hören eines Textes Notizen zu machen. So können Sie später leichter auf die Informationen zurückgreifen.

Beim Lesen

Auf den ersten Blick scheint es ziemlich leicht, sich beim Lesen eines Textes Notizen zu machen. Trotzdem fällt es vielen schwer, wirklich kurze, sinnvolle Stichpunkte zu notieren. Oft führt die Sorge, etwas Wichtiges auszulassen, dazu, dass ganze Sätze des Originaltextes abgeschrieben werden. Damit verliert man nicht nur Zeit, sondern es wird später auch schwierig, seinen Text in eigenen Worten zu formulieren.

Hier einige Tipps, damit Sie diese Falle umgehen:

- Geben Sie Ihren Notizen eine Überschrift, die Ihr Thema klar umreißt, z. B. *Effects of genetic engineering on the environment*.
- Gehen Sie den Text durch und filtern Sie die wesentlichen Unterthemen heraus, die Sie als Überschriften verwenden können. Denken Sie daran, unter den Überschriften genug Platz für Ihre Stichpunkte zu lassen.
- Halten Sie Ausschau nach Signalen wie Hervorhebungen, Wiederholung und bedeutungstragenden Adjektiven wie *huge, incredible, devastating* usw. Diese zeigen, was der Verfasser für wichtig hält.
- Notieren Sie nur Stichwörter, nicht ganze Sätze.
- Verdeutlichen Sie den logischen Aufbau der Informationen, z. B. indem Sie bestimmte Punkte in einer Liste untereinanderschreiben, Themen durch Leerzeilen voneinander abheben oder die wichtigsten Begriffe unterstreichen.
- Kontrollieren Sie, ob Sie alle notwendigen Informationen zusammengetragen haben. Vergessen Sie nicht, dass sie oft über den gesamten Text verstreut sind.

► Detailverständnis, S. 108

Beim Hören

In diesem Fall ist es schwieriger Notizen zu machen, da man oft sehr schnell schreiben muss. Man muss sich auf das Wesentliche konzentrieren und sollte Abkürzungen verwenden, damit man den Faden nicht verliert. Tipps dazu siehe oben in dem Abschnitt „Das Hörverständnis üben".

► Das Hörverständnis üben, S. 111

▶ Umgang mit unbekannten Vokabeln, S. 109

Mind Mapping

Eine Mind Map ist eine sinnvolle Methode, Begriffe und Angaben übersichtlich in einem Netz um einen Oberbegriff herum anzuordnen. Sie eignet sich z. B. zum Vokabellernen, zum Brainstorming, zum Ideensammeln und zur Vorbereitung eines Aufsatzes oder einer Präsentation.

Materialien: Ein großes Blatt (z. B. DIN A3), farbige Stifte.

1. Schritt: Schreiben Sie den Oberbegriff (wenn es um Wortfelder geht) bzw. das Thema (wenn es um eine Ideensammlung geht) deutlich und groß in die Mitte.

2. Schritt: Schreiben Sie die wichtigsten Begriffe zum Thema um den Oberbegriff herum; sie sollten durch starke „Äste" mit dem Oberbegriff verbunden sein.

3. Schritt: Fügen Sie nach demselben Prinzip weitere Wörter und Ideen zu den einzelnen Unterthemen hinzu. Je spezieller, desto kleiner die Verzweigungen, d.h. der Weg vom Thema nach außen führt vom Allgemeinen zum Speziellen. Sie können jederzeit und überall neue Ideen hinzufügen.

4. Schritt: Heben Sie wichtige Begriffe durch farbige Markierungen und Symbole hervor.

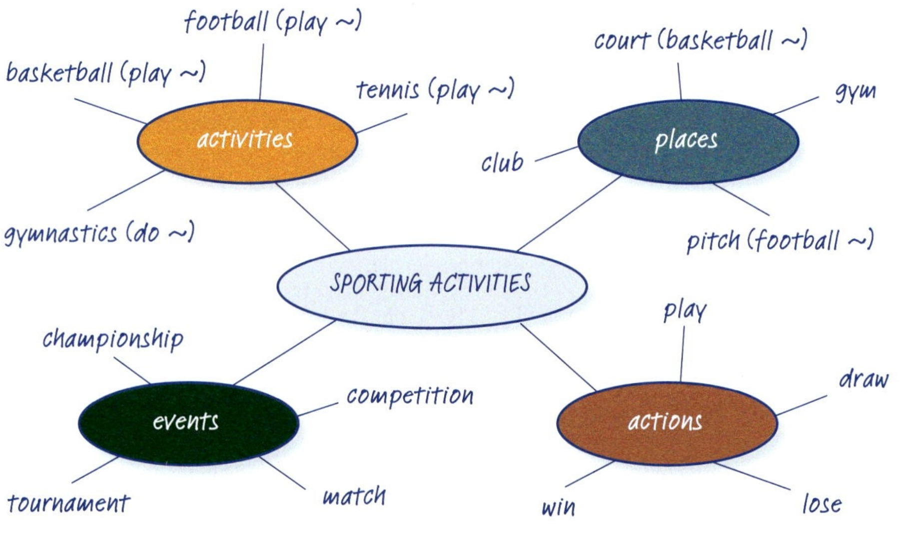

▶ Lesen schwieriger Texte, S. 108

Fragen zum Text beantworten

Bevor Sie mit dem Schreiben beginnen, vergewissern Sie sich, dass Sie den gesamten Text verstanden haben. (Nicht jedes Wort ist wichtig – überlegen Sie sich, ob Sie die Bedeutung des Satzes auch verstehen, ohne jedes Wort zu kennen.) Lesen Sie die Aufgabenstellung immer genau, um zu verstehen, worauf es bei der Beantwortung genau ankommt – ein häufiger Fehler ist das „Vorbeischreiben" an der Frage. Achten Sie auch darauf, keine Informationen zu „verpulvern", die Sie möglicherweise für die Beantwortung einer anderen Frage benötigen.

- Wenn Sie im Buch nichts anstreichen dürfen, machen Sie sich Notizen in Form von Stichpunkten und Listen, anstatt ganze Sätze aus dem Text herauszuschreiben. In der Klassenarbeit bzw. Prüfung sollten Sie die wichtigsten Passagen im Text markieren. Am besten markieren Sie alles, was für eine Textverständnisfragen wichtig ist, mit einer bestimmten Farbe, und nehmen dann eine andere Frage für die nächste Textverständnisfrage.
- Verwenden Sie in der Antwort die Zeitform der Fragestellung.
- Verwenden Sie so viele Synonyme und Umschreibungen der Begriffe und Formulierungen aus dem Text wie möglich, z. B. *recently – in recent years; violent crime – crime involving violence; think – believe; to a great extent – greatly; when she was a child – in her childhood* usw.
- Suchen Sie Signale im Text wie Hervorhebungen, Wiederholungen und bedeutungstragende Adjektive und Adverbien wie *absolutely, unbelievably, amazing.* Dies sind Signale dafür, was der Verfasser für wichtig hält.
- Versuchen Sie nicht, Ihre eigene Meinung einzubringen, wenn dies nicht in der Fragestellung gefordert ist.

Formulierungen für das Schreiben über den Text
- *According to the author, …*
- *The article goes on to say that …*
- *The text says that …*
- *The author makes the point that …*

Aus dem Text zitieren

Wenn Sie wirklich einmal eine wichtige Aussage aus dem Text zitieren möchten, um einen Punkt zu unterstreichen, so tun Sie dies nicht, indem Sie einfach die Formulierung des Textes übernehmen, sondern zeigen Sie, dass Sie bewusst zitieren und dies auch sprachlich deutlich machen können. Zitieren Sie in Ihrer Antwort höchstens einmal aus dem Text.

Zitate in die Antwort einbauen
- *To quote the author, …*
- *The problem discussed in the article is that teenagers are becoming 'increasingly fixated with their weight.'*
- *Sandra Goodwin describes it as 'disappointing and frustrating' that the figures are so high.*
- *'It is disappointing,' Martin Bloomberg is quoted as saying, 'that … .'*

Eine Stellungnahme (*comment*) schreiben

Bei einer Stellungnahme geht es darum, Ihre Meinung zu einem bestimmten Thema darzulegen. Wichtig ist, dass Ihre Meinung begründet und mit Beispielen belegt ist.

1. Schritt: Machen Sie sich genau bewusst, worüber Sie schreiben sollen. Lesen Sie die Aufgabenstellung mehrmals durch.

2. Schritt: Machen Sie sich Notizen. Ordnen Sie Ihre Stichwörter übersichtlich an, z. B. in einer Mind Map, einer Liste oder einer Übersicht.

▸ Note Making, S. 113
▸ Mind Mapping, S. 114

3. Schritt: Schreiben Sie einen Einleitungssatz, der sich auf die Aufgabenstellung beziehen sollte.

▸ Einen Text sinnvoll gliedern, S. 118

4. Schritt: Behandeln Sie jedes Argument in einem Absatz. Handelt es sich um ein Pro-/Kontra-Thema, können Sie erst die Pro- und dann die Kontra-Argumente anführen. Verdeutlichen Sie Ihre Argumentation durch die Verwendung von Strukturwörtern; hierzu siehe die Liste auf der hinteren Umschlagklappe dieses Buches (*Language for writing*).

5. Schritt: Bringen Sie Ihre Argumentation in einem prägnanten Schlusssatz auf den Punkt.

Eine Stellungnahme einleiten
- *In the following I shall deal with the the problem/subject/issue of …*
- *I would like to discuss …*
- *I intend to present arguments in favour of … and against …*

Eine Stellungnahme abschließen
- *All in all, I think it can be said that …*
- *In conclusion, I would like to say that …*
- *I would like to conclude by saying that …*

Einen Text zusammenfassen

▸ Fragen zum Text beantworten, S. 114
▸ Mediation, S. 122

Die Fähigkeit, einen gelesenen Text zusammenzufassen, ist nicht nur wichtig, um den Text richtig zu verstehen, sondern sie hilft auch bei anderen Situationen, in denen Sie Informationen aus einem Text auf das Wesentliche reduzieren müssen. Zu solchen Situationen gehören z. B. die Beantwortung von Textverständnisfragen oder eine Mediation.

▸ Detailverständnis, S. 108
▸ Umgang mit unbekannten Vokabeln, S. 109

1. Schritt: Lesen Sie den Text so oft wie möglich, bis Sie sicher sind, alles verstanden zu haben.

2. Schritt: Fassen Sie in ein oder zwei einleitenden Sätzen zusammen, worum es in dem Text geht, z. B.: *This article is about genetic modification. It deals with the advantages it could bring to farming, especially in underdeveloped countries.*

3. Schritt: Machen Sie sich bewusst, welche Informationen für den Leser wichtig sind, indem Sie *Wh*-Fragen beantworten: *Who? What? When? Where? Why?*, z. B.:
- *Who: geneticist Yang Huanming*
- *What: decoded the rice genome*

▸ Note Making, S. 113

4. Schritt: Machen Sie sich Notizen in Form von Stichwörtern.

5. Schritt: Schreiben Sie Ihren Text. Beachten Sie dabei folgende Punkte:
- Lassen Sie Unwesentliches weg. Dazu gehören etwa Beispiele, Aufzählungen, Namen, Zitate usw.
- Verwenden Sie so weit wie möglich Ihre eigenen Worte.
- Vermeiden Sie es, zu dem Text Stellung zu nehmen. Dies gehört in der Regel nicht zur Aufgabenstellung.
- Denken Sie daran, Zitate in indirekte Rede umzuwandeln.

▸ Reported speech, S. 130

6. Schritt: Kontrollieren Sie Ihren Text auf Fehler und vergewissern Sie sich, dass Sie alle wichtigen Aspekte des Textes berücksichtigt haben.

Einen Aufsatz schreiben

Im Laufe der Oberstufe, in der Abiturprüfung und auch später, z. B. im Studium, werden Sie immer wieder Aufsätze zu unterschiedlichsten Themen schreiben müssen. Es ist sinnvoll, sich von Anfang an einige Regeln zu eigen zu machen, um das Vorgehen möglichst zu automatisieren und sich gleich auf den Inhalt konzentrieren zu können. Dies ist besonders wichtig, wenn es – wie in der Abiturprüfung – auf die Zeit ankommt.

1. Schritt: Verschaffen Sie sich Klarheit über Ihr Thema. Welche Aspekte gehören dazu, welche nicht?

2. Schritt: Machen Sie ein Brainstorming, indem Sie alle Ideen aufschreiben, die Ihnen zum Thema in den Kopf kommen. Wichtig: Die Ideen sollten Sie gleich in eine Struktur bringen, um nicht in einem Wust von ungeordnetem Gekritzel zu enden. Zur Strukturierung eignen sich z. B. Listen oder Mind Maps.

▸ Note Making, S. 113
▸ Mind Mapping, S. 114

3. Schritt: Überlegen Sie sich einen Aufbau für Ihren Text. Dies kann z. B. in Form einer Mind Map geschehen, die Sie nummerieren, um die Reihenfolge der Ideen zu verdeutlichen. Eine andere Möglichkeit ist eine Übersicht (*outline*) wie die folgende:

Should old towns be closed to private vehicles?
Einleitung: Umreißen des Themas
Hauptteil: Ausführung zum Thema, z. B.:
1. *Disadvantages for business*
   1.1 *Job losses*
      1.1.1 *retail trade*
      1.1.2 *fewer tourists*
         1.1.2.1 *less money for tourist attractions*
         1.1.2.2 *job losses in cafés etc.*
   1.2 *What about town centre residents, delivery vehicles etc.?*
2. *Advantages, positive effects on town and people*
…
Schluss: Zusammenfassung, Fazit

4. Schritt: Schreiben Sie Ihren Text. Lassen Sie Platz für Korrekturen, Änderungen oder Ergänzungen. Wichtig: Verdeutlichen Sie Ihre Argumentation durch die Verwendung von Strukturwörtern; hierzu siehe die Liste auf der hinteren Umschlagklappe dieses Buches (*Language for writing*) und den Abschnitt „Einen Text sinnvoll gliedern".

▸ Einen Text sinnvoll gliedern, S. 118

5. Schritt: Überprüfen Sie Ihren Entwurf auf:
- **Rechtschreibfehler** (z. B. gleichlautende Wörter wie *there/their, meet/meat* usw.)
- **Grammatikfehler** (z. B. Gebrauch der Zeitformen; *-ly*-Endung für Adverbien)
- **Wortwahl** (z. B. Wiederholungen; *False friends* wie „aktuell" ≠ *actual*, „eventuell" ≠ *eventual*, „spenden" ≠ *spend*, „zum Schluss" ≠ *at last*)
- **Satzbau** (z. B. unvollständige Antworten, die mit *Because* beginnen)
- **Gedankenführung** (z. B. Klarheit des Ausdrucks; Verwendung von Strukturwörtern wie *However, On the other hand, In addition, As a result* usw.)

Einen Text sinnvoll gliedern

Wann immer es darum geht, einen zusammenhängenden Text zu schreiben, sei es eine Antwort auf eine Frage zum Text, ein Aufsatz, eine Zusammenfassung o. Ä., ist es ganz wichtig, seine Gedanken in einen logischen Zusammenhang zu bringen, damit der Leser den Faden nicht verliert. Dies alles gilt ebenso für mündliche Präsentationen, nur werden Sie dabei Ihre Materialien nicht Wort für Wort ablesen, sondern frei sprechen. Daher ist es wichtig, Formulierungen für die Gliederung auch mündlich parat zu haben.

Die wichtigsten Strukturwörter finden Sie auf der hinteren Umschlagklappe dieses Buches (*Language for writing*). Im Folgenden sehen Sie einige Beispiele, wie man diese Formulierungen in einen Text einbauen kann.

Argumente gliedern

- *In his text 'The world's changing energy supplies' Knapp discusses many aspects of energy and the environment. Firstly, he states that … Secondly/Then he goes on to say that … Another point he makes is that … Finally, …*

Eine Begründung anführen

- *Due to / Because of / As a result of all the discussions about renewable sources of energy …*
- *Renewable energy has been talked about a lot. Therefore, the public …*
- *Renewable energy has been talked about a lot, so the public …*

Aspekte ergänzen

- *Brian Knapp states that many renewable sources of energy include high development costs. In addition, / Moreover, he points out that they these energy forms still only offer a small amount of the world's rising energy requirements.*
- *In addition to / Besides / As well as mentioning the high development costs of many renewable forms of energy, Knapp points out that they these energy forms still only offer a small amount of the world's rising energy requirements.*

Einen Gegensatz ausdrücken

- *Although the demand for cheap energy is continuing to rise, our current main sources of energy – fossil fuels – are running out.*
- *In spite of the rising demand for cheap energy, our current main sources of energy are running out.*
- *While/Whereas the demand for cheap energy is continuing to rise, our current main sources of energy are running out.*
- *Our current main sources of energy are running out. However, / But nevertheless, the demand for cheap energy is continuing to rise.*
- *On the one hand, our current main sources of energy are running out; on the other hand, the demand for cheap energy is continuing to rise.*

Beispiele anführen

- *The writer is of the opinion that nuclear fusion is a safe energy source compared with other energy sources, for example / for instance / such as / e.g. …*

Ein Fazit ziehen

- *As a consequence, / All in all, / Consequently, Brian Knapp thinks that …*
- *To sum up / To conclude, I would like to say that …*

Diese Strukturwörter (*connectors*) sollten Sie sich so zu eigen machen, dass Sie sie möglichst in jedem Text verwenden. Dadurch gewöhnen Sie sich eine genaue und logische Ausdrucksweise an. Achten Sie auch beim Lesen von Texten auf Strukturwörter; so können Sie der Gedankenführung leichter folgen.

Die Arbeitsergebnisse präsentieren

Die Fähigkeit, wirkungsvoll vor einem Publikum zu referieren, ist wichtig im Berufsleben und zunehmend auch in der Schule. Dabei kommt es nicht nur auf den Inhalt an, sondern auch darauf, wie anschaulich Sie den Inhalt „verpacken", d.h. dass Sie Ihren Vortrag leicht nachvollziehbar gliedern, abwechslungsreich gestalten und lebendig illustrieren.

Vor der Präsentation

1. Schritt: Bereiten Sie Ihr Thema gründlich vor und machen Sie sich dabei schon Notizen auf Englisch.

2. Schritt: Prüfen Sie Ihre Stichpunkte sprachlich und vergewissern Sie sich, dass Sie alles richtig aussprechen (anhand der Lautschrift in einem Wörterbuch oder der Aussprachebeispiele in gängigen Online-Wörterbüchern oder auf Wörterbuch-CD-ROMs).

3. Schritt: Überlegen Sie sich, wie Sie Ihren Vortrag interessanter und lebendiger machen können (Anschauungsmaterial, Audiobeispiele, Anekdoten usw.).

4. Schritt: Organisieren Sie alle Hilfsmittel, die Sie benötigen (OHP, Flipchart usw.).

5. Schritt: Üben Sie die Präsentation, am besten vor Zuhörern.

Während der Präsentation

1. Schritt: Steigen Sie nicht gleich mitten ins Thema ein, sondern geben Sie einen Überblick über Ihre Präsentation.

2. Schritt: Machen Sie es den Zuhörern leicht, indem Sie sich klar ausdrücken, kurze Sätze benutzen und langsam sprechen.

3. Schritt: Die Zuhörer bleiben am ehesten interessiert, wenn Sie Ihre Präsentation so abwechslungsreich wie möglich gestalten: Ziehen Sie zwischendurch Anschauungsmaterial (OHP, Beamer usw.) heran und teilen Sie Handouts aus. Wenn Sie Folien benutzen, halten Sie sie klar und übersichtlich, anstatt sie mit Grafiken zu überladen.

4. Schritt: Achten Sie auf Ihre Körpersprache: Wenden Sie sich dem Publikum zu, halten Sie Blickkontakt mit den Zuhörern, sprechen Sie langsam und deutlich und benutzen Sie Gesten, um den Inhalt zu verdeutlichen.

5. Schritt: Fassen Sie zum Schluss das Wichtigste zusammen. Bedanken Sie sich bei den Zuhörern für ihre Aufmerksamkeit und ermuntern Sie sie, Fragen zu stellen.

Interpretation von Bildern und Karikaturen

Am besten eignen Sie sich einen Grundstock an Formulierungen zur Beschreibung und Interpretation von Bildern und Karikaturen an. Achten Sie darauf, sich auf die wesentlichen Bildaussagen zu konzentrieren, anstatt sich in Details zu verlieren. Halten Sie die folgenden Schritte ein, um ihre Antwort sinnvoll zu gliedern:

1. Schritt: **Beschreibung des Bildes.** Betrachten Sie alle Einzelheiten der Bildvorlage, aber beschränken Sie sich bei der Beschreibung auf die Elemente, die für die Aussage wichtig sind.
Verwenden Sie bei der Beschreibung der Bildinhalte das *Present progressive* (außer bei Verben, die gewöhnlich nicht in dieser Zeitform

▸ Present progressive, S. 125

vorkommen). Zu dem Cartoon auf S. 17 könnten Sie z. B. schreiben: *The cartoon shows a mother and child outside a supermarket. The child is wearing a hoodie. There is a sign outside which says 'No hoodies'. A security guard is pointing at the sign …* Aber Vorsicht: Das *Present progressive* gilt nur für die Handlungen und Situationen, die im Bild dargestellt sind, nicht für die Verben, mit denen Sie den Cartoon beschreiben und interpretieren (*The cartoon* ***shows/describes*** *… / It* ***seems*** *as if the person on the left …*).

2. Schritt: **Interpretation des Bildes.** Wenn Ihnen das Bild nicht viel sagt, können Sie dies in Ihre Interpretation miteinbeziehen, indem Sie es als *ambiguous* oder *unclear* bezeichnen.

3. Schritt: **Stellungnahme zur Bildaussage.** Bringen Sie die Hauptaussage der Bildvorlage auf den Punkt und/oder beziehen Sie Stellung, indem Sie z. B. die Wirkung des Bildes auf den Betrachter beurteilen.

4. Schritt: **Vergleich der Bildvorlage mit dem Text** (wenn die Aufgabenstellung dies erfordert). Gehen Sie zum Text zurück und suchen Sie die Passagen heraus, die im Zusammenhang mit der Bildvorlage von Bedeutung sind. Beurteilen Sie, ob die Bildvorlage mit der Aussage des Textes in Einklang steht oder ihr widerspricht.

1. Beschreibung des Bildes

- *In the foreground/background/centre there is …*
- *The speech bubble* (Sprechblase) / *thought bubble* (Denkblase) / *caption* (Bildunterschrift) / *label* (Aufschrift) *says that …*
- *On the left/right you can see …*
- *The scene depicts/shows …*
- *The … looks as if …*
- *The person on the left appears to … / It seems as if the person …*
- *The prime minister is wearing/holding …*

2. Interpretation der Bildaussage

- *The picture / cartoon deals with the recent discussion of …*
- *I think the cartoonist's / artist's / photographer's use of irony / exaggeration is intended to create … / is aimed at making … / conveys …*
- *The person in the centre represents / symbolises / shows …*
- *This indicates / shows / reveals that …*
- *The cartoonist / artist / photographer criticises / wants to express the idea that …*
- *Because the foreground / background is …, the impression is given that …*
- *From the way the people are depicted it is obvious that …*
- *The point of the cartoon seems to be that …*

3. Stellungnahme, Beschreibung der Wirkung auf den Betrachter

- *I agree with the cartoonist / artist, but …*
- *Because of …, the picture touches me / leaves me cold.*
- *I think the … is a symbol of …*
- *The … helps to create a … atmosphere, which forces you to / has the effect of …*

4. Vergleich der Bildvorlage mit einem Text

- *While the text says that …, the cartoon / picture shows / makes the point that …*
- *In the text we found out that …*
- *The cartoon / picture illustrates the facts / information in the text in the following way.*
- *The cartoon / picture gives a completely different opinion about the information in the text.*

Interpretation von Grafiken, Diagrammen und Tabellen

Wie im Falle von Cartoons ist es auch bei Grafiken, Diagrammen und Tabellen sinnvoll, einen Grundstock an Formulierungen zur Beschreibung und Interpretation parat zu haben. Halten Sie die folgenden Schritte ein, um ihre Antwort sinnvoll zu gliedern:

1. Schritt: **Beschreibung der Vorlage.** Hier geht es nicht darum, alle Details aufzuzählen, sondern zu beschreiben, worum es in der Vorlage geht und welche Daten dargestellt werden.

2. Schritt: **Zusammenfassung der dargestellten Tendenzen, Entwicklungen bzw. Größen.** Welche Schlussfolgerungen ergeben sich aus den Daten? Kann man zusammenfassend ein Ergebnis oder Fazit formulieren?

3. Schritt: **Vergleich der Vorlage mit dem Text** (wenn die Aufgabenstellung dies erfordert). Gehen Sie zum Text zurück und suchen Sie die Passagen heraus, die im Zusammenhang mit der Grafik von Bedeutung sind. Beurteilen Sie, ob die dargestellten Daten mit der Aussage des Textes in Einklang stehen oder ihr widersprechen.

Typen von Diagrammen

Tabelle (*table*)

	USA	UK
1995	495	105
2005	718	85

Kurvendiagramm (*graph, line graph*)

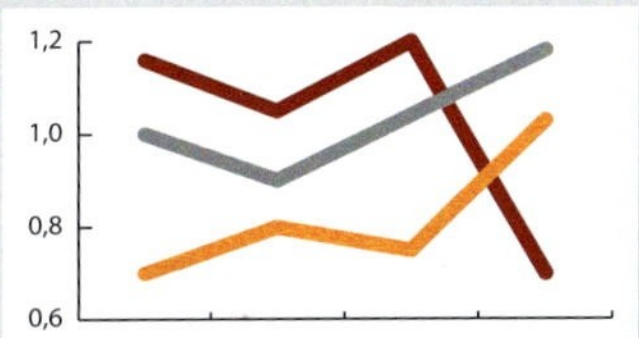

Balkendiagramm (*bar chart*)

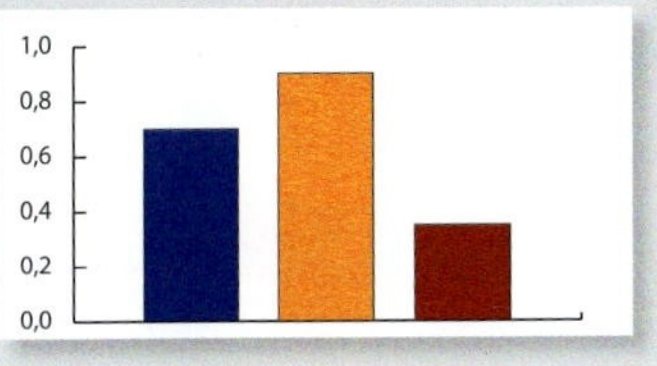

Kreis-/Tortendiagramm (*pie chart*)

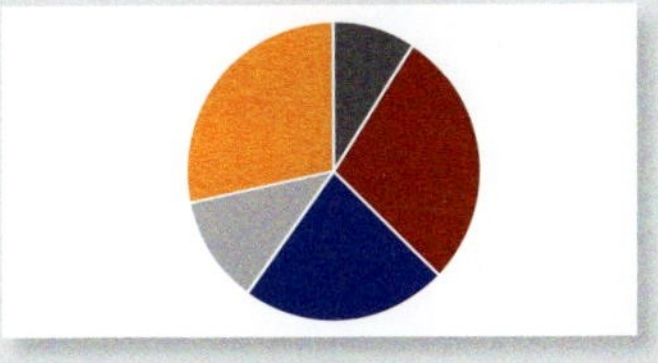

Sprechen über Zahlen und Mengenangaben (*values, amounts*)

- *more / less than ...*
- *no less than ...*
- *eighty-five per cent (said that ...)*
- *On the other hand, almost ...*

Sprechen über Proportionen (*proportions, shares, percentages*)

- *(over) half of*
- *more / less than one third / quarter of ...*
- *the (vast) majority of*
- *a mere third of ...*

Sprechen über Entwicklungen (*developments*) und Tendenzen (*tendencies*)

- *a huge / sharp increase / decrease*
- *a small / slight rise / dip*
- *levels out, remains constant*
- *drastically, gradually, sharply, steadily*
- *rises / increases / hits a maximum*
- *drops / decreases / falls / plunges*
- *over a period of ...*
- *between 1998 and 2004*

Vergleich der Informationen aus einer Grafik mit einem Text

- *While the text says that ..., the diagram shows that ...*
- *The graph illustrates the facts / information in the text in the following way.*
- *The diagram gives a completely different opinion about the information in the text.*

INTERAKTION

Gruppengespräche und Diskussionen führen

Ob es um Gruppengespräche, Diskussionen oder Rollenspiele geht: Machen Sie das meiste daraus, indem Sie die folgenden Punkte beherzigen.

- Lernen Sie die Formulierungen auf der hinteren Umschlagklappe dieses Buches (*Language for speaking*). Klappen Sie diese während des Unterrichts aus. Die Formulierungen helfen Ihnen, sich klar und logisch auszudrücken.
- Bereiten Sie sich inhaltlich vor, indem Sie sich einzelne Aspekte des Themas nochmal in Stichworten ins Gedächtnis rufen und Schlüsselbegriffe auf Englisch notieren.
- Legen Sie sich, wenn genügend Zeit ist, ein paar Fragen/Antworten zum Thema zurecht.
- Bleiben Sie immer ruhig und denken Sie nach, bevor Sie sprechen.
- Bleiben Sie beim Thema und schweifen Sie nicht ab.
- Gehen Sie auf Ihre Gesprächspartner ein und halten Sie Blickkontakt.
- Beteiligen Sie sich und hören Sie nicht bloß still zu: Gruppenarbeit ist eine hervorragende Gelegenheit zum freien Sprechen.

Melden Sie sich auch immer mal wieder spontan zu Wort und lassen Sie Ausdrücke einfließen, die Interesse, Überraschung, Skepsis usw. äußern – so etwas macht das Gespräch gleich viel lebendiger:

Sich zu Wort melden
- *Can I just say that …*
- *Well, if you ask me …*

Jemand anderen ins Gespräch einbringen
- *What do you think, Sven / Svenja?*

Verständnis, Erstaunen usw. ausdrücken

Ach so. / Ah ja.	*I see. / Right. / Oh, right.*
Oh je!	*Oh dear!*
Echt?	*Really?*
Gut. / Okay.	*Fine.*
Alles klar.	*OK then.*
Das ist doch wohl nicht dein Ernst!	*You're kidding!*

MEDIATION

Mediation

Schriftliche Mediation bedeutet das sinngemäße Übertragen von Texten in eine andere Sprache für jemanden, der das Original nicht versteht. Wichtig bei einer Mediation ist immer die Konzentration auf das Wesentliche, im Unterschied zur Übersetzung. Einzelheiten sind bei einer Mediation ebenso zweitrangig wie stilistische Feinheiten.

1. Schritt: Lesen Sie genau, **für welche Situation** Sie den Text zusammenfassen müssen und **für wen**. Meist bestimmt die jeweilige Situation, worauf es ankommt.

2. Schritt: Lesen Sie den gesamten Text durch, ohne sich dabei auf Einzelwörter zu konzentrieren. Ignorieren Sie unbekannte Vokabeln wenn möglich, oft sind sie für das Verständnis des Hauptinhalts nicht wesentlich.

3. Schritt: Lesen Sie nochmals, worauf es in der Aufgabenstellung ankommt und in welcher Form die Lösung abgefasst sein soll. Wenn es einzelne Fragen gibt, markieren Sie die für die jeweiligen Fragen wichtigen Textpassagen in unterschiedlichen Farben.

4. Schritt: Fassen Sie die Hauptpunkte des Textes zusammen. Drücken Sie sich klar und verständlich aus; vereinfachen Sie die Sprache des Originals, indem Sie sich darauf konzentrieren, **was** gesagt wird, nicht **wie** es gesagt wird.

5. Schritt: Lesen Sie Ihren Text nochmals durch und vergewissern Sie sich, dass der Inhalt des Originals angemessen und verständlich ausgedrückt ist.

Übersetzung

Im Gegensatz zur Mediation ist bei der Übersetzung jedes Wort des Originaltextes wichtig. Oft muss im Deutschen jedoch eine andere Satzkonstruktion gewählt werden. Besonders knifflig sind z. B. die folgenden Konstruktionen; übersetzen Sie die Beispielsätze ins Deutsche:

- **Partizipialkonstruktionen**
  z. B. *The jobs done by women are often badly paid. / Some people say that feminism has been a great success pointing to the progress in the last 30 years.*
- **Konstruktionen mit Gerundium**
  z. B. *I avoided looking at her. / She achieved her aims by working very hard.*
- **Passivkonstruktionen**
  z. B. *He was offered a good job. / He is said to be rich.*

Außerdem muss häufig die Wortart geändert werden, z. B. *There is a need to …* (Es ist notwendig, zu …) oder *She used to work in France.* (Früher arbeitete sie in Frankreich.).

Eine weitere Schwierigkeit sind kleinere Partikel und Ausdrücke, die sich vom Deutschen oft unterscheiden, z. B. *after all, as, as to, as for, at all, at least, however, neither … nor, not … either, not … until, unless.*

1. Schritt: Lesen Sie den gesamten Text einmal zügig durch.

2. Schritt: Lesen Sie den Text nun Wort für Wort und schlagen Sie schwierige Wörter nach. Vergewissern Sie sich, dass Sie den Satzbau jedes Satzes richtig erfasst haben (siehe die Liste schwieriger Konstruktionen oben).

3. Schritt: Fertigen Sie eine Rohfassung an, die Sie am besten doppelzeilig schreiben, um Korrekturen einfügen zu können.

4. Schritt: Bevor Sie die Reinschrift anfertigen, prüfen Sie Ihren Text auf:
Rechtschreib- und Grammatikfehler (z. B. Partizipien, Gerundien, Zeitenfolge)
Ausdruck (z. B. Sätze, an denen man noch das englische Original erkennt)
Verständlichkeit (z. B. zu lange oder verschachtelte Sätze)
Vollständigkeit (ausgelassene Wörter oder Satzteile).

GRAMMAR SUMMARY

The simple present

1 I **go** to the disco once a week.
2 We **live** in Bavaria.
3 Mr Brown **teaches** us English every day.
4 **I don't like** chocolate.
5 **Does** he **like** chocolate?

- Man gebraucht das **simple present** für regelmäßige, sich wiederholende Ereignisse oder Handlungen (1, 3) und für Dauerzustände (2, 4, 5).
- Mit Ausnahme der 3. Person Singular (*he, she, it*) hat das **simple present** dieselbe Form wie der Infinitiv (1, 2).
  ⚠ Die **3. Person Singular** endet auf *-(e)s* (3).
- Ist **kein Hilfsverb** im Satz vorhanden, werden **Verneinung** und **Fragen** mit der entsprechenden Form von *to do* gebildet (4, 5).

Das **simple present** wird häufig mit den folgenden **Zeitangaben** benutzt:

- *always, never, often, rarely, seldom, sometimes*
- *generally, mostly, normally, regularly, usually*
- *every day/week/month/..., every morning/afternoon/...*
- *on Mondays/Tuesdays/..., on weekdays*
- *in (the) summer/winter/...*
- *at Christmas/Easter, at weekends*

The present progressive

1 **I'm calling** to say that Ben's ill.
2 He**'s staying** in bed today.
3 The computer **isn't working**.
4 **Are** you **sleeping**?

- Man benutzt das **present progressive** (auch **present continuous** genannt) für Vorgänge oder Handlungen, die im Moment des Sprechens oder Schreibens passieren und noch nicht abgeschlossen sind (1, 3, 4).
- Es wird auch für vorübergehende Situationen gebraucht (2).
- Das **present progressive** wird mit dem Präsens von *to be* und der *-ing*-Form des Vollverbs gebildet.
- Da beim **present progressive** immer ein Hilfsverb vorhanden ist, wird die **Verneinung** mit *not/n't* gebildet (3).
- Fragen werden durch Umstellung gebildet (4).

Das **present progressive** wird oft mit den folgenden **Zeitangaben** benutzt:

at the moment, at present, now, this week/month

⚠ Diese Verben bilden normalerweise **keine progressive-Form**:

be, believe, doubt, feel (meinen), *hate, hear, imagine, know, like/dislike, love, mean, notice, prefer, realize, recognize, remember, see* (begreifen), *seem, suppose, think* (meinen), *understand, want, wish*

The simple past

1 We **wanted** to go to the USA last year.
2 She **went** on a school trip to London.
3 Jasmin **did not enjoy** her holiday in Rimini last summer.
4 Where **did** you **go** last year?

- Man benutzt das **simple past**, um über Vergangenes zu berichten.
- Das **simple past** wird auch gebraucht, wenn man sagen will, **wann** etwas geschehen ist (1, 3, 4).
- Bei **regelmäßigen** Verben wird das **simple past** durch das Anhängen von *-ed* an den Infinitiv gebildet (1).
  ⚠ Die unregelmäßigen Verben haben eine Sonderform (2), die man sich merken – auswendig lernen! – muss.
- Ist **kein Hilfsverb** im Satz vorhanden, bildet man die **Verneinung** und **Fragen** mit *did/didn't* (3, 4).

► Irregular Verbs (p. 156)

Das **simple past** wird häufig mit den folgenden **Zeitangaben** benutzt:

- *yesterday, the day before yesterday, the week/month/... before last*
- *last night/week/month/summer/December/Easter/...*
- *two/three/... hours/days/years/... ago*
- *in 2005 / in the 20th century...*
- *at that time, in those days*

The past progressive

1 The teacher **was talking** to Heather **during the break**.
2 The tourists **were taking** photos when a lion (suddenly) **sprang** towards them.
3 I **wasn't doing** anything particular when he **came** around.
4 **Were** you **having** breakfast when I **phoned**?

- Wenn man ausdrücken möchte, dass eine Handlung zu einem bestimmten Zeitpunkt oder während eines bestimmten Zeitraumes in der Vergangenheit **im Gange** war, benutzt man das **past progressive** (auch **past continuous** genannt)(1).
- Das **past progressive** wird auch benutzt, um zu verdeutlichen, dass eine Handlung im Gange war, als ein neues Ereignis (plötzlich) eintrat (2, 3, 4).
- Man bildet das **past progressive** mit *was/were* und der *-ing*-Form des Vollverbs (1).
- Die **Verneinung** wird mit *was not / wasn't* bzw. *were not / weren't* gebildet (3).
- **Fragen** bildet man durch Umstellung (4).
  ⚠ Einige Verben haben **keine progressive-Form** (siehe die Liste unter **present progressive**).

► The present progressive (p. 125)

The present perfect

1 I**'ve bought** a new car.
2 I **haven't seen** the new film yet.
3 How long **have** you **had** it?
4 We**'ve had** snow **for** two weeks.
5 She**'s had** a cold **since** December.

- Wenn man ausdrücken will, dass etwas geschehen ist, ohne dass der genaue Zeitpunkt des Ereignisses wichtig ist, wird das **present perfect** benutzt (1, 2).

- Man gebraucht das **present perfect** auch, um zu sagen, seit wann oder wie lange ein Zustand oder eine Handlung schon andauert (3–5). Dafür wird sehr oft *for* bzw. *since* verwendet. (Im Deutschen steht dafür „seit" plus Gegenwart.)
- Das **present perfect** wird mit *have/has* und der 3. Form des Vollverbs gebildet (1, 4, 5).
- Die **Verneinung** wird durch das Einfügen von *not/n't* unmittelbar nach *have/has* gebildet (2).
- **Fragen** bildet man durch Umstellung (3).

Das **present perfect** wird oft mit den folgenden Zeitangaben benutzt:

- *already, still (not), (not) yet*
- *(not) ever, just, lately, never, recently*
- *so far this week/month/…, till/until now*

The present perfect progressive

1 I**'ve been learning** English since I was 10.
2 They**'ve not been speaking** to each other lately.
3 **Has** he **been singing** in the choir for long?

- Das **present perfect progressive** (auch **present perfect continuous**) benutzt man für Handlungen und Vorgänge, die in der Vergangenheit begonnen haben und zum Zeitpunkt des Sprechens bzw. Schreibens noch nicht beendet sind.
- Das **present perfect progressive** wird mit *have/has been* und der *-ing*-Form des Vollverbs gebildet (1).
- Die **Verneinung** bildet man durch das Einfügen von *not/n't* unmittelbar nach *have/has* (2).
- **Fragen** werden durch Umstellung gebildet (3).
  ⚠ Einige Verben haben normalerweise **keine progressive-Form**. (Siehe die Liste unter **present progressive**, S. 125.)

▸ The present progressive (S. 125)

The past perfect

1 Laura couldn't pay. She **had forgotten** her purse.
2 Nina **had** already **left** the coffee bar by the time I arrived.
3 When I visited John in hospital, he **had been** there for ten days.

- Mit Hilfe des **past perfect** drückt man aus, dass zwei Handlungen oder Vorgänge in der Vergangenheit aufeinander folgten (1, 2). Die Handlung, die zeitlich voranging, steht im **past perfect**.
- Das **past perfect** wird auch verwendet, um auszudrücken, dass ein Zustand vor einem Zeitpunkt der Vergangenheit begann und zu diesem Zeitpunkt noch andauerte (3).
  ⚠ Wenn zwei oder mehrere kurze Handlungen in der Vergangenheit direkt aufeinander folgen, wird für alle Handlungen das **simple past** verwendet:
  The cat ***ran*** *out when Joanne* ***opened*** *the door.*

The past perfect progressive

1 Rod **had been travelling** for three months when he ran out of money.
2 When I found Mary, I could see that she **had been crying**.

- Das **past perfect progressive** wird verwendet, wenn man ausdrücken will, dass eine Handlung oder ein Vorgang vor einem Zeitpunkt in der Vergangenheit begonnen hatte und bis (oder fast bis) zu diesem Zeitpunkt andauerte.

The future

A will

1 In the future people **will use** public transport more often.
2 We can only hope that everyone **will accept** this shift in attitudes.
3 You've forgotten your purse? Don't worry. I**'ll lend** you some money.
4 Ms Smith **will not be** at the meeting this afternoon.
5 I **won't come** either.
6 **Will** he **get** the job?

- Das **will future** benutzt man, um Vorhersagen zu machen (1) oder Vermutungen über die Zukunft zu äußern (2).
- Man benutzt es auch, wenn man sich spontan zu etwas entschließt, Angebote oder Versprechen macht (3).
- Das **will future** wird mit *will* + Infinitiv des Vollverbs gebildet. Es hat für alle Personen die gleiche Form (1–3).
- Die **Verneinung** bildet man durch das Einfügen von *not* unmittelbar nach *will*. Im gesprochenen Englisch sagt man häufig *won't* (4, 5).
- **Fragen** werden durch Umstellung gebildet (6).

Das **will future** kommt häufig mit den folgenden einleitenden Verben und Ausdrücken vor:

- *believe, expect, forecast, hope, imagine, suppose, think*
- *It's clear/obvious that ..., There's no doubt that ...*

B going to

1 Look at these clouds. It**'s going to rain** soon.
2 This time **I'm going to get** good marks in the class test.
3 Tom **isn't going to work** at the club any more.
4 When **are** you **going to sit** your driving test?

- Das **going to future** benutzt man für Ereignisse und Situationen, die nach Meinung des Sprechers bald eintreten werden (weil es bereits Anzeichen dafür gibt) (1).
- Es wird auch für Pläne und Absichten gebraucht (2).
- Das **going to future** wird mit *am/is/are* + *going to* + Infinitiv gebildet (1, 2).
- Die **Verneinung** bildet man durch das Einfügen von *not/n't* unmittelbar nach *am/is/are* (3).
- **Fragen** werden durch Umstellung gebildet (4).

  ⚠ Der **Gebrauch des Futurs** hängt in gewissem Maße von der Absicht oder Sichtweise des Sprechers ab. Dies gilt insbesondere für das **going to future** und für zukünftige Ereignisse. Daher ist es im Zweifelsfall ratsam, das neutralere **will future** zu benutzen.

C The present progressive / the simple present

1 We**'re leaving** the house at 10.30.
2 The bus **goes** at 11 o'clock.

- Man kann das **present progressive** auch **mit einer Zeitbestimmung der Zukunft** (*at 10.30, this afternoon, on Sunday*) für bereits feststehende Pläne und Verabredungen verwenden (1).
- Genau wie im Deutschen wird auch im Englischen das **simple present mit einer Zeitangabe** benutzt, um fest terminierte Vorgänge (Fahrpläne, Stundenpläne, Programme usw.) anzugeben (2).

Modal auxiliary verbs

1 He **can speak** several languages.
2 You **must accept** your new situation.
3 We **needn't go** to work today.
4 **May** I **interrupt** you?

- Um zu sagen, was geschehen kann, muss, darf, soll usw., benutzt man ein modales Hilfsverb in Verbindung mit einem Vollverb (1–4).

⚠ Im Englischen steht ein Hilfsverb – anders als im Deutschen – nie ohne Vollverb:
– Lena kann Spanisch. → *Lena can speak Spanish.* NICHT: ~~can Spanish~~

- Modale Hilfsverben – nicht jedoch die Ersatzverben (siehe unten) – haben bei allen Personen immer die gleiche Form, einschließlich der 3. Person Singular (keine *-s*-Endung) (1, 2).
- Die **Verneinung** wird durch das Einfügen von *not/n't* unmittelbar nach dem Hilfsverb gebildet (3).
- **Fragen** bildet man durch Umstellung (4).
- Abgesehen von *could* (wenn es für eine Fähigkeit gebraucht wird) kann man modale Hilfsverben nur im Präsens und – mit einer geeigneten Zeitangabe – mit zukünftiger Bedeutung benutzen, zum Beispiel:
  – *You **can go** home now.* (Präsens)
  *You **can go** home an hour early tomorrow.* (Futur)
  – *I **must write** these letters now.* (Präsens)
  *I **must write** a long report next week.* (Futur)

⚠ Um ein modales Hilfsverb z. B. in der Vergangenheit zu verwenden, muss ein geeignetes Ersatzverb gebraucht werden:

must *The provider **had to block** access to the internet last December.*
can *I **couldn't start** the car yesterday.* (Fähigkeit)
*We **weren't allowed to go** home early last Friday.* (Erlaubnis)

Übersicht der modalen Hilfsverben nach Funktion

Funktion	Modale(s) Hilfsverb(en)	
Fähigkeit	*He **can** speak several languages.* *The first satellites **could** only transmit sound.*	
Möglichkeit	*With your qualifications you **could** work abroad.* *The boss **may** come in at any moment.* *He **might** ask you what you are doing.*	
Bitte	***Can** I have a word with Ms Sims, please?* ***Could** I speak to Ms Sims, please?* ***May** I interrupt you?* ***Might** I ask you a personal question?*	(neutral) (höflich) (betont höflich) (äußerst höflich)
Erlaubnis	*You **can** go in now.* *The boss is free. You **may** go in now.*	(neutral) (gefällig)
Verbot	*We **mustn't** be late for work tomorrow.*	
Pflicht	*You **must** wear a hard hat in the factory.*	
Wahl	*Most shop workers **needn't** work on Sundays.*	
Empfehlung	*You **should** get better qualifications.* *You **ought to** get better qualifications.* *You **must** get better qualifications.*	(neutral) (betont) (streng)

Reported speech

A Aussagesätze

1 Some people **claim** that 'servant' robots **are putting** people out of work.
2 The speaker **reminded** his audience that there **were** some jobs robots **couldn't do**.

- Wenn man einem Dritten berichten möchte, was während eines Gespräches gesagt wurde, benutzt man die **indirekte Rede**.
- Bei Verwendung der indirekten Rede benutzt man ein einleitendes Verb wie *claim, say, remind, answer, think, mention* usw., um zu verdeutlichen, dass eine Äußerung wiedergegeben wird.
- Steht das einleitende Verb in der Vergangenheit – also *said, answered, mentioned* usw. –, dann verschieben sich die Zeiten wie folgt:

direkte Rede		indirekte Rede
simple present *she works hard*	→	**simple past** *she worked hard*
present progressive *she is working hard*	→	**past progressive** *she was working hard*
simple past *she worked hard*	→	**past perfect** *she had worked hard*
past progressive *she was working hard*	→	**past perfect progressive** *she had been working hard*
present perfect *she has worked hard*	→	**past perfect** *she had worked hard*
present perfect progressive *she has been working hard*	→	**past perfect progressive** *she had been working hard*
past perfect *she had worked hard*		(keine Verschiebung) –
past perfect progressive *she had been working hard*		(keine Verschiebung) –
will *she will work hard*	→	**would** *she would work hard*
am/is/are going to *she is going to work hard*	→	**was/were going to** *she was going to work hard*
would/might etc. *she would work hard*		(keine Verschiebung) –
would have/might have etc. *she had been working hard*		(keine Verschiebung) –

⚠ Die modalen Hilfsverben werden folgendermaßen verschoben:

Modalverb	Bedeutung	indirekte Rede
can	Fähigkeit	*could, was/were able to*
can	Erlaubnis	*was/were allowed to*
may	Möglichkeit	*might*
may	Erlaubnis	*was/were allowed to*
must	Pflicht	*had to*
mustn't	Verbot	*was/were not allowed to*
needn't	freie Wahl	*did not/didn't have to*

- Außer wenn man über ein Gespräch, das am selben Tag stattgefunden hat, berichtet, müssen fast alle **Zeit-** und einige **Ortsangaben** entsprechend der folgenden Tabelle geändert werden. (Angaben, die nicht aufgeführt sind, bleiben unverändert.)

direkte Rede		**indirekte Rede**
today	→	*on that day*
tomorrow	→	*the next day*
yesterday	→	*the day before*
the day after tomorrow	→	*two days later*
the day before yesterday	→	*two days before*
next day/Friday/week/Christmas/…	→	*the following day/Friday/week/Christmas/…*
last Friday/week/summer/…	→	*the Friday/week/summer/… before*
two years/months/weeks/…ago	→	*two years/months/weeks/… before*
now, at present	→	*then*
at the moment	→	*at that moment*
at this time	→	*at that time*
here	→	*there*
in this place	→	*at that place*
this	→	*that*
these	→	*those*

B Fragesätze

1 A member of the audience **asked what had led** to the widespread use of robots in factories.
2 She **wanted to know if/whether** her job **was endangered**.

- Bei indirekten **Fragen** unterscheidet man zwischen Fragen mit Fragewort (1) und Fragen ohne Fragewort (2).
- Bei Fragen **mit Fragewort** wird das Fragewort übernommen (1).
- Bei Fragen **ohne Fragewort** benutzt man *if* bzw. *whether* (= ob), um zu verdeutlichen, dass es sich um eine Frage handelt (2).
- Alle anderen Änderungen erfolgen wie bei den Aussagesätzen (siehe **Aussagesätze** oben).

C Bitten, Aufforderungen und Befehle

1 Lucy **asked the engineer to show her** the robot.
2 He **told her not to go** too close to it.

- **Bitten** werden meist durch *asked* (= bitten) (1), **Aufforderungen** und **Befehle** durch *told* (= sagen) (2) eingeleitet.
- Bei **positiven Sätzen** erscheint das Verb als *to* + Infinitiv (1).
- Bei **negativen Sätzen** setzen wir *not* unmittelbar vor *to* (2).

⚠ Die beiden Verben *to tell* und *to ask* stehen immer mit einem Objekt, das die angesprochene Person erwähnt (1, 2). Ist dies vom Kontext her nicht erkennbar, wird einfach ein passender Begriff eingesetzt:

– *Jack said, 'Ann, can you tell Carol to give me a ring, please?'*
– *Jack* **asked Ann** *to tell Carol to give him a ring.*
– *Ben said, 'Don't enter the studio when the red light is on.'*
– *Ben* **told everybody** *not to enter the studio when the red light was on.*

The passive

1 Measures **are being introduced** to reduce traffic pollution.
2 Pollution **is caused by** some thoughtless people.

- Ist der Verursacher einer Handlung unbekannt oder zweitrangig, benutzt man das Passiv. Im Vordergrund steht also das Ergebnis des Vorgangs (1).
- Möchte man den Verursacher doch angeben, benutzt man einen *by agent* (2).
  ⚠ Der Verursacher wird mit *by* – auf keinen mit Fall *from*! – eingeleitet.
- Das Passiv wird mit einer Zeitform von *to be* und der 3. Form des Vollverbs gebildet:

Zeit	Zeitform von *to be*	3. Form
simple present	*am/is/are*	*caused*
present progressive	*am/is/are being*	*introduced*
simple past	*was/were*	*buried*
past progressive	*was/were being*	*built*
present perfect	*has/have been*	*installed*
***will*-Futur**	*will be*	*blocked*
***going to*-Futur**	*am/is/are going to be*	*sacked*

- Beim Gebrauch von modalen Hilfsverben wird nach folgendem Muster verfahren:

bei Aussagen	Hilfsverb + *to be* + 3. Form	*must be displayed*
bei Fragen	Hilfsverb + Subjekt + *to be* + 3. Form	*Can … be persuaded?*

⚠ Das Verb *to be* bleibt im Infinitiv immer unverändert.

The impersonal passive

1 **It is said that** petrol should cost more.
2 He **is thought** to have gone to hospital.

- Das **impersonal passive** wird vor allem dann benutzt, wenn man sich objektiv bzw. unbeteiligt ausdrücken möchte. Daher kommt diese Struktur oft in Polizeiberichten, seriösen Zeitungsartikeln usw. vor.
- Bei Verben des Berichtens, Denkens usw. benutzt man häufig das Satzmuster:
  – *It is/was/…* + 3. Form des einleitenden Verbs + *that*-Satz (1).
  Hier sind weitere Beispiele dieses Musters:
  Aktiv *Some **say** that companies which cause pollution should be heavily fined.*
  Passiv ***It is said that** companies which cause pollution should be heavily fined.*
  Aktiv *Experts **recommended** that more be spent on public transport.*
  Passiv ***It was recommended** that more be spent on public transport.*
- Um das Subjekt des *that*-Satzes zu betonen, kann man folgendes Muster benutzen:
  – Subjekt + *is/was/…* + 3. Form + *to be* + andere Satzteile (2):
  Aktiv *Many **believe** that the minister is thinking of raising fuel taxes.*
  Passiv *The minister **is believed to be** thinking of raising fuel taxes.*
  ⚠ Der *by agent* wird in solchen Passivsätzen folgendermaßen verwendet:
  Aktiv *The speaker felt that the idea was too radical.*
  Passiv *The idea was felt to be too radical **by** the speaker.*

Conditionals

1 If we **invest** in new technology, a lot of people **will lose** their jobs.
2 If more people **took part** in re-training schemes, they **wouldn't have to worry** about finding new employment.
3 We **won't have** political censorship if we **don't start** to censor the internet.
4 **Will** we soon **have** political censorship if we **start** to censor the internet?

- Ein **Konditionalsatz** besteht aus zwei Teilen: dem ***if*-Teil** und dem **Hauptteil**. Der ***if*-Teil** drückt eine **Bedingung** aus, der Hauptteil eine **Folge**.
- Bei **Konditionalsätzen** kommen folgende **Zeitmuster** am häufigsten vor:

Typ I	*If + simple present*	+	*will*-future
Typ II	*If + simple past*	+	*would* + Infinitiv
Typ III	*If + past perfect*	+	*would have* + 3. Form des Verbs

- Je nach Sinn kann der *if*-Teil, der Hauptteil oder beide Teile des Satzes **verneint** werden (2, 3).
- Bei **Fragen** kann nur der **Hauptteil** zu einer Frage geformt werden. Dann steht dieser Teil **an erster Stelle** (4).
- *if*-Sätze werden gemäß der **Wahrscheinlichkeit** der zu erwartenden Folge eingesetzt:
  Typ I: Folge (fast) sicher.
  *If we **invest in** new technology, a lot of people **will lose** their jobs.*
  D.h. viele Leute werden (vermutlich) ihre Stellen verlieren, da wir (sehr wahrscheinlich) in die neue Technologie investieren werden.
  Typ II: Folge theoretisch möglich, aber kaum wahrscheinlich.
  *If we **invested in** new technology, a lot of people **would lose** their jobs.*
  D.h. es ist kaum zu erwarten, dass viele Leute ihre Stellen verlieren werden, da wir (wahrscheinlich) nicht in die neue Technologie investieren werden.
  Typ III: Folge unmöglich, da die Bedingung nicht erfüllt wurde und in bereits in der Vergangenheit liegt.
  *If we **had invested in** new technology, a lot of people **would have lost** their jobs.*
  D.h. der Sprecher weiß schon, dass keiner den Job verloren hat, da wir in die neue Technologie nicht investiert haben.

Gerund/Infinitive

1 Max **enjoys playing** football.
2 Can you **afford to buy** that DVD collection?
3 Cem and Julie **continued to meet** even though they had spilt up.
4 Cem and Julie **continued meeting** even though they had split up.
5 Alison **normally likes going** to parties, but **today** she would **prefer to stay** at home.

- Nach einigen Verben folgt immer die *-ing*-Form (**gerund**) (1).
  Am wichtigsten sind:

admit, avoid, consider, deny, enjoy, finish, imagine, mention, mind (etwas dagegen haben), *miss, practise, risk, suggest*

- **Nach einigen Verben** folgt immer der Infinitiv (**infinitive**) (2).
  Die **wichtigsten** Verben dieser Gruppe sind:

afford, choose, decide, expect, hope, mean, promise, refuse, want

⚠ Nach den Verben *begin, continue, intend* und *start* können der **Infinitiv** oder die **-*ing*-Form beliebig benutzt werden** (3, 4).

- Einige Verben werden **je nach Bedeutung** entweder mit dem **Infinitiv** oder mit der **-*ing*-Form** benutzt. Die **wichtigsten** Verben dieser Gruppe sind:

like, dislike, love, hate, prefer

- Wenn von einer **allgemeingültigen Situation** die Rede ist, folgt auf diese Verben die -*ing*-**Form**. Handelt es sich aber um eine **Ausnahmesituation**, dann verwendet man den **Infinitiv** (5).

advise, allow, encourage, forbid, permit, recommend

Handelt es sich um einen **konkreten Einzelfall**, wird mit diesen Verben ein **Objekt + Infinitiv** verwendet.
*I strongly **advise you to** be more polite to people.*
Wenn es sich aber um eine **allgemeine Situation** handelt, dann steht das nachfolgende Verb in der **-*ing*-Form.**
*Most firms don't **allow smoking** in their offices.*

forget/remember

Die Struktur ***forget/remember* + -*ing*-Form** bezieht sich auf die Vergangenheit. Sie drückt etwa die Idee „Ich werde nie vergessen …“ aus.
⚠ „Vergangenheit“ bezieht sich hier nicht auf *forget/remember*, sondern auf das nachfolgende Verb.
*I still **remember getting** my first bicycle.*
*I'll never **forget going** to the Rock against Hunger concert last year.*

Die Struktur ***forget/remember* + Infinitiv** dagegen bezieht sich auf die Zukunft. Sie drückt etwa die Idee aus „Ich darf nicht vergessen, etwas zu tun“ bzw. „ich habe noch etwas zu tun, weil ich es bis jetzt vergessen habe“.
*Dad, please **remember / don't forget to pick me up** from the station.*
*Oh dear. I **forgot / didn't remember to pick Sally up** from the station.*

regret

Die Struktur ***regret* + -*ing*-Form** drückt Bedauern über eine vergangene Situation bzw. einen vergangenen Vorfall aus. Häufig geht es dabei um verpasste Chancen.
*I really **regret leaving** school without qualifications.*
*I know they will **regret buying** such a big, expensive car.*

Die Struktur ***regret* + Infinitiv** – fast immer mit einem Verb des Mitteilens wie *inform, say, tell* kombiniert – drückt eine schlechte Nachricht aus.
*I **regret to say** that I can't attend the meeting tomorrow.*
*We **regret to inform** you that the vacancy has now been filled.*

stop

Bedeutet stop „aufhören, etwas zu tun“, steht das nachfolgende Verb in der **-*ing*-Form.**
Bedeutet aber stop „kurz anhalten, um etwas anderes zu tun“, folgt ein Verb im **Infinitiv.**
*For heaven's sake **stop shouting** at me.*
*I'm a little late because I **stopped to give** somebody a lift.*

try

Bedeutet *try* „etwas ausprobieren“, steht das nachfolgende Verb in der **-*ing*-Form.**
Bedeutet aber *try* „sich anstrengen, etwas zu tun“, folgt ein Verb im **Infinitiv.**
*I **tried phoning** Ellie, but she wasn't at home.*
*We**'ll try to repair** your computer by the weekend.*

Adjectives and adverbs

1 John has a **new** DVD player.
2 He always buys **expensive** equipment.
3 My computer has become **very slow**.
4 That CD sounds **terrible**.
5 We can make printouts **quickly** and **cheaply**.

- Um **Personen** oder **Sachen** näher zu beschreiben, benutzt man **Adjektive** (1–4).
- Adjektive stehen **unmittelbar** vor Substantiven oder **unmittelbar nach** einer Form von *be* (bzw. *become* oder *seem*, die *be* ersetzen können) (3).
- **Adjektive** können mit Verben wie *feel, look* (aussehen), *sound, smell* und *taste* eine **sinnliche Wahrnehmung** ausdrücken (4).
- Um einen **Tätigkeitsverb** näher zu beschreiben, setzt man ein Adverb **unmittelbar hinter das Verb** bzw. Verb + Objekt (5).
  ⚠ Im Englischen können ein Verb und sein Objekt – anders als im Deutschen – nicht durch ein Adverb getrennt werden. Also NICHT: ~~We can make quickly printouts~~.
- Adverbien werden auch benutzt, um **Adjektive**, **andere Adverbien** und **ganze Sätze** näher zu bestimmen:
  MP3 players have become ***surprisingly cheap****.* (Adverb + Adjektiv)
  My fax machine prints out ***terribly slowly****.* (Adverb + Adverb)
  Luckily *Gerd left a message on my mailbox.* (Satzadverb)
- Die meisten Adverbien werden durch Anhängen von *-ly* an das Adjektiv gebildet (5). Eine kleine Anzahl von Adverbien haben dieselbe Form wie Adjektive; die häufigsten sind *fast, hard, early late, long, daily.*

▸ Word order (S. 135)

Comparison of adjectives and adverbs

1 A hundred years ago life was **slower** and people may have been **happier**.
2 Which technological innovation is the **most/least important**?
3 Today you can copy data **more easily than** ever before.

- **Einsilbige** und **zweisilbige Adjektive**, die auf *-y* enden – zum Beispiel *easy, happy* und *lucky* –, werden mit *-(i)er/-(i)est* gesteigert (1).
- **Mehrsilbige Adjektive** und **Adverbien**, die auf *-ly* enden, werden mit *more/most* gesteigert (2, 3).
  ⚠ Die Adverbien, die dieselbe Form wie das entsprechende Adjektiv haben (*fast, hard, early* usw.), werden mit *-er/-est* gesteigert.
- Um Personen oder Sachen im Satz miteinander zu vergleichen, gibt es folgende Möglichkeiten:

– Kein Unterschied	***as** good **as***	genau so gut wie
– Unterschied	***not as** good **as***	nicht so gut wie
– Unterschied	***better than***	besser als

Word order – positions of adverbs of time, place and frequency

1 She goes shopping **every week**.
2 They play in a club **in Doherty Street**.
3 **Last year** we went to India for our holidays.
4 Paul and Emily went to **the USA last year**.
5 She **always finishes** school early on Fridays.

6 He **is never** at home when I call.
7 I like to stay at home **now and then**.
8 Gina acted **strangely at the party last night**.

- Zeitangaben (Wann?) und Ortsangaben (Wo?, Wohin?) stehen in der Regel am Satzende (1, 2).
- Um die Zeit eines bestimmten Ereignisses hervorzuheben, kann man die Zeitangabe an die erste Stelle setzen (3).
- Stehen eine Zeitangabe und eine Ortsangabe zusammen am Satzende, dann gilt die Reihenfolge Ort vor Zeit (alphabetisch merken: O vor Z!) (4).
- Besteht eine Häufigkeitsangabe aus einem Wort, z.B. *always, often, sometimes*, steht sie unmittelbar vor dem Vollverb (5).
- Lautet das Vollverb *to be*, steht das Adverb **direkt dahinter** (6).
- Besteht die Häufigkeitsangabe aus mehreren Wörtern, z.B. *every day, now and then*, steht sie wie eine Zeitangabe am Satzende (7).
- Adverbien der Art und Weise stehen in der Regel am Satzende. Kommen noch Zeit- oder Ortsadverbien hinzu, lautet die Reihenfolge: Art und Weise – Ort – Zeit (AOZ) (8).

Relative clauses and contact clauses

1 Car manufacturers are designing cars **which/that** can use hydrogen fuel cells.
2 Wildernesses are being spoiled by tourists **who/that** want to go to 'unspoiled' places.
3 Tony filled in a Dateline questionnaire **(which/that)** he found on the Internet.
4 Fred Foley is a paparazzo **whose** photos sell for huge sums of money.
5 Call centre employees, most of **whom** come from India, work long hours.
6 Some non-GM crops are attacked by pests **against which** they have no resistance.

- Relativsätze werden benutzt, um den Hauptsatz durch zusätzliche Informationen genauer zu bestimmen.
- Für **Sachen** benutzt man das Relativpronomen *which* bzw. *that* (1) und für Personen *who* bzw. *that* (2).
- Steht das Relativpronomen für das **Objekt des Hauptsatzes**, dann kann man es weglassen (3). Solche Relativsätze heißen **contact clauses**.
- Um **Besitz** bzw. **Zugehörigkeit** anzuzeigen, gebraucht man *whose* unmittelbar vor dem **Substantiv** bei Personen und Sachen (4).
- Steht eine **Präposition** vor dem **Relativpronomen**, wird *whom* für Personen und *which* für Sachen benutzt (5, 6). In solchen Fällen ist der Gebrauch von *that* nicht möglich.

Defining and non-defining relative clauses

1 The first Europeans **who** settled in Australia came from Britain.
2 Sydney, **which** is famous for its unusually designed opera house, is situated on the south-eastern coast of Australia.

- Im **ersten Beispielsatz** ist der Sinn des Hauptsatzes *The first Europeans came from Britain* ohne den Relativsatz *who settled in Australia* offensichtlich falsch bzw. unvollständig. Relativsätze dieser Art – die wesentlich für das Verständnis des gesamten Satzes sind – nennt man **defining relative clauses** (notwendige oder bestimmende Relativsätze).
- Im **zweiten Beispielsatz** ist die Aussage des Hauptsatzes *Sydney is situated on the south-eastern coast of Australia* ohne den Relativsatz völlig verständlich, weil der Relativsatz *which is famous for its unusually designed opera house* eine zusätzliche, also nebensächliche, Information enhält. Daher werden solche Relativsätze

non-defining relative clauses (nicht notwendige oder nicht bestimmende Relativsätze) genannt.

⚠ Notwendige Relativsätze werden immer **ohne** trennende **Kommas** benutzt. Dies signalisiert, dass sie fester Bestandteil der Hauptaussage sind.

Participle constructions

1 Malaria, preventable with a treated bed net **costing** less than one pound, is endemic.
2 Many men believe that any work **involved** with cooking is a woman's chore.
3 **Losing** more and more people to AIDS, Africa now needs effective help more urgently than ever before.
4 **Burdened** with declining life-expectancy, large parts of Africa are caught in a poverty trap.
5 **Having fetched** water from a river for many years, some women in developing countries are now happy to be able to use the Hippo Roller.
6 **Despite facing** extreme destitution, many rural residents haven't given up hope.
7 Donors should invest in projects that help local inhabitants become self-supporting, **thereby making** sure that the money isn't wasted.
8 Poor infrastructure is a key barrier to economic growth in Nepal, **thus causing** huge additional costs to the transport of commercial goods.
9 Life is becoming hard in the developing countries, **with** many small farmers **going** out of business.
10 AIDS represents a major challenge to sub-Saharan Africa, currently **killing** more than two million people every year.

Die englische Sprache ist geprägt durch häufige Verwendung von Partizipialkonstruktionen. Diese ermöglichen einen eleganteren Sprachfluss. Partizipialkonstruktionen verkürzen

- Relativsätze; dabei kann entweder das **present participle** (1) oder das **past participle** (2) verwendet werden.
- adverbiale Nebensätze; in diesen Fällen unterscheidet man zwischen Partizipialkonstruktionen ohne Konjunktion (3–5) und solchen mit Konjunktion (6–9). In Sätzen ohne Konjunktion ist der Inhalt des Satzes auch ohne eine solche klar. Dagegen sind Konjunktionen nötig, um zu verhindern, dass der logische Zusammenhang des Satzes verloren geht. Zum Beispiel wird der Inhalt von Satz 6 unklar, wenn die Konjunktion *despite* ausgelassen wird.
- Wie bei der Verkürzung von Relativsätzen kommen auch bei der Verkürzung von adverbialen Nebensätzen das **present participle** (3, 6–9) und das **past participle** (4) zur Anwendung. Darüber hinaus wird hier auch noch das **perfect participle** verwendet (5), und zwar um die Vorzeitigkeit der Handlung im Nebensatz auszudrücken. *(Nachdem sie jahrelang Wasser aus dem Fluss geholt hatten, …)*
- Schließlich verknüpft man mit einer Partizipialkonstruktion zwei Hauptsätze zu einem einzigen Satz, und zwar ausnahmslos mittels **present participle** (10).

Countable and uncountable nouns

1 Visit our website for more **information** on our firm. NICHT ~~informations~~
2 Have you read the paper today? The political **news** is interesting. NICHT ~~news are~~
3 Where can I get some **advice**? NICHT ~~an advice~~

- Einige wichtige **Substantive** sind **zählbar im Deutschen**, **nicht jedoch im Englischen**. Diese Substantive können also nicht ohne weiteres mit dem unbestimmten Artikel *a/an* oder mit einem Zahlwort benutzt werden.
  Hier ist eine Liste solcher Wörter, die Sie auswendig lernen sollten:

  advice, baggage, damage, data, equipment, evidence, furniture, garbage (Abfall), *information, knowledge, luck, luggage, machinery, news, progress, research, rubbish, work (housework, homework)*

- Um diese Substantive im Plural zu verwenden, muss *some, a bit of* bzw. *a piece of* hinzugefügt werden (3).

The definite article

1 **Sociologists** say that **violence** is increasing among young people.
2 Is **the current trend** partly caused by **the violent films** they watch?
3 **Most sentences** are not tough enough.
4 Nearly **half the prisoners** in **British prisons** are under 25.
5 **Spring** is my favourite season but **the spring** we're having this year is more like **winter**.
6 We had **breakfast** late this morning so we came to school **by car** instead of **by bus**.
7 They are thinking of legalizing soft drugs in **the Netherlands**.

- Hat ein Substantiv eine allgemeine, uneingeschränkte Bedeutung – also „alle ohne Ausnahme" – dann steht es ohne Artikel (1, 5).
- Ist die Bedeutung eines Substantives auf bestimmte Fälle eingeschränkt, benutzt man den Artikel (2, 5).
- Ferner wird der Artikel in den folgenden Fällen und Wendungen im Englischen – z. T. anders als im Deutschen – nicht gebraucht:
  - bei *most* in der Bedeutung „die meisten" (3),
  - bei öffentlichen Gebäuden im allgemeinen Sinn (4),
  - bei Mahlzeiten (6),
  - bei Verkehrsmitteln (6),
  - bei Straßennamen,
  - bei Tageszeiten, Wochentagen, Monaten und Jahreszeiten im allgemeinen Sinn (5).
- Der Artikel wird verwendet nach *all* und *half* (4) und mit den Pluralnamen von Staaten (7).

  ⚠ Der bestimmte Artikel steht im Englischen (viel) seltener als im Deutschen. Daher: *When in doubt, leave it out!*

UNIT WORD LIST

Dieses Wörterverzeichnis enthält alle in *Crossover 1* eingeführten, in den Texten angegebenen Vokabeln in der Reihenfolge ihres Erscheinens.

TOPIC 1 Young People in Britain and America

TEXT 1 Spare Time – Making the Most of it

page 7

award [ə'wɔ:d]	prize, sth given as a reward for good work	*Auszeichnung, Preis*
community [kə'mju:nəti]	the group of people living in a particular local area	*Gemeinschaft*
to fancy oneself as sth ['fænsi wʌnself əz]	to think that one is sth (often when one is not)	*sich für etw halten*
residential [ˌrezɪ'denʃl]	with accommodation	*mit Übernachtung*
to take the plunge [ˌteɪk ðə 'plʌndʒ]	to decide to do sth, esp. after thinking about it for a long time	*den Sprung wagen*
to wipe sth out [ˌwaɪp 'aʊt]	to use up or take away sth completely	*etw zunichte machen*
to benefit sth ['benɪfɪt]	to improve sth, to be helpful to sth	*etw nützen, zugute kommen*
able-bodied [ˌeɪbl'bɒdid]	opp. disabled	*gesund, tauglich, nicht behindert*
regardless of [rɪ'gɑ:dləs əv]	without considering, no matter what	*unabhängig von*
to fit the bill [ˌfɪt ðə 'bɪl]	to be right for a particular task or situation	*der/die Richtige sein*

page 9

netball ['netbɔ:l]	sport in which players score by throwing a ball through a net at the top of a post	*Korbball*
to compete [kəm'pi:t]	to take part in a game or sport and try to win	*gegeneinander kämpfen*

TEXT 2 The School Uniform Debate

page 10

to indicate ['ɪndɪkeɪt]	to show, to suggest	*besagen, hinweisen auf*
to make the case [ˌmeɪk ðə 'keɪs]	to argue, to give the theory	*die These vertreten*
performance [pə'fɔ:məns]	how well sb does (eg. in an exam)	*Leistung*
crusade [kru:'seɪd]	long campaign for or against sth	*Kreuzzug*
comprehensive [ˌkɒmprɪ'hensɪv]	including all the most important information	*umfassend*
to conduct [kən'dʌkt]	to organise or carry out	*durchführen*
to date [tə 'deɪt]	up until now	*bis heute*
achievement [ə'tʃi:vmənt]	something done well, something gained using one's own skill	*Leistung*
research [rɪ'sɜ:tʃ]	careful study to find new information	*Studie, Untersuchung*
principal ['prɪnsəpl]	*(AE)* BE: headteacher	*Schulleiter/in*

page 11

to curb [kɜ:b]	to reduce, to control	*eindämmen*
prevalent ['prevələnt]	widespread, common	*gängig, verbreitet*
resistance [rɪ'zɪstəns]	attitude where sb is against sth	*Widerstand*

page 12

to be required to [bi rɪ'kwaɪəd tə]	to be needed to or expected to	*es wird von jdm erwartet*
to shape [ʃeɪp]	to influence the development of	*gestalten, festlegen*

page 13

overly ['əʊvəli]	excessively, too	*übermäßig*
baggy ['bægi]	opp. tight	*ausgebeult, herabhängend*
scarf [skɑ:f]	cloth worn around the neck or over the hair	*Kopftuch, Schal*
dog collar ['dɒg kɒlə]	band with studs or spikes worn around the neck	*Nietenhalsband*
stud [stʌd]	small piece of metal worn as earring or other piercing	*Piercing*

TEXT 3 Teenagers are Trouble?

page 16

supposedly [sə'pəʊzɪdli]	thought to be	*angeblich*
reputation [ˌrepju'teɪʃn]	what people in general think of sb or sth	*Ruf*
garment ['gɑːmənt]	piece of clothing	*Kleidungsstück*
fashion statement ['fæʃn steɪtmənt]	something worn to draw attention to oneself	*Ausdruck eines modischen Stils, Statement*
shoplifting ['ʃɒplɪftɪŋ]	stealing goods from a shop	*Ladendiebstahl*
to be up to no good [bi ˌʌp tə nəʊ 'gʊd]	to be doing something bad	*nichts Gutes im Schilde führen*
to insult [ɪn'sʌlt]	to offend, to say nasty things to	*beleidigen*
to clutch [klʌtʃ]	to hold on tightly to	*umklammern*
target ['tɑːgɪt]	here: victim	*Ziel*
assumption [ə'sʌmpʃn]	sth that sb thinks is true although they have no proof	*Annahme*
to provoke [prə'vəʊk]	to cause a particular reaction, to give rise to	*provozieren*
to taunt [tɔːnt]	to tease, to say nasty things to	*verhöhnen*
to intimidate [ɪn'tɪmɪdeɪt]	to frighten, to threaten	*einschüchtern*
vicious circle [ˌvɪʃəs 'sɜːkl]	a situation in which one problem causes another problem which makes the first problem worse and so on	*Teufelskreis*
to be down to sth [bi 'daʊn tə]	to be the result of, to be caused by	*an etw liegen*
to portray [pɔː'treɪ]	to represent, to describe	*darstellen*
to blame sb for sth ['bleɪm fə]	to say that sb has done sth bad	*jdm/etw die Schuld an etw geben*

page 18

widespread ['waɪdspred]	common to many places or among many people	*weit verbreitet*
despite [dɪ'spaɪt]	in spite of	*ungeachtet dessen*
survey ['sɜːveɪ]	investigation, research using questionnaires	*Umfrage*
offender [ə'fendə]	lawbreaker, person who does sth wrong	*Straftäter/in*
regarding [rɪ'gɑːdɪŋ]	concerning, about	*bezüglich, betreffend*
to claim [kleɪm]	to say to be true	*behaupten, verkünden*
binge [bɪndʒ]	excess of a particular activity (eg. drinking)	*Sauforgie*

TEXT 4 Part-time Jobs

page 21

to dread [dred]	to fear, to be very afraid of	*fürchten*
my stomach churns [maɪ 'stʌmək tʃɜːnz]	to feel disgusted	*mir dreht sich der Magen um*
stench [stentʃ]	stink, strong unpleasant smell	*Gestank*
dungeon ['dʌndʒən]	underground prison, esp. in a castle	*Kerker*
to escape [ɪ'skeɪp]	to get away from	*entfliehen, entkommen*
lettuce ['letɪs]	plant with leaves often used to make salads	*(grüner) Salat*
remotely [rɪ'məʊtli]	slightly	*entfernt, im Entferntesten*
to clock on [ˌklɒk 'ɒn]	to record the time one starts work (usually by putting a card in a machine)	*(den Arbeitsbeginn) stempeln*
greasiness ['griːzinəs]	oiliness	*Schmierigkeit, Öligkeit*
surroundings (pl.) [sə'raʊndɪŋz]	environment, things all around	*Umgebung*
to sizzle ['sɪzl]	to make a noise like food frying	*brutzeln*
to crackle ['krækl]	to make short sharp noises (eg. like wood burning)	*knistern*
to gush out [ˌgʌʃ 'aʊt]	to flow suddenly and quickly	*herausschießen, heraussprudeln*
to vomit ['vɒmɪt]	to be sick, to throw up	*erbrechen*
essentials (pl.) [ɪ'senʃlz]	necessities, things that are needed	*Notwendigkeiten, das Wesentliche*

page 22

to hold down a job [həʊld ˌdaʊn ə 'dʒɒb]	to have a job for some time	*einer Arbeit nachgehen*
food outlet ['fuːd aʊtlet]	place where food is sold ready to eat	*Imbiss*
occupation [ˌɒkju'peɪʃn]	job, type of work	*Tätigkeit*

TEXT 5 Calorie Countdown

page 24

eating disorders (pl.) [ˌiːtɪŋ dɪsˈɔːdəz]	health problems related to sb's eating habits	*Essstörungen*
skinny [ˈskɪni]	very thin	*mager, dürr*
to starve oneself [ˈstɑːv wʌnself]	to eat very little or no food (usually when trying to lose weight)	*hungern*
short-term [ˌʃɔːt ˈtɜːm]	opp. long-term	*kurzfristig*
gain [geɪn]	achievement, improvement	*Zugewinn*
stick-thin [ˌstɪkˈθɪn]	extremely thin	*spindeldürr*
gruesome [ˈgruːsəm]	horrible, grim	*grausig*
insomnia [ɪnˈsɒmniə]	condition where sb finds it impossible to get to sleep	*Schlaflosigkeit*
sick [sɪk]	unhealthy, perverse	*krank, pervers*
comfort [ˈkʌmfət]	sth that makes sb feel better when worried or upset	*Trost*
reassurance [ˌriːəˈʃʊərəns]	sth that helps reduce sb's doubts or worries	*Bestätigung*
mood swing [ˈmuːd swɪŋ]	sudden change in sb's emotions or attitude	*Stimmungsschwankung*
weird [wɪəd]	strange, mysterious	*seltsam*
obsessive [əbˈsesɪv]	thinking about one thing much more often or for much longer than is normal	*zwanghaft, besessen*
assessment [əˈsesmənt]	examination	*Beurteilung, Prüfung*
to reveal [rɪˈviːl]	to show, to make known	*offenbaren, verraten*
potassium [pəˈtæsiəm]	chemical element (K)	*Kalium*
to plummet [ˈplʌmɪt]	to fall quickly	*fallen*
to contract [kənˈtrækt]	to get or catch (eg. an illness)	*erkranken an, sich zuziehen*
self-aware [ˈself əweə]	conscious of one's self (both the body and the mind)	*seiner selbst bewusst*
honourable [ˈɒnərəbl]	worthy of respect or praise	*ehrenhaft*
disgusted [dɪsˈgʌstɪd]	unpleasantly shocked	*angewidert*
miserable [ˈmɪzrəbl]	very sad, deeply unhappy	*elend, unglücklich*
failure [ˈfeɪljə]	opp. success	*Versager/in*
to put sb off [ˌpʊt ˈɒf]	to discourage sb, to make sb lose interest in sth	*jdn abschrecken*
fuel [ˈfjuːəl]	sth that produces power or energy	*Treibstoff*

page 26

underfed [ˌʌndəˈfed]	having not had enough to eat	*unterernährt*
medieval [ˌmediˈiːvl]	from the Middle Ages (about AD600 to AD1450)	*mittelalterlich*
forehead [ˈfɔːhed]	part of the face between the eyes and the hair	*Stirn*
Virgin Mary [ˌvɜːdʒɪn ˈmæri]	mother of Jesus	*Jungfrau Maria*
desirable [dɪˈzaɪərəbl]	sexually attractive	*begehrenswert*
well-nourished [ˌwel ˈnʌrɪʃt]	healthy and well fed	*gut genährt*
by no means [baɪ ˌnəʊ ˈmiːnz]	in no way, not at all	*keineswegs*

TEXT 6 Intercultural Relationships

page 29

to let sb down [ˌlet ˈdaʊn]	to disappoint sb, to fail to do what sb hoped or expected	*jdn im Stich lassen*
odd [ɒd]	strange	*seltsam*
as far as sb is concerned [əz fɑːr əz sʌmbədi ɪz kənˈsɜːnd]	in sb's opinion	*was jdn betrifft*
to maintain [meɪnˈteɪn]	to keep, to hold on to	*aufrechterhalten, bewahren*
to get on with sb [ˌget ˈɒn wɪð]	to be friendly with sb, to have a good relationship with sb	*sich gut mit jdm verstehen*
to be fond of sb [bi ˈfɒnd əv]	to like sb, to be close to sb	*jdn gern haben*
to cancel [ˈkænsl]	to call off	*absagen*
straight [streɪt]	directly, honestly	*offen, direkt*

page 32

large-scale [ˈlɑːdʒskeɪl]	involving many people or things	*in großem Umfang*
diverse [daɪˈvɜːs]	varied	*vielfältig*
dazzling [ˈdæzlɪŋ]	brilliant	*schillernd*
tension [ˈtenʃn]	situation where there are problems or bad feelings between different people or groups	*Spannung*
to feel comfortable with [fiːl ˈkʌmftəbl wɪð]	to feel at ease with sth, to not worry about sth	*mit etw gut zurechtkommen*

TEXT 7 A Gap Year in the US

page 34

gap year ['gæp jɪə]	year between school and university (often spent travelling or working)	*Zeitraum zwischen Schule und Studium*
sheltered ['ʃeltəd]	protected from the more difficult or unpleasant parts of life	*behütet*
to face sth [feɪs]	to have to deal with sth	*vor etw stehen*
high rope ['haɪ rəʊp]	*(AE)* BE: tightrope	*Hochseil*
pond probe ['pɒnd prəʊb]	investigation to see what lives in a pond (ie. a small area of still water)	*Teichuntersuchung*
corporate ['kɔːpərət]	business	*Firmen-, Unternehmens-*
reward [rɪ'wɔːd]	sth given for sb's hard work or good results	*Belohnung, Lohn*
chief executive [ˌtʃiːf ɪg'zekjətɪv]	person who has the highest rank in a company	*Vorstandschef/in*
height [haɪt]	high place	*Höhe*
initial [ɪ'nɪʃl]	first	*erste(r, s)*
placement ['pleɪsmənt]	job, work experience	*Praktikum*
counsellor ['kaʊnsələ]	*(AE)* person who is in charge at a summer camp	*Betreuer/in*
log cabin [ˌlɒg 'kæbɪn]	small house made of wooden logs	*Blockhütte*
sibling ['sɪblɪŋ]	brother or sister	*Bruder, Schwester, Geschwister*
prospective [prə'spektɪv]	future	*zukünftig*
to throw oneself in at the deep end [θrəʊ wʌnself ˌɪn ət ðə diːp 'end]	to take on a difficult task that you are not fully prepared for	*ins kalte Wasser springen*

page 36

a variety of [ə və'raɪəti əv]	different kinds of, a number of	*eine Vielzahl von*
to pursue [pə'sjuː]	to try to do sth over a period of time	*verfolgen*
range [reɪndʒ]	variety, spectrum	*Spektrum, Bandbreite*
mountain range ['maʊntən reɪndʒ]	line or group of mountains	*Bergkette, Gebirgszug*
to range (from … to) ['reɪndʒ frəm tə]	to include a number of different things	*reichen, sich erstrecken (von … bis zu)*
abroad [ə'brɔːd]	in or to a foreign country	*im/ins Ausland*

TOPIC 2 Regions in Britain and the US – and a Changing City

TEXT 1 Robbie Coltrane's Glasgow

page 39

grid [grɪd]	pattern of straight lines crossing to form squares	*Gitternetz*
tremendous [trɪ'mendəs]	great, really good	*enorm, großartig*
refurbishment [rɪ'fɜːbɪʃmənt]	work on a building to improve it	*Renovierung*
feel [fiːl]	atmosphere, mood	*Atmosphäre*
roll [rəʊl]	small round bread	*Brötchen*
weirdo ['wɪədəʊ]	*(slang)* someone who looks odd or acts in an odd way	*komischer Kauz*
to take sth for granted [ˌteɪk fə 'grɑːntɪd]	to be so used to sth that you do not really notice it or appreciate it any more	*etw für selbstverständlich halten*
to be more vocal about sth [bi mɔː 'vəʊkl əbaʊt]	to speak more loudly about sth	*etw lauter sagen*
astonishing [ə'stɒnɪʃɪŋ]	hard to believe, very surprising	*erstaunlich*
notorious [nəʊ'tɔːriəs]	famous (often for sth bad)	*notorisch, (berühmt-) berüchtigt*
stylish ['staɪlɪʃ]	fashionable, well-dressed	*elegant, stilvoll*
to dress to the nines [ˌdres tə ðə 'naɪnz]	to dress very smartly	*sich in Schale werfen*
woe betide you [ˌwəʊ bɪ'taɪd juː]	*(humorous)* there will be trouble	*wehe dir*
grub [grʌb]	*(slang)* food	*(umgs.) Essen*
scallywag ['skæliwæg]	*(slang)* person (usually a child) who does sth bad but not very serious	*Schlingel, frecher Bursche*
to flog [flɒg]	*(slang)* to sell	*verhökern*
old fart [ˌəʊld 'fɑːt]	*(slang, taboo)* person who is boring or stupid (and often old)	*(umgs.) alter Sack*
disaffected [ˌdɪsə'fektɪd]	disillusioned, dissatisfied	*desillusioniert*

page 41		
shipyard ['ʃɪpjɑ:d]	place where ships are built and repaired	*Schiffswerft*
to line [laɪn]	to be in rows or lines along sth	*säumen*
decline [dɪ'klaɪn]	decrease over time	*Rückgang, Niedergang*
poverty ['pɒvəti]	state of being poor	*Armut*
to mark [mɑ:k]	to show, to signal (eg. a change)	*prägen*
landmark ['lændmɑ:k]	important (esp. in a historical sense)	*wegweisend, historisch*
to host [həʊst]	to organise an event to which other people are invited	*veranstalten, ausrichten*
previous ['pri:viəs]	before, in the past	*vorher, zuvor*
derelict ['derəlɪkt]	no longer used or maintained (usually referring to buildings or land)	*heruntergekommen, baufällig*
fortune ['fɔ:tʃu:n]	good and bad things that happen to sb or sth	*Schicksal*
to thrive [θraɪv]	to do very well, to be continuously successful	*florieren*
glossy ['glɒsi]	smooth and shiny	*glänzend, Hochglanz-*
abuse [ə'bju:z]	use of sth in a way that is wrong or dangerous	*Missbrauch*

TEXT 2 Poor Diet in Glasgow's East End

page 43		
life expectancy ['laɪf ɪkspektənsi]	how long sb is expected to live	*Lebenserwartung*
comparable ['kɒmpərəbl]	similar	*vergleichbar*
lifespan ['laɪfspæn]	amount of time that sb is alive	*Lebensdauer*
profoundly [prə'faʊndli]	deeply, very	*zutiefst*
concerned [kən'sɜ:nd]	worried	*besorgt*
can't be bothered (to do sth) [ˌkɑ:nt bi 'bɒðəd]	to not want to spend time or energy doing sth	*keine Lust haben (etw zu tun)*
to pick up the pieces [ˌpɪk ʌp ðə 'pi:sɪz]	to get things back to normal after sth has gone wrong	*die Scherben aufsammeln, etw wiedergutmachen*
page 44		
to be on benefits [ˌbi ɒn 'benɪfɪts]	to get money from the government (eg. because you are sick or have no job)	*Unterstützung bekommen*
to rely on [rɪ'laɪ ɒn]	to depend on sth, to need sth	*sich auf etw verlassen*
convenience food [kən'vi:niəns fu:d]	food that can be cooked very quickly and easily (often frozen or in a can)	*Fertiggericht(e)*
ability [ə'bɪləti]	possibility to do sth	*Möglichkeit*
to flourish ['flʌrɪʃ]	to thrive, to do well	*florieren, gedeihen*
victim ['vɪktɪm]	person who suffers as a result of sth that has happened	*Opfer*
circumstance ['sɜ:kəmstəns]	condition, situation	*Umstand*
to sort out [ˌsɔ:t 'aʊt]	to deal with, to resolve	*in Ordnung bringen*
to be called to account [bi ˌkɔ:l tə ə'kaʊnt]	to make sb explain why they have done sth wrong	*zur Rechenschaft gezogen werden*
to pin one's hopes on sth [ˌpɪn wʌnz 'həʊps ɒn]	to rely on sth for success	*seine ganze Hoffnung auf etw setzen*
it's not rocket science [ɪts nɒt 'rɒkɪt saɪəns]	*(slang)* it's not very difficult	*es ist keine hohe Wissenschaft*
daft [dɑ:ft]	silly, funny	*doof*
to afford sth [ə'fɔ:d]	to have enough money for sth	*sich etw leisten*
undertaker ['ʌndəteɪkə]	person whose job it is to organise funerals and prepare dead bodies before they are buried	*Leichenbestatter*
to take sth in your stride [ˌteɪk ɪn jə 'straɪd]	to stay positive when a bad thing happens	*sich keine Gedanken um etw machen*
page 46		
disease [dɪ'zi:z]	illness, infection	*Erkrankung*
obese [əʊ'bi:s]	so fat that it is unhealthy	*fettleibig*
to be at play [ˌbi ət 'pleɪ]	to have an influence, to play a role	*mit hineinspielen, eine Rolle spielen*
to deep-fry ['di:p fraɪ]	to cook food in hot oil that covers it completely	*frittieren*
pie [paɪ]	pastry baked in a dish with a sweet or savoury filling	*Pastete; Kuchen*
brisk [brɪsk]	lively	*rege*
ongoing ['ɒngəʊɪŋ]	continuing, still happening	*im Gange, laufend*

TEXT 3 A Short History of Scotland

page 47

to decline [dɪ'klaɪn]	to decrease, to become smaller or less important	*zurückgehen*
due to sth ['dju: tə]	because of sth	*aufgrund von etw*
agriculture ['ægrɪkʌltʃə]	farming	*Landwirtschaft*
clearance ['klɪərəns]	removal, emptying	*Räumung*
entire [ɪn'taɪə]	whole	*ganz*
be reborn [bi ˌri:'bɔ:n]	to become active or useful again	*wieder aufleben*

page 48

mutual ['mju:tʃuəl]	common	*gemeinsam*
to roam sth [rəʊm]	to wander, to travel without a definite aim	*durch etw ziehen*

page 51

act [ækt]	law	*Gesetz*
struggle ['strʌgl]	fighting to achieve sth	*Auseinandersetzung, Kampf*
warfare ['wɔ:feə]	fighting that goes on in a war	*Krieg, Kriegsführung*
to irritate ['ɪrɪteɪt]	to annoy	*ärgern*
to comprise [kəm'praɪz]	to consist of, to be made up of	*umfassen, bestehen aus*
to devolve sth to sb [dɪ'vɒlv tə]	to give sth (e.g. power or responsibility) to sb	*etw jdm übertragen*
framework ['freɪmwɜ:k]	structure, system	*Rahmen, Grundlage*
outright ['aʊtraɪt]	complete, total	*total, gänzlich, völlig*
to fail [feɪl]	to be unsuccessful	*scheitern*
domestic policy [dəˌmestɪk 'pɒləsi]	opp. foreign policy	*Innenpolitik*

TEXT 4 American Regions and Cities

page 52

to estimate ['estɪmeɪt]	to form an idea of sth (e.g. a quantity or price) without calculating it exactly	*schätzen*
census ['sensəs]	official process of collecting facts about the population	*Volkszählung*

TEXT 5 Out and About in the American Midwest

page 55

adolescence [ˌædə'lesns]	puberty, teenage years	*Jugend, Pubertät*
to moan about sth ['məʊn əbaʊt]	to complain	*über etw jammern*
dump [dʌmp]	*(slang)* unpleasant place, place where there is nothing to do	*Müllkippe; Kaff*
to settle down [ˌsetl 'daʊn]	to find a place to live	*sesshaft werden*
interstate ['ɪntəsteɪt]	*(US)* main road running from one state to the next; UK: motorway	*etwa: Autobahn (in den USA)*
hub [hʌb]	centre	*Zentrum, Knotenpunkt*
tournament ['tʊənəmənt]	competition between different people or teams	*Turnier*
hayseed ['heɪsi:d]	*(AE, slang)* person from the countryside who does not know much about culture or modern life	*Landpomeranze*
to accost [ə'kɒst]	to go and speak to sb (esp. in a rude or threatening way)	*ansprechen*
snide [snaɪd]	indirectly nasty or critical	*abfällig*
to negotiate [nɪ'gəʊʃieɪt]	to get through or past something that is in the way	*bewältigen*
revolving door [ˌrɪvɒlvɪŋ 'dɔ:]	door which turns in a circle as people walk through it	*Drehtür*
remote [rɪ'məʊt]	isolated, far away from other places	*abgelegen*
hamlet ['hæmlət]	very small village	*kleines Dorf*
delirious [dɪ'lɪriəs]	mad, unable to think or speak properly because of extreme emotion	*im Delirium, Taumel*
to insist [ɪn'sɪst]	to demand	*darauf bestehen*
(bowling) alley ['bəʊlɪŋ æli]	place where people can go bowling (ie. roll a ball at skittles to try to knock them down)	*Kegelbahn (Gebäude)*
warped ['wɔ:pt]	bent, twisted, out of shape	*verzogen, verbogen*
lane [leɪn]	narrow strip along which bowling balls are rolled	*Kegelbahn*
chipped ['tʃɪpt]	damaged by having small pieces broken off	*abgestoßen*
soda ['səʊdə]	*(AE)* sweet fizzy drink	*Limonade*
to sigh [saɪ]	to breathe out deeply (eg. to show happiness or sadness)	*seufzen*
inordinate [ɪn'ɔ:dɪnət]	far more than is normal	*außerordentlich*
approach [ə'prəʊtʃ]	movement nearer to sb or sth	*Herankommen*
to zip [zɪp]	*(slang)* to move very fast	*sausen*
rear-view mirror [ˌrɪəvju: 'mɪrə]	mirror in which the driver can see what is behind them	*Rückspiegel*

haze [heɪz]	air that is hard to see through (often because of very hot weather)	*Dunst(schleier), Schwaden*

page 57

bite to eat [ˌbaɪt tə 'iːt]	*(slang)* snack, small meal	*Happen zu essen*
spare tire [ˌspeə 'taɪə]	*(AE)* extra wheel for a car; BE: spare tyre	*Ersatzreifen*
to patch [pætʃ]	to mend (by covering a hole in sth)	*flicken*
homemade diner [ˌhəʊmmeɪd 'daɪnə]	(esp. *AE*) small cheap restaurant	*einfache Imbissstube*
rawhide ['rɔːhaɪd]	*(AE, slang)* rough, tough (like a cowboy)	*raubeinig*
bunch [bʌntʃ]	*(slang)* group, gang	*Gruppe, Haufen*
raspy ['rɑːspi]	croaky, rough-sounding (eg. voice)	*rau*
plain [pleɪn]	large area of flat land	*Ebene*
regard [rɪ'gɑːd]	respect, care	*Respekt, Beachtung*
to boom [buːm]	to make a loud deep sound	*dröhnen, donnern*
cherry pie ['tʃeri paɪ]	pastry filled with cherries	*Kirschkuchen*
scoop [skuːp]	amount picked up by a scoop (ie. a big round spoon for serving ice cream etc.)	*Kugel*
to rustle sth up [ˌrʌsl 'ʌp]	*(slang)* to make sth (eg. some food) quickly and unplanned	*etw organisieren, fertigmachen*
raw [rɔː]	not cooked	*roh*
to yell [jel]	to shout loudly	*schreien*

TEXT 6 On the Road in the US

page 58

storied ['stɔːrid]	legendary	*legendär, sagenumwoben*
expanse [ɪk'spæns]	large open area (eg. of land or water)	*Fläche, Weite*
to festoon [fe'stuːn]	to decorate, to hang	*schmücken, behängen; aufhängen*
sound [saʊnd]	deep, peaceful (describing sleep)	*fest*
rude [ruːd]	sudden and unexpected (in a negative sense)	*unsanft*
to jolt [dʒəʊlt]	to move suddenly, to give sb a sudden shock	*aufrütteln*
haggard ['hægəd]	looking very tired	*ausgezehrt*
bleak [bliːk]	sad-looking, empty	*öde, trostlos*
trolley ['trɒli]	*(AE)* BE: tram	*Straßenbahn*
to shroud [ʃraʊd]	to cover, to hide	*umhüllen, einhüllen*
to stumble ['stʌmbl]	to trip over, to walk unsteadily	*stolpern, torkeln*
bum [bʌm]	(esp. *AE, slang*) person who has no home and no job and asks other people for money	*Penner/in*
dime [daɪm]	coin worth ten cents	*(US) Zehncentstück*
dawn [dɔːn]	time of early morning when the first sunlight appears in the sky	*Morgendämmerung*
to dig [dɪg]	*(slang)* to really like sth	*(umgs.) auskosten, mögen, genießen*
shack [ʃæk]	small roughly built building usually made of wood or metal	*Baracke*
treed [triːd]	covered with trees	*bewaldet*
profuse [prə'fjuːs]	in large amounts	*üppig*
slope [sləʊp]	surface that is higher at one end than at the other	*Abhang*
to descend [dɪ'send]	to go down, to fall	*sich herabsenken, hinunterkommen*
cottonwood ['kɒtnwʊd]	type of poplar tree with seeds that look as if they are covered in cotton	*Pappel*
to brood [bruːd]	*(literary)* to be sad or mysterious	*brüten*
peak [piːk]	highest point	*Gipfel*
foothill ['fʊthɪl]	small hill or mountain around the base of other bigger mountains	*Ausläufer, Vorgebirge*
to advance [əd'vɑːns]	to move forward	*herankommen*
patch [pætʃ]	small area of land (esp. one where a particular plant is grown)	*Landstück, Beet*
to spin [spɪn]	to turn round quickly	*sich drehen, herumwirbeln*
dizzy ['dɪzi]	feeling as if everything is spinning around	*schwindlig*
bulge [bʌldʒ]	round lump or swelling	*Wölbung*
bulk [bʌlk]	main part of sth	*Ausmaß, Masse*
gloomy ['gluːmi]	dark in a depressing way	*düster*

page 60

naval ['neɪvl]	connected to the navy (ie. the part of the armed forces that fights at sea)	*Marine-*
to service ['sɜːvɪs]	to examine and repair	*warten*
fleet [fliːt]	a group of ships	*Flotte*
to contribute to [kən'trɪbjuːt tə]	to give (usually sth useful)	*beitragen zu*

page 61

gentle ['dʒentl]	calm and kind	*sanft, gutmütig*
love-in ['lʌvɪn]	party where people show sexual attraction and love for each other freely (esp. amongst the hippies of the 1960s)	*Liebesrausch*

TOPIC 3 The Media Today

TEXT 1 Virtual Friends?

page 62

likes (pl.) [laɪks]	things that sb likes	*Vorlieben*
relationship [rɪ'leɪʃnʃɪp]	emotional connection between two people	*Beziehung*
to hook up with sb [ˌhʊk 'ʌp wɪð]	*(slang)* to meet, to communicate with	*sich mit jdm zusammentun*
like-minded [ˌlaɪk 'maɪndɪd]	with similar interests and opinions	*gleich gesinnt*
appeal [ə'piːl]	what makes sth popular or attractive	*Reiz*
crucial ['kruːʃl]	essential, extremely important	*entscheidend*
adolescent [ˌædə'lesnt]	of the time between childhood and adulthood	*jugendlich*
ease [iːz]	lack of difficulty	*Leichtigkeit*
asset ['æset]	sth useful or valuable	*Wert, Vermögen*
upwards of ['ʌpwədz əv]	more than, over	*über, mehr als*
akin to sth [ə'kɪn tə]	like sth, similar to sth	*einer Sache ähnlich*
reach [riːtʃ]	extent of influence	*Sphäre, Bereich*
to want [wɒnt]	need	*brauchen*
compassion [kəm'pæʃn]	sympathy	*Mitleid*
envy ['envi]	jealousy, wanting what sb else has	*Neid*
pal [pæl]	*(slang)* friend, mate	*Kumpel*

page 65

venture ['ventʃə]	project or activity (esp. one that is risky)	*Unternehmen*
to measure ['meʒə]	to check how big/high etc sth is or how many of sth there are	*messen*
to respond [rɪ'spɒnd]	to answer, to react	*reagieren, antworten*

TEXT 2 The TV Business

page 66

to touch up [ˌtʌtʃ 'ʌp]	to make small changes to sth to make it better	*retuschieren, ausbessern*
icicle ['aɪsɪkl]	pointed piece of ice	*Eiszapfen*
snowdrift ['snəʊdrɪft]	mass of snow piled up by the wind	*Schneewehe*
to double for ['dʌbl fə]	to represent, to serve as	*(im Film) darstellen*
set [set]	place where a TV show or film is filmed	*Szenenbild, Set*
lot [lɒt]	piece of ground, site	*Gelände*
prime time ['praɪm taɪm]	time of day when the largest number of people are watching TV	*Hauptsendezeit*
grip [grɪp]	power, control	*Griff, Kontrolle*
conglomerate [kən'glɒmərət]	big company formed by joining together smaller companies	*Konzern*

page 67

to pick at sth ['pɪk ət]	to eat sth slowly and only in small amounts	*in etw herumstochern*
beneficiary [ˌbenɪ'fɪʃəri]	person who benefits from sth	*Nutznießer*
sustained [sə'steɪnd]	continuing without decreasing	*anhaltend*
to recall [rɪ'kɔːl]	to remember	*sich erinnern an*
to have the edge [ˌhəv ði 'edʒ]	small advantage	*einen Vorteil haben*
to dwarf [dwɔːf]	to make sth look smaller in comparison with sth else	*in den Schatten stellen*
formidable ['fɔːmɪdəbl]	impressive (esp. in a way which makes people feel respect or fear)	*gewaltig, enorm*
array [ə'reɪ]	range, collection	*Ansammlung*

gadget ['gædʒɪt]	device (usually small, often electronic) that does sth useful	*Gerät*
to flicker ['flɪkə]	to keep going on and off	*flimmern*
to captivate ['kæptɪveɪt]	to fascinate, to keep sb interested	*faszinieren, fesseln*
poll [pəʊl]	survey	*Umfrage*
to eat into ['i:t ɪntə]	to take away from sth (esp. time or money)	*verringern, angreifen*

page 68

conversely [kən'vɜ:sli]	in contrast, on the contrary	*umgekehrt*

TEXT 3 snd me a txt (Send Me a Text Message)

page 70

craze [kreɪz]	interest common to many people (esp. one that does not last very long)	*Mode, Fimmel*
to dump sb [dʌmp]	*(slang)* to end a relationship with	*(umgs.) mit jdm Schluss machen*
to evade [ɪ'veɪd]	to avoid, to escape from	*sich einer Sache entziehen*
to chat sb up [ˌtʃæt 'ʌp]	*(slang)* to talk to sb to whom one is attracted	*jdn anquatschen, anbaggern*
to edit ['edɪt]	to make changes to a text	*bearbeiten, überarbeiten*
brave [breɪv]	not afraid, able to do sth that is difficult or dangerous	*mutig*
abbreviation [əˌbri:vi'eɪʃn]	short form of a word or group of words	*Abkürzung*

page 71

to creep into sth ['kri:p ɪntə]	to start to appear in sth, to slowly affect sth	*sich in etw einschleichen*
to argue with sb ['ɑ:gju: wɪð]	to speak to sb in an angry way because they do not agree with you	*sich mit jdm streiten*
to get lost [ˌget 'lɒst]	*(slang)* to go away	*(umgs.) abhauen*

page 73

to emerge [ɪ'mɜ:dʒ]	to appear, to become known	*aufkommen*
impact ['ɪmpækt]	effect	*Auswirkung*
to innovate ['ɪnəveɪt]	to create new things or new ways of doing sth	*erneuern*
component [kəm'pəʊnənt]	part	*Bestandteil*
appropriate [ə'prəʊpriət]	suitable, acceptable in a particular situation	*angemessen*

TEXT 4 Criticising the Media

page 74

nutritional value [njuˌtrɪʃənl 'vælju:]	measure of how good a food is for the body (ie. of what it contains)	*Nährwert*
to gawk [gɔ:k]	*(slang)* to look at sb/sth for a long time in a way that is rude or stupid	*gaffen*
worshipful ['wɜ:ʃɪpfl]	showing deep respect for sb/sth	*verehrend, vergötternd*
disgusting [dɪs'gʌstɪŋ]	sickening, shocking, extremely unpleasant	*widerlich*
to behold [bɪ'həʊld]	*(literary)* to see, to look at	*beobachten, sehen*
warrior ['wɒriə]	person who fights in a war or battle	*Krieger*
to rake it in [ˌreɪk ɪt 'ɪn]	to earn large amounts of money	*abkassieren*
smart [smɑ:t]	clever, intelligent	*clever, raffiniert*
filthy ['fɪlθi]	very dirty	*schmutzig*
rotten ['rɒtn]	*(slang)* dishonest, unfair	*verdorben, korrupt*
to kid sb [kɪd]	*(slang)* to make sb believe sth that is not really true	*jdm etwas vormachen*
to chop [tʃɒp]	to cut sth into small pieces	*(zer)hacken*
counter ['kaʊntə]	surface in a shop over which goods are sold	*Ladentisch, Theke*
fame [feɪm]	state of being well known	*Ruhm*
conspiracy [kən'spɪrəsi]	secret plan by a group of people to do sth bad	*Verschwörung, Komplott*
lowest common denominator [ləʊɪst ˌkɒmən dɪ'nɒmɪneɪtə]	sth simple that interests the largest possible number of people	*kleinster gemeinsamer Nenner*
con [kɒn]	*(slang)* swindle, nasty trick	*Schwindel*
homespun ['həʊmspʌn]	home-made	*selbst gestrickt, einfach*
as opposed to [əz ə'pəʊzd tə]	in contrast to	*im Gegensatz zu*
hollow ['hɒləʊ]	empty, without real meaning	*hohl*
fertility [fə'tɪləti]	ability to produce good results or new ideas	*Fruchtbarkeit*

page 76

literacy ['lɪtərəsi]	ability to read and write, education	*die Fähigkeit, lesen und schreiben zu können, Bildung*
to reject [rɪ'dʒekt]	to say no to, to refuse to consider or accept sth	*ablehnen, zurückweisen*
condescending [ˌkɒndɪ'sendɪŋ]	treating others as less important	*herablassend*
to resolve [rɪ'zɒlv]	to settle	*entscheiden, klären*
to proliferate [prə'lɪfəreɪt]	to increase in number very quickly	*wachsen, sich verbreiten*

TEXT 5 Reporting the Royals – the Quality and Popular Press in Britain

page 78

to attempt [ə'tempt]	to try	*versuchen*
to ward off [ˌwɔːd 'ɒf]	to protect oneself against	*abwehren, abwenden*
bout [baʊt]	short period when there is a lot of a particular thing or activity (esp. sth unpleasant)	*Runde, Phase*
off limits [ˌɒf 'lɪmɪts]	not allowed (to be discussed)	*tabu*
extract ['ekstrækt]	short piece taken from a text	*Auszug*
to prevent [prɪ'vent]	to stop sth happening, to avoid	*verhindern*
exhaustive [ɪg'zɔːstɪv]	very thorough, taking all possibilities into account	*umfassend, gründlich*
inquiry [ɪn'kwaɪəri]	official investigation	*Untersuchung*
conclusive [kən'kluːsɪv]	proving sth, finding one definite answer	*eindeutig*
desire [dɪ'zaɪə]	strong wish	*Wunsch, Sehnsucht*

page 79

torment ['tɔːment]	extreme suffering or unhappiness	*Qual*
candid ['kændɪd]	honest, open	*offen*
in tribute to [ɪn 'trɪbjuːt tə]	act to show respect (esp. for a dead person)	*zu Ehren von*
anniversary [ˌænɪ'vɜːsəri]	day that is an exact number of years after a particular event	*Jahrestag*
to air [eə]	to broadcast, to show on TV	*ausstrahlen, senden*
to be done with sth [bi 'dʌn wɪð]	to be finished with sth	*mit etw fertig sein*

page 81

appearance [ə'pɪərəns]	arrival	*Erscheinung*
forthcoming [ˌfɔːθ'kʌmɪŋ]	going to happen soon	*bevorstehend*
to pursue [pə'sjuː]	to follow, to chase	*verfolgen*
fair game [feə 'geɪm]	allowed, considered acceptable (e.g. as a target)	*erlaubt*
to profile ['prəʊfaɪl]	to write a description of, to report the most important information on	*berichten über, darstellen*
embarrassing [ɪm'bærəsɪŋ]	making one feel shy, ashamed or awkward	*peinlich*
to remain [rɪ'meɪn]	to continue to be	*bleiben*

TEXT 6 Reporting a War

page 82

to embed [ɪm'bed]	to send sb (eg. a journalist) to travel with the army and report on the fighting	*einbetten*

page 83

to push in [ˌpʊʃ 'ɪn]	*(military)* to move quickly through an area	*hineinstoßen, eindringen*
eternity [ɪ'tɜːnəti]	an extremely long time	*Ewigkeit*
to crouch [kraʊtʃ]	to get close to the ground by bending your knees	*(sich) niederkauern*
shell [ʃel]	metal object filled with explosives which is thrown or fired from a gun	*Granate*
shrapnel ['ʃræpnəl]	small pieces of metal that fly out of a bomb when it explodes	*Bombensplitter*
at the outset [ət ði 'aʊtset]	at the start, in the beginning	*am Anfang*
to inhibit [ɪn'hɪbɪt]	to limit, to reduce	*hemmen, einschränken*
curious ['kjʊəriəs]	wanting to know about sth	*neugierig*
fraud [frɔːd]	sb who cheats	*Betrüger/in*
to witness ['wɪtnəs]	to see, to experience	*(mit)erleben*
to cease [siːs]	to stop, to end	*aufhören, eingestellt werden*
to rough it ['rʌf ɪt]	*(slang)* to live in a way that is uncomfortable (often for a short time)	*primitiv leben*
sheet [ʃiːt]	thin cloth that covers a bed	*Betttuch, Laken*

utter ['ʌtə]	complete	*völlig*
callous ['kæləs]	cruel, not caring how other people feel	*gefühllos, abgebrüht*
to perpetrate ['pɜːpətreɪt]	to carry out or do (sth bad)	*begehen, verüben*
generosity [ˌdʒenə'rɒsəti]	giving freely, opp. meanness	*Großzügigkeit*
enraged [ɪn'reɪdʒd]	extremely angry	*wütend*
composure [kəm'pəʊʒə]	calmness, control over one's emotions	*Fassung*
dignity ['dɪgnəti]	calmness which is worthy of respect	*Würde*
splendour ['splendə]	impressive beauty	*Glanz, Pracht*
filth [fɪlθ]	dirt	*Schmutz, Dreck*
want [wɒnt]	need	*Not*
to trap [træp]	to keep sb in a bad situation or dangerous place	*einschließen, fangen*
accurate ['ækjərət]	correct, truthful	*genau*

TOPIC 4 The State We're In – USA and UK

TEXT 1 Young People and Politics

page 86

to grab sth [græb]	to take advantage of sth (eg. an opportunity)	*etw ergreifen*
charity ['tʃærəti]	organisation to help people in need	*Wohltahrtsorganisation*
to back [bæk]	to support	*unterstützen*
valid ['vælɪd]	based on truth, worthy of consideration	*berechtigt*
to regain [rɪ'geɪn]	to get back (sth)	*wiedererlangen*
unresponsive [ʌnrɪ'spɒnsɪv]	not reacting or giving the response hoped for	*unempfänglich, gleichgültig*
citizenship education ['sɪtɪznʃɪp edʒuˌkeɪʃn]	learning about being part of the community and one's duty as a citizen	*Staatsbürgerkunde*
peer [pɪə]	member of the nobility (ie. people of high social rank)	*Mitglied des Hochadels*
put one's weight behind sth [ˌpʊt wʌnz 'weɪt bɪhaɪnd]	to use all one's power to support sth	*sich für etw stark machen*
bill [bɪl]	written suggestion for a new law which parliament will discuss	*Gesetzentwurf*
burden ['bɜːdn]	sth that sb must deal with but that causes them worry or difficulty	*Last*

page 89

threshold ['θreʃhəʊld]	level or point at which sth changes or a new stage begins	*Schwelle*

TEXT 2 The Most Powerful Leader in the World

page 91

drive [draɪv]	energy, enthusiasm	*Energie, Schwung*
cunning ['kʌnɪŋ]	cleverness that allows sb to trick other people	*Schläue*
commanding [kə'mɑːndɪŋ]	comprehensive	*hier: umfassend*
law degree ['lɔː dɪgriː]	qualification got by students who study law at university	*ein Universitätsabschluss in Jura*
résumé ['rezjumeɪ]	*(AE)* BE: CV (curriculum vitae)	*Lebenslauf*
to raise [reɪz]	to collect (usually for a particular project)	*hier: sammeln*
ticket ['tɪkɪt]	list of candidates supported by a political party	*Wahlliste*
to gather ['gæðə]	to bring together	*um sich versammeln*
devoted [dɪ'vəʊtɪd]	loyal, always supporting and trustworthy	*hingebungsvoll*
primary ['praɪməri]	*(US)* local election to choose a candidate for another more important election	*Vorwahl*
caucus ['kɔːkəs]	*(US)* party conference to choose candidates or decide on policies (ie. political plans)	*Parteikonferenz zur Wahlvorbereitung*
running mate ['rʌnɪŋ meɪt]	*(US)* person chosen by a candidate in an election to have the next highest position if they win	*Vizekandidat*
to deliver [dɪ'lɪvə]	to bring with oneself	*hier: mitbringen*
bottom line [ˌbɒtəm 'laɪn]	the most important thing to consider, the essential point	*das Entscheidende*
national convention [ˌnæʃnəl kən'venʃn]	*(US)* party meeting to choose a candidate for the next presidential election	*Nominierungsparteitag*
unpledged [ʌn'pledʒd]	(esp. *AE*) not yet decided which political party to support	*(noch) nicht verpflichtet*
electoral college [ɪˌlektərəl 'kɒlɪdʒ]	*(US)* group of people who elect the president and vice-president based on votes from people in each state	*Wahlmännergremium*

popular vote [ˌpɒpjələ 'vəʊt]	total votes from ordinary people	*Gesamtzahl der abgegebenen Stimmen bundesweit*
to recite [rɪ'saɪt]	to say sth that you have learned (usually in front of other people)	*aufsagen*
oath [əʊθ]	official promise	*Eid*
inauguration [ɪˌnɔːgjə'reɪʃn]	when a new leader is officially introduced	*Amtseinführung*
solemn ['sɒləm]	serious	*ernst, feierlich; hier: aufrichtig*
to affirm [ə'fɜːm]	to say firmly	*bekräftigen*
to execute ['eksɪkjuːt]	to do sth successfully	*ausüben*
page 93		
to pass a law [ˌpɑːs ə 'lɔː]	to agree on a new law by voting	*ein Gesetz verabschieden*
to veto ['viːtəʊ]	to use one's official power to stop sth happening	*sein Veto einlegen, ablehnen*
to segregate ['segrɪgeɪt]	to separate people (eg. because of their race or religion) and treat them differently	*trennen*
to exercise ['eksəsaɪz]	to use (eg. power or rights)	*ausüben*
to appoint [ə'pɔɪnt]	to choose sb to do a particular job or task	*ernennen*
to be subject to sth [bi 'sʌbdʒekt tə]	depending on sth in order to be finished	*einer Sache unterliegen*
approval [ə'pruːvl]	agreement, permission	*Genehmigung, Zustimmung*
to hold in check [ˌhəʊld ɪn 'tʃek]	to keep under control, to limit	*unter Kontrolle halten*

TEXT 3 The British Electoral System

page 94		
proportional representation [prəˌpɔːʃənl reprɪzen'teɪʃn]	voting system in which each party gets a number of seats in parliament related to the number of votes they get	*Verhältniswahlrecht*
constituency [kən'stɪtjuənsi]	area where people vote for their own representative in parliament	*Wahlkreis*
page 95		
electorate [ɪ'lektərət]	group of people in a country or area who have the right to vote in elections	*Wähler, Wählerschaft*
eventual [ɪ'ventʃuəl]	at the end of a period of time	*letztendlich, schließlich*
to cast one's vote [ˌkɑːst wʌnz 'vəʊt]	to vote	*seine Stimme abgeben*
victorious [vɪk'tɔːriəs]	winning, successful	*siegreich*
essentially [ɪ'senʃəli]	basically, in most ways	*im Wesentlichen*
to occur [ə'kɜː]	to happen, to come about	*vorkommen, sich ereignen*
page 96		
legislation [ˌledʒɪs'leɪʃn]	laws	*Gesetzgebung*
noble ['nəʊbl]	from a family with a high rank in society, aristocratic	*adlig*
hereditary [hə'redɪtri]	passed on to sb's child when they die	*erblich, Erb-*
peerage ['pɪərɪdʒ]	the rank of a peer	*Adelsstand*
to retain [rɪ'teɪn]	to keep, to continue to have	*bewahren, behalten*
to scrap [skræp]	to get rid of sth, to cancel sth (esp. sth that is no longer useful or needed)	*abschaffen, aufgeben*

TEXT 4 Putting Politics Online

page 98		
to make a point [ˌmeɪk ə 'pɔɪnt]	to give an opinion	*ein Anliegen vorbringen, ein Argument anbringen*
earnest ['ɜːnɪst]	requiring much effort and time	*gewissenhaft, ernsthaft*
polling day ['pəʊlɪŋ deɪ]	day when people vote in an election	*Wahltag*
to rack sth up [ˌræk 'ʌp]	to collect, to receive	*auf etw kommen*
cutback ['kʌtbæk]	reduction (eg. in money spent on sth)	*Kürzung*
to oblige [ə'blaɪdʒ]	to force (often by law)	*verpflichten*
to disclose [dɪs'kləʊz]	to reveal, to give information on sth that was previously not known	*bekannt geben*
embarrassment [ɪm'bærəsmənt]	feeling of shame or awkwardness	*Peinlichkeit, Ärgernis*
to submit [səb'mɪt]	to give (eg. a document) to sb in power so they can consider it	*einreichen*
page 99		
to be opposed to sth [bi ə'pəʊzd tə]	to be against sth, to disagree with sth	*gegen etw sein*

response [rɪ'spɒns]	reaction	*Reaktion*
inheritance [ɪn'herɪtəns]	things (usually money, houses etc.) that one receives from sb when they die	*Erbschaft*
to repeal [rɪ'pi:l]	to scrap (ie. a law)	*aufheben*
national anthem [ˌnæʃnəl 'ænθəm]	official song of a country (sung on special occasions)	*Nationalhymne*
to trouble ['trʌbl]	to worry, to concern	*beunruhigen, bedrücken*
sanguine ['sæŋgwɪn]	optimistic, confident about the future	*zuversichtlich*

page 100

surgery ['sɜ:dʒəri]	time when people can meet and talk to their MP	*Sprechstunde*

TEXT 5 Politics and Personal Responsibility

page 102

bare [beə]	uncovered	*entblößt, nackt*
to be struck by sth [bi 'strʌk baɪ]	to have suddenly (ie. an idea or thought)	*jdn überkommen*
convenient [kən'vi:niənt]	useful and easy	*bequem*
mercury ['mɜ:kjəri]	chemical element (Hg) that is a poisonous silver liquid metal	*Quecksilber*
salmon ['sæmən]	a large fish that is used for food	*Lachs*
to gasp [gɑ:sp]	to breathe in quickly (usually as a sign of shock or pain)	*den Atem verschlagen*
wasteful ['weɪstfl]	using more of sth than one really needs	*verschwenderisch*
self-obsessed [ˌself əb'sest]	thinking only about oneself	*von sich selbst besessen, egozentrisch*
to dwell on sth ['dwel ɒn]	to keep thinking about sth	*sich den Kopf über etw zerbrechen*
nasty ['nɑ:sti]	bad, unpleasant	*schlimm, scheußlich*

page 103

backdrop ['bækdrɒp]	conditions in which an event takes place	*Hintergrund*
challenge ['tʃæləndʒ]	difficult task that tests sb's skills	*Herausforderung*
to strive [straɪv]	to try very hard	*nach etw streben, bemüht sein etw zu tun*
consumerism [kən'sju:mərɪzəm]	behaviour of customers choosing products to buy	*Konsumverhalten*
purchase ['pɜ:tʃəs]	sth bought	*Kauf, Anschaffung*
free-range [ˌfri:'reɪndʒ]	connected with a way of farming that lets animals move around freely	*frei laufend*
appliance [ə'plaɪəns]	machine that does a specific task (usually used in the home)	*Gerät*
hermit ['hɜ:mɪt]	person who lives a simple life on their own without social contact	*Einsiedler/in*

page 104

consumption [kən'sʌmpʃn]	buying and using products	*Konsum, Verbrauch*
straightforward [ˌstreɪt'fɔ:wəd]	simple, easy, not complicated	*einfach*
to verify ['verɪfaɪ]	to show that sth is true	*nachweisen, bestätigen*

A–Z WORD LIST

Dieses Wörterverzeichnis enthält alle in *Crossover 1* eingeführten, in den Texten angegebenen Vokabeln in alphabetischer Reihenfolge.

A

a variety of 36 eine Vielzahl von
abbreviation 70 Abkürzung
ability 44 Möglichkeit
able-bodied 7 gesund, tauglich, nicht behindert
abroad 36 im/ins Ausland
abuse 41 Missbrauch
to accost 55 ansprechen
accurate 83 genau
achievement 10 Leistung
act 51 Gesetz
adolescence 55 Jugend, Pubertät
adolescent 62 jugendlich
to advance 58 herankommen
to affirm 91 bekräftigen
to afford sth 44 sich etw leisten
agriculture 47 Landwirtschaft
to air 79 ausstrahlen, senden
akin to sth 62 einer Sache ähnlich
anniversary 79 Jahrestag
appeal 62 Reiz
appearance 81 Erscheinung
appliance 103 Gerät
to appoint 93 ernennen
approach 55 Herankommen
appropriate 73 angemessen
approval 93 Genehmigung, Zustimmung
to argue with sb 71 sich mit jdm streiten
array 67 Ansammlung
as far as sb is concerned 29 was jdn betrifft
as opposed to 74 im Gegensatz zu
assessment 24 Beurteilung, Prüfung
asset 62 Wert, Vermögen
assumption 16 Annahme
astonishing 39 erstaunlich
to be at play 46 mit hineinspielen, eine Rolle spielen
at the outset 83 am Anfang
to attempt 78 versuchen
award 7 Auszeichnung, Preis

B

to back 86 unterstützen
backdrop 103 Hintergrund
baggy 13 ausgebeult, herabhängend
bare 102 entblößt, nackt
to behold 74 erblicken, sehen
beneficiary 67 Nutznießer
to benefit sth 7 etw nützen, zugute kommen
to be on benefits 44 Unterstützung bekommen
bill 86 Gesetzentwurf
binge 18 Sauforgie
bite to eat 57 Happen zu essen
to blame sb for sth 16 jdm/etw die Schuld an etw geben
bleak 58 öde, trostlos
to boom 57 dröhnen, donnern
can't be bothered (to do sth) 43 keine Lust haben (etw zu tun)
bottom line 91 das Entscheidende
bout 78 Runde, Phase
(bowling) alley 55 Kegelbahn (Gebäude)
brave 70 mutig
brisk 46 rege
to brood 58 brüten
bulge 58 Wölbung
bulk 58 Ausmaß, Masse
bum 58 Penner/in
bunch 57 Gruppe, Haufen
burden 86 Last
by no means 26 keineswegs

C

to be called to account 44 zur Rechenschaft gezogen werden
callous 83 gefühllos, abgebrüht
to cancel 29 absagen
candid 79 offen
to captivate 67 faszinieren, fesseln
to cast one's vote 95 seine Stimme abgeben
caucus 91 Parteikonferenz zur Wahlvorbereitung
to cease 83 aufhören, eingestellt werden
census 52 Volkszählung
challenge 103 Herausforderung
charity 86 Wohlfahrtsorganisation
to chat sb up 70 jdn anquatschen, anbaggern
cherry pie 57 Kirschkuchen
chief executive 34 Vorstandschef/in
chipped 55 abgestoßen
to chop 74 (zer)hacken
circumstance 44 Umstand
citizenship education 86 Staatsbürgerkunde
to claim 18 behaupten, verkünden
clearance 47 Räumung
to clock on 21 (den Arbeitsbeginn) stempeln
to clutch 16 umklammern
comfort 24 Trost
commanding 91 hier: umfassend
community 7 Gemeinschaft
comparable 43 vergleichbar
compassion 62 Mitleid
to compete 9 gegeneinander kämpfen
component 73 Bestandteil
composure 83 Fassung
comprehensive 10 umfassend
to comprise 51 umfassen, bestehen aus
con 74 Schwindel
concerned 43 besorgt
conclusive 78 eindeutig
condescending 76 herablassend
to conduct 10 durchführen
conglomerate 66 Konzern
conspiracy 74 Verschwörung, Komplott
constituency 94 Wahlkreis
consumerism 103 Konsumverhalten
consumption 104 Konsum, Verbrauch
to contract 24 erkranken an, sich zuziehen
to contribute to 60 beitragen zu
convenience food 44 Fertiggericht(e)
convenient 102 bequem
conversely 68 umgekehrt
corporate 34 Firmen-, Unternehmens-
cottonwood 58 Pappel
counsellor 34 Betreuer/in
counter 74 Ladentisch, Theke
to crackle 21 knistern
craze 70 Mode, Fimmel
to creep into sth 71 sich in etw einschleichen
to crouch 83 (sich) niederkauern
crucial 62 entscheidend
crusade 10 Kreuzzug
cunning 91 Schläue
to curb 11 eindämmen
curious 83 neugierig
cutback 98 Kürzung

D

daft 44 doof
to date 10 bis heute
dawn 58 Morgendämmerung
dazzling 32 schillernd
decline 41 Rückgang, Niedergang
to decline 47 zurückgehen
to deep-fry 46 frittieren
delirious 55 im Delirium, Taumel
to deliver 91 hier: mitbringen
derelict 41 heruntergekommen, baufällig
to descend 58 sich herabsenken, hinunterkommen
desirable 26 begehrenswert
desire 78 Wunsch, Sehnsucht
despite 18 ungeachtet dessen
to devolve sth to sb 51 etw jdm übertragen
devoted 91 hingebungsvoll
to dig 58 (umgs.) auskosten, mögen, genießen
dignity 83 Würde
dime 58 (US) Zehncentstück
disaffected 39 desillusioniert
to disclose 98 bekannt geben
disease 46 Erkrankung
disgusted 24 angewidert
disgusting 74 widerlich
diverse 32 vielfältig
dizzy 58 schwindlig
dog collar 13 Nietenhalsband
domestic policy 51 Innenpolitik

to be done with sth 79 mit etw fertig sein
to double for 66 (im Film) darstellen
to be down to sth 16 an etw liegen
to dread 21 fürchten
to dress to the nines 39 sich in Schale werfen
drive 91 Energie, Schwung
due to sth 47 aufgrund von etw
dump 55 Müllkippe; Kaff
to dump sb 70 (umgs.) mit jdm Schluss machen
dungeon 21 Kerker
to dwarf 67 in den Schatten stellen
to dwell on sth 102 sich den Kopf über etw zerbrechen

E

earnest 98 gewissenhaft, ernsthaft
ease 62 Leichtigkeit
to eat into 67 verringern, angreifen
eating disorders *(pl.)* 24 Essstörungen
to have the edge 67 einen Vorteil haben
to edit 70 bearbeiten, überarbeiten
electoral college 91 Wahlmänner-gremium
electorate 95 Wähler, Wählerschaft
embarrassing 81 peinlich
embarrassment 98 Peinlichkeit, Ärgernis
to embed 82 einbetten
to emerge 73 aufkommen
enraged 83 wütend
entire 47 ganz
envy 62 Neid
to escape 21 entfliehen, entkommen
essentially 95 im Wesentlichen
essentials *(pl.)* 21 Notwendigkeiten, das Wesentliche
to estimate 52 schätzen
eternity 83 Ewigkeit
to evade 70 sich einer Sache entziehen
eventual 95 letztendlich, schließlich
to execute 91 ausüben
to exercise 93 ausüben
exhaustive 78 umfassend, gründlich
expanse 57 Fläche, Weite
extract 78 Auszug

F

to face sth 34 vor etw stehen
to fail 51 scheitern
failure 24 Versager/in
fair game 81 erlaubt
fame 74 Ruhm
to fancy oneself as sth 7 sich für etw halten
fashion statement 16 Ausdruck eines modischen Stils, Statement
feel 39 Atmosphäre
to feel comfortable with 32 mit etw gut zurechtkommen
fertility 74 Fruchtbarkeit
to festoon 58 schmücken, behängen; aufhängen
filth 83 Schmutz, Dreck
filthy 74 schmutzig
to fit the bill 7 der/die Richtige sein
fleet 60 Flotte
to flicker 67 flimmern
to flog 39 verhökern
to flourish 44 florieren, gedeihen
to be fond of sb 29 jdn gern haben
food outlet 22 Imbiss
foothill 58 Ausläufer, Vorgebirge
forehead 26 Stirn
formidable 67 gewaltig, enorm
forthcoming 81 bevorstehend
fortune 41 Schicksal
framework 51 Rahmen, Grundlage
fraud 83 Betrüger/in
free-range 103 frei laufend
fuel 24 Treibstoff

G

gadget 67 Gerät
gain 24 Zugewinn
gap year 34 Zeitraum zwischen Schule und Studium
garment 16 Kleidungsstück
to gasp 102 den Atem verschlagen
to gather 91 um sich versammeln
to gawk 74 gaffen
generosity 83 Großzügigkeit
gentle 61 sanft, gutmütig
to get lost 71 (umgs.) abhauen
to get on with sb 29 sich gut mit jdm verstehen
gloomy 58 düster
glossy 41 glänzend, Hochglanz-
to grab sth 86 etw ergreifen
greasiness 21 Schmierigkeit, Öligkeit
grid 39 Gitternetz
grip 66 Griff, Kontrolle
grub 39 (umgs.) Essen
gruesome 24 grausig
to gush out 21 herausschießen, heraussprudeln

H

haggard 58 ausgezehrt
hamlet 55 kleines Dorf
hayseed 55 Landpomeranze
haze 55 Dunst(schleier), Schwaden
height 34 Höhe
hereditary 96 erblich, Erb-
hermit 103 Einsiedler/in
high rope 34 Hochseil
to hold down a job 22 einer Arbeit nachgehen
to hold in check 93 unter Kontrolle halten
hollow 74 hohl
homemade diner 57 einfache Imbissstube
homespun 74 selbst gestrickt, einfach
honourable 24 ehrenhaft
to hook up with sb 62 sich mit jdm zusammentun
to host 41 veranstalten, ausrichten
hub 55 Zentrum, Knotenpunkt

I

icicle 66 Eiszapfen
impact 73 Auswirkung
in tribute to 79 zu Ehren von
inauguration 91 Amtseinführung
to indicate 10 besagen, hinweisen auf
inheritance 99 Erbschaft
to inhibit 83 hemmen, einschränken
initial 34 erste(r, s)
to innovate 73 erneuern
inordinate 55 außerordentlich
inquiry 78 Untersuchung
to insist 55 darauf bestehen
insomnia 24 Schlaflosigkeit
to insult 16 beleidigen
interstate 55 etwa: Autobahn (in den USA)
to intimidate 16 einschüchtern
to irritate 51 ärgern

J

to jolt 58 aufrütteln

K

to kid sb 74 jdm etwas vormachen

L

landmark 41 wegweisend, historisch
lane 55 Kegelbahn
large-scale 32 in großem Umfang
law degree 91 ein Universitätsabschluss in Jura
legislation 96 Gesetzgebung
to let sb down 29 jdn im Stich lassen
lettuce 21 (grüner) Salat
life expectancy 43 Lebenserwartung
lifespan 43 Lebensdauer
like-minded 62 gleich gesinnt
likes *(pl.)* 62 Vorlieben
to line 41 säumen
literacy 76 die Fähigkeit, lesen und schreiben zu können, Bildung
log cabin 34 Blockhütte
lot 66 Gelände
love-in 61 Liebesrausch
lowest common denominator 74 kleinster gemeinsamer Nenner

M

to maintain 29 aufrechterhalten, bewahren
to make a point 98 ein Anliegen vorbringen, ein Argument anbringen
to make the case 10 die These vertreten
to mark 41 prägen
to measure 65 messen
medieval 26 mittelalterlich
mercury 102 Quecksilber

miserable 24 elend, unglücklich
to moan about sth 55 über etw jammern
mood swing 24 Stimmungsschwankung
mountain range 36 Bergkette, Gebirgszug
mutual 48 gemeinsam

N

nasty 102 schlimm, scheußlich
national anthem 99 Nationalhymne
national convention 91 Nominierungsparteitag
naval 60 Marine-
to negotiate 55 bewältigen
netball 9 Korbball
noble 96 adlig
notorious 39 notorisch, (berühmt-) berüchtigt
nutritional value 74 Nährwert

O

oath 91 Eid
obese 46 fettleibig
to oblige 98 verpflichten
obsessive 24 zwanghaft, besessen
occupation 22 Tätigkeit
to occur 95 vorkommen, sich ereignen
odd 29 seltsam
off limits 78 tabu
offender 18 Straftäter/in
old fart 39 (umgs.) alter Sack
ongoing 46 im Gange, laufend
to be opposed to sth 99 gegen etw sein
outright 51 total, gänzlich, völlig
overly 13 übermäßig

P

pal 62 Kumpel
to pass a law 93 ein Gesetz verabschieden
patch 58 Landstück, Beet
to patch 57 flicken
peak 58 Gipfel
peer 86 Mitglied des Hochadels
peerage 96 Adelsstand
performance 10 Leistung
to perpetrate 83 begehen, verüben
to pick at sth 67 in etw herumstochern
to pick up the pieces 43 die Scherben aufsammeln, etw wiedergutmachen
pie 46 Pastete; Kuchen
to pin one's hopes on sth 44 seine ganze Hoffnung auf etw setzen
placement 34 Praktikum
plain 57 Ebene
to plummet 24 fallen
poll 67 Umfrage
polling day 98 Wahltag
pond probe 34 Teichuntersuchung
popular vote 91 Gesamtzahl der abgegebenen Stimmen bundesweit
to portray 16 darstellen
potassium 24 Kalium
poverty 41 Armut
prevalent 11 gängig, verbreitet
to prevent 78 verhindern
previous 41 vorher, zuvor
primary 91 Vorwahl
prime time 66 Hauptsendezeit
principal 10 Schulleiter/in
to profile 81 berichten über, darstellen
profoundly 43 zutiefst
profuse 58 üppig
to proliferate 76 wachsen, sich verbreiten
proportional representation 94 Verhältniswahlrecht
prospective 34 zukünftig
to provoke 16 provozieren
purchase 103 Kauf, Anschaffung
to pursue 36, 81 verfolgen
to push in 83 hineinstoßen, eindringen
to put sb off 24 jdn abschrecken
put one's weight behind sth 86 sich für etw stark machen

R

to rack sth up 98 auf etw kommen
to raise 91 hier: sammeln
to rake it in 74 abkassieren
range 36 Spektrum, Bandbreite
to range (from … to) 36 reichen, sich erstrecken (von … bis zu)
raspy 57 rau
raw 57 roh
rawhide 57 raubeinig
reach 62 Sphäre, Bereich
rear-view mirror 55 Rückspiegel
reassurance 24 Bestätigung
to be reborn 47 wieder aufleben
to recall 67 sich erinnern an
to recite 91 aufsagen
refurbishment 39 Renovierung
to regain 86 wiedererlangen
regard 57 Respekt, Beachtung
regarding 18 bezüglich, betreffend
regardless of 7 unabhängig von
to reject 76 ablehnen, zurückweisen
relationship 62 Beziehung
to rely on 44 sich auf etw verlassen
to remain 81 bleiben
remote 55 abgelegen
remotely 21 entfernt, im Entferntesten
to repeal 99 aufheben
reputation 16 Ruf
to be required to 12 es wird von jdm erwartet
research 10 Studie, Untersuchung
residential 7 mit Übernachtung
resistance 11 Widerstand
to resolve 76 entscheiden, klären
to respond 65 reagieren, antworten
response 99 Reaktion
résumé 91 Lebenslauf
to retain 96 bewahren, behalten
to reveal 24 offenbaren, verraten
revolving door 55 Drehtür
reward 34 Belohnung, Lohn
to roam sth 48 durch etw ziehen
rocket science, it's not ~ 44 es ist keine hohe Wissenschaft
roll 39 Brötchen
rotten 74 verdorben, korrupt
to rough it 83 primitiv leben
rude 58 unsanft
running mate 91 Vizekandidat
to rustle sth up 57 etw organisieren, fertigmachen

S

salmon 102 Lachs
sanguine 99 zuversichtlich
scallywag 39 Schlingel, frecher Bursche
scarf 13 Kopftuch, Schal
scoop 57 Kugel
to scrap 96 abschaffen, aufgeben
to segregate 93 trennen
self-aware 24 seiner selbst bewusst
self-obsessed 102 von sich selbst besessen, egozentrisch
to service 60 warten
set 66 Szenenbild, Set
to settle down 55 sesshaft werden
shack 58 Baracke
to shape 12 gestalten, festlegen
sheet 83 Betttuch, Laken
shell 83 Granate
sheltered 34 behütet
shipyard 41 Schiffswerft
shoplifting 16 Ladendiebstahl
short-term 24 kurzfristig
shrapnel 83 Bombensplitter
to shroud 58 umhüllen, einhüllen
sibling 34 Bruder, Schwester, Geschwister
sick 24 krank, pervers
to sigh 55 seufzen
to sizzle 21 brutzeln
skinny 24 mager, dürr
slope 58 Abhang
smart 74 clever, raffiniert
snide 55 abfällig
snowdrift 66 Schneewehe
soda 55 Limonade
solemn 91 ernst, feierlich; aufrichtig
to sort out 44 in Ordnung bringen
sound 58 fest
spare tire 57 Ersatzreifen
to spin 58 sich drehen, herumwirbeln
splendour 83 Glanz, Pracht
to starve oneself 24 hungern
stench 21 Gestank
stick-thin 24 spindeldürr
stomach, my ~ churns 21 mir dreht sich der Magen um
storied 58 legendär, sagenumwoben
straight 29 offen, direkt
straightforward 104 einfach
to strive 103 nach etw streben, bemüht sein etw zu tun
to be struck by sth 102 jdn überkommen
struggle 51 Auseinandersetzung, Kampf
stud 13 Piercing
to stumble 58 stolpern, torkeln
stylish 39 elegant, stilvoll
to be subject to sth 93 einer Sache unterliegen
to submit 98 einreichen
supposedly 16 angeblich
surgery 100 Sprechstunde
surroundings *(pl.)* 21 Umgebung
survey 18 Umfrage
sustained 67 anhaltend

T

to take sth for granted 39 etw für selbstverständlich halten
to take sth in your stride 44 sich keine Gedanken um etw machen
to take the plunge 7 den Sprung wagen

target 16 Ziel
to taunt 16 verhöhnen
tension 32 Spannung
threshold 89 Schwelle
to thrive 41 florieren
to throw oneself in at the deep end 34 ins kalte Wasser springen
ticket 91 Wahlliste
torment 79 Qual
to touch up 66 retuschieren, ausbessern
tournament 55 Turnier
to trap 83 einschließen, fangen
treed 58 baumbewachsen
tremendous 39 enorm, großartig
trolley 58 Straßenbahn
to trouble 99 beunruhigen, bedrücken

U

underfed 26 unterernährt
undertaker 44 Leichenbestatter
unpledged 91 (noch) nicht verpflichtet
unresponsive 86 unempfänglich, gleichgültig
to be up to no good 16 nichts Gutes im Schilde führen
upwards of 62 über, mehr als
utter 83 völlig

V

valid 86 berechtigt
venture 65 Unternehmen
to verify 104 nachweisen, bestätigen
to veto 93 sein Veto einlegen, ablehnen
vicious circle 16 Teufelskreis
victim 44 Opfer
victorious 95 siegreich
Virgin Mary 26 Jungfrau Maria
vocal, to be more ~ about sth 39 etw lauter sagen
to vomit 21 erbrechen

W

want 83 Not
to want 62 brauchen
to ward off 78 abwehren, abwenden
warfare 51 Krieg, Kriegsführung
warped 55 verzogen, verbogen
warrior 74 Krieger
wasteful 102 verschwenderisch
weird 24 seltsam
weirdo 39 komischer Kauz
well-nourished 26 gut genährt
widespread 18 weit verbreitet
to wipe sth out 7 etw zunichte machen
to witness 83 (mit)erleben
woe betide you 39 wehe dir
worshipful 74 verehrend, vergötternd

Y

to yell 57 schreien

Z

to zip 55 sausen

IRREGULAR VERBS

be – was/were – been	*sein*
beat – beat – beaten	*schlagen, besiegen*
become – became – become	*werden*
begin – began – begun	*anfangen, beginnen*
behold – beheld – beheld	*erblicken, beobachten, sehen*
bind – bound – bound	*binden*
break – broke – broken	*brechen*
build – built – built	*bauen*
burn – burned/burnt – burned/burnt	*(ver)brennen*
buy – bought – bought	*kaufen*
cast – cast – cast	*(seine Stimme) abgeben; werfen*
catch – caught – caught	*fangen, verstehen*
choose – chose – chosen	*(aus)wählen*
come – came – come	*kommen*
cost – cost – cost	*kosten*
creep – crept – crept	*(ein)schleichen*
cut – cut – cut	*schneiden*
do – did – done	*tun, machen*
deal – dealt – dealt	*sich befassen; handeln; austeilen*
draw – drew – drawn	*zeichnen*
dream – dreamt – dreamt	*träumen*
drink – drank – drunk	*trinken*
drive – drove – driven	*fahren*
dwell – dwelt/dwelled – dwelt/dwelled	*sich den Kopf zerbrechen*
eat – ate – eaten	*essen*
fall – fell – fallen	*fallen*
feed – fed – fed	*füttern, ernähren*
feel – felt – felt	*(sich) fühlen, empfinden*
fight – fought – fought	*kämpfen*
find – found – found	*finden*
fit – fit/fitted – fit/fitted	*passen*
fly – flew – flown	*fliegen*
forget – forgot – forgotten	*vergessen*
freeze – froze – frozen	*(ge)frieren*
get – got – got (AE gotten)	*bekommen*
give – gave – given	*geben*
go – went – gone	*gehen, fahren*
grow – grew – grown	*wachsen*
hang – hung – hung	*hängen*
have – had – had	*haben*
hear – heard – heard	*hören*
hide – hid – hidden	*(sich) verstecken*
hit – hit – hit	*schlagen; treffen auf*
hold – held – held	*halten, festhalten*
hurt – hurt – hurt	*verletzen, weh tun*
keep – kept – kept	*behalten*
know – knew – known	*kennen, wissen*
lay – laid – laid	*legen*
lead – led – led	*führen*
learn – learnt/learned – learnt/learned	*lernen*
leave – left – left	*abfahren, verlassen, weggehen*
let – let – let	*lassen*
lie – lay – lain	*liegen*
light – lit – lit	*anzünden, beleuchten*
lose – lost – lost	*verlieren*
make – made – made	*machen*
mean – meant – meant	*meinen, bedeuten*
meet – met – met	*treffen*
pay – paid – paid	*bezahlen*
put – put – put	*setzen, stellen, legen*
quit – quit/quitted – quit/quitted	*verlassen, aufhören*
read – read – read	*lesen*
ride – rode – ridden	*reiten, fahren*
rise – rose – risen	*(an)steigen*
ring – rang – rung	*läuten, klingeln*
run – ran – run	*laufen, rennen*
say – said – said	*sagen*
see – saw – seen	*sehen*
seek – sought – sought	*suchen*
sell – sold – sold	*verkaufen*
send – sent – sent	*senden, schicken*
set – set – set	*setzen, stellen*
shake – shook – shaken	*schütteln*
show – showed – shown	*zeigen*
shut – shut – shut	*schließen*
sing – sang – sung	*singen*
sink – sank/sunk – sunk/sunken	*sinken*
sit – sat – sat	*sitzen*
sleep – slept – slept	*schlafen*
smell – smelt/smelled – smelt/smelled	*riechen*
speak – spoke – spoken	*sprechen*
spell – spelt/spelled – spelt/spelled	*buchstabieren*
spend – spent – spent	*ausgeben, verbringen*
spin – spun – spun	*sich drehen, herumwirbeln*
stand – stood – stood	*stehen*
steal – stole – stolen	*stehlen*
strive – strove/strived – striven/strived	*streben (nach)*
swim – swam – swum	*schwimmen*
take – took – taken	*nehmen*
teach – taught – taught	*unterrichten, beibringen*
tell – told – told	*sagen, erzählen*
think – thought – thought	*denken*
thrive – thrived/throve – thrived/thriven	*florieren*
throw – threw – thrown	*werfen*
understand – understood – understood	*verstehen*
wake – woke/waked – woken/waked	*aufwachen, wecken*
wear – wore – worn	*tragen*
win – won – won	*gewinnen*
write – wrote – written	*schreiben*

GEOGRAPHICAL NAMES

Africa [ˈæfrɪkə] Afrika
America [əˈmerɪkə] Amerika
Austin [ˈɒstɪn] *Hauptstadt von Texas*
Baghdad [bæɡˈdæd] Bagdad
Barras [ˈbærəs] Flohmarkt in Glasgow
Basra [ˈbæsrə] *Stadt im Südosten des Irak*
Bathgate [ˈbɑːθɡeɪt] *Schottischer Ort in der Nähe von Edinburgh*
Beverly Hills [ˌbevəli ˈhɪlz] *Stadt im County Los Angeles*
Boston [ˈbɒstən] *Hauptstadt von Massachussetts*
Brighton [ˈbraɪtn] *Stadt in Südostengland*
Brooklyn [ˈbrʊklɪn] *Stadtteil von New York*
California [ˌkæləˈfɔːniə] Kalifornien
Canada [ˈkænədə] Kanada
Cannes [kæn] *Stadt im Südosten Frankreichs*
Chicago [ʃɪˈkɑːɡəʊ] *Stadt in Illinois*
Cologne [kəˈləʊn] Köln
Colorado [ˌkɒləˈrɑːdəʊ] *Staat in den USA*
Denver [ˈdenvə] *Hauptstadt des US-Bundesstaates Colorado*
Des Moines [dɪˈmɔɪn] *Hauptstadt des US-Bundesstaates Iowa*
Devon [ˈdevn] *Grafschaft im Südwesten Englands*
Dog Water [ˈdɒɡ wɔːtə] *Kleines Dorf in der Nähe von Des Moines*
Downing Street [ˈdaʊnɪŋ striːt] *Straße in London, in der sich der Amtssitz des Premierministers befindet*
Dunceville [ˈdʌnsvɪl] *Kleines Dorf in der Nähe von Des Moines*
Edinburgh [ˈedɪnbərə] *Hauptstadt Schottlands*
Edlington [ˈedlɪŋtən] *Ort im Norden Englands*
Essex [ˈesɪks] *Grafschaft im Südosten Englands*
Europe [ˈjʊərəp] Europa
Falkirk [ˈfɔːlkɜːk] *Schottische Industriestadt nordöstlich von Glasgow*
FL = Florida [ˈflɒrɪdə] *Bundesstaat im Südosten der USA*
France [frɑːns] Frankreich
Frisco = San Francisco [ˈfrɪskəʊ/ˌsæn frənˈsɪskəʊ] Stadt in Kalifornien
Germany [ˈdʒɜːməni] Deutschland
Glasgow [ˈɡlɑːsɡəʊ] *Stadt in Westschottland*
Grand Island [ˌɡrænd ˈaɪlənd] *Stadt in Nebraska*
(Great) Britain [ˌɡreɪt ˈbrɪtn] Großbritannien
Greece [ɡriːs] Griechenland
Greenhithe [ˈɡriːnhaɪð] *Dorf in der Grafschaft Kent*
Guam [ˈɡuəm] *Insel im pazifischen Ozean*
Hampstead [ˈhæmpstɪd] *Vorort von London*
Hollywood [ˈhɒliwʊd] *Stadtteil im Nordwesten von Los Angeles*
Illinois [ˌɪləˈnɔɪ] *Bundesstaat im Mittleren Westen der USA*
India [ˈɪndiə] Indien
Iraq [ɪˈrɑːk] Irak
Ireland [ˈaɪələnd] Irland
Irvine [ˈɜːvɪn] *Ort im Südwesten Schottlands*
Kennesaw [ˈkenɪsɔː] *Stadt in Georgia, USA*
Kent [kent] *Grafschaft im Südosten Englands*
Kuwait [kʊˈweɪt] *Staat am Persischen Golf*
Leicestershire [ˈlestəʃə] *Grafschaft in England*
Lewis [ˈluːɪs] *Schottische Inselhälfte der Äußeren Hebriden*
Linwood [ˈlɪnwʊd] *Schottischer Ort in der Nähe von Glasgow*
Liverpool [ˈlɪvəpuːl] *Stadt im Nordosten Englands*
Lochaber [lɒˈxɑːbə] *Ehem. Grafschaft in der schottischen Hochebene*
London [ˈlʌndən] *Britische Hauptstadt*
Los Angeles [lɒs ˈændʒəliːz] *Stadt im Südwesten Kaliforniens*
Manchester [ˈmæntʃɪstə] *Stadt im Nordwesten Englands*
Massachusetts [ˌmæsəˈtʃuːsɪts] *US-Bundesstaat in Neuengland*
Memphis [ˈmemfɪs] *Stadt in Tennessee*
Methil [ˈmeθɪl] *Ort im Südosten Schottlands*
Miami [maɪˈæmi] *Stadt in Florida (USA)*
Mill City [ˌmɪl ˈsɪti] *Verbindung aus „Marin City" und „Mill Valley", zwei Orte bei San Francisco*
Milton Keynes [ˌmɪltn ˈkiːnz] *Stadt in Südengland*
Milwaukee [mɪlˈwɔːki] *Stadt in Wisconsin*
Minneapolis [ˌmɪniˈæpəlɪs] *Stadt im Südosten von Minnesota*
Nebraska [nəˈbræskə] *Bundesstaat im mittleren Westen der USA*
New Jersey [ˌnjuː ˈdʒɜːzi] *Bundesstaat an der Ostküste der USA*
New York [ˌnjuː ˈjɔːk] *Bundesstaat an der Ostküste der USA*
New York (City) [ˌnjuː jɔːk ˈsɪti] *größte Stadt in den USA*
Newton Abbot [ˌnjuːtn ˈæbɪt] *Ort in Devon*
Northern Ireland [ˌnɔːðən ˈaɪələnd] Nordirland
Norwich [ˈnɒrɪdʒ] *Stadt im Osten Englands*
Nova Scotia [ˌnəʊvə ˈskəʊʃə] Neuschottland, an der Atlantikküste gelegene Provinz Kanadas
Oakland [ˈəʊklənd] *Stadt in Kalifornien*
Orlando [ɔːˈlændəʊ] *Stadt in Florida*
Pakistan [ˌpækɪˈstɑːn] Pakistan
Paris [ˈpærɪs] *Hauptstadt Frankreichs*
Puerto Rico [ˌpwɜːtəʊ ˈriːkəʊ] *Gebiet im Bereich der Westindischen Inseln*
Rhine [raɪn] Rhein
Clyde [klaɪd] Fluss in Schottland
Sacramento [ˌsækrəˈmentəʊ] *Hauptstadt von Kalifornien*
San Francisco [ˌsæn frənˈsɪskəʊ] *Stadt in Kalifornien*
Scotland [ˈskɒtlənd] Schottland
Scottish Lowlands [ˌskɒtɪʃ ˈləʊləndz] Schottische Tiefebene
Seattle [siˈætl] *Stadt im Westen des Staates Washington*
Shettleston [ˈʃetlstn] *Vorort von Glasgow*
Skye [skaɪ] *Schottische Insel*
Spain [speɪn] Spanien
Staffordshire [ˈstæfədʃə] *Grafschaft in den West Midlands von England*
Stoke Newington [ˌstəʊk ˈnjuːɪŋtən] *Bezirk in London*
Sutherland [ˈsʌðələnd] *Ehem. Grafschaft in der schottischen Hochebene*
Tennessee [ˌtenəˈsiː] *Stadt im Südosten der USA*
Texas [ˈteksəs] *Bundesstaat im Süden der USA*
Troy [trɔɪ] Troja
UK = United Kingdom [ˌjuː ˈkeɪ/juˌnaɪtɪd ˈkɪŋdəm] Vereinigtes Königreich (Großbritannien und Nordirland)
Umm Qasr [ˌʊm kəˈzɑːr] *Hafenstadt im Irak*
US(A) = United States (of America) [ˌjuː es ˈeɪ/juˌnaɪtɪd steɪts əv əˈmerɪkə] Vereinigte Staaten (von Amerika)
Virgin Islands [ˌvɜːdʒɪn ˈaɪləndz] Jungferninseln
Wales [weɪlz] *Landesteil des Vereinigten Königreichs*
Warwickshire [ˈwɒrɪkʃə] *Grafschaft in den englischen West Midlands*
Wester Ross [ˌwestə ˈrɒs] *Gebiet an der Westküste Schottlands*
Westminster [ˈwestmɪnstə] *Stadtbezirk in London*
Wisconsin [wɪsˈkɒnsɪn] *Bundesstaat im Nordosten der USA*
Zimbabwe [zɪmˈbɑːbwi] *Simbabwe*

BILDQUELLEN

Cover: Fotosearch RF

RF-Fotos:
Alamy: S. 10-Darren Greenwood, S. 38/1 Findlay , S. 52/4 J. Arnold Images; C.Buckstegen: S. 13/1/2/3, S. 71/2; Corbis S. 37; Gettyimages: S. 33/2, S. 27/2 Stockbyte; S. 68-Image Source Black; Comstock:S. 27/5; Konrad Gabriel: S. 43; H. Goebel: S. 56/4, S. 74/2; V. Maly: S. 27/4; Mauritius: S. 71/4; Istockphoto: S. 56/1/2/3/5/6/7/8, S. 59/1/2/3/4; S. 70; S. 74/1; S. 94; S. 40

RM-Fotos:
Archiv für Kunst und Geschichte: S. 47/1-akg-images; S. 47/2

Alamy: S. 6/2-Angela Hampton; S. 9-Mike Booth; S. 15/5-Janine Wiedel; S. 31-Konrad Zelazowski; S. 38/2-Edward Moss; S. 38/4-R. Harding Picture Library; S. 47/4-The Print Collector; S. 47/6-Yadid Lewy; S. 51-Chris Willson; S. 52/1-John Henshall, S. 52/2-C. Pefley; S. 52/3-J. Arnold Images; S. 52/5-pictures dimensions; S. 80-Stephen Bisgrove; S. 90/2-Classic image; S. 90/5-Pictorial Press; S. 98/1-Paul Glendell; S. 98/2-Julio Rito; S. 98/3-Martin Jenkinson; S. 103/2-Keith Brofsky

Contentmine: S. 39/2-KPA Collection

Corbis: S. 15/1-Mika; S. 15/3-Peter Turnley; S. 15/4-Bettmann; S. 20-Ariel Skelley; S. 23/1-Charles Platiau; S. 26/1-Michel Arnaud; S. 26/2-National Gallery Collection; S. 26/3-Sunset Boulevard; S. 39/1-Rune Hellestad; S. 58/2-Bettmann;S. 61-Henry Diltz; S. 78-Tim Graham; S. 90/1-Brooks Kraft; S. 90/3-Owen Franken; S. 90/4-Bettmann; S. 93/1-Thierry Tronnel; S. 93/2-Wally McNamee; S. 95-Bettmann

Fotofinder: S. 6/1-Thomas Imo/photothek.net; S. 6/3-Mark Edwards/Still Pictures; S. 15/2-VISUM/ The ImageWorks; S. 33/3-Mark Edwards/Still Pictures; S. 33/4-Clay McLachlan/IPN

GettyImages:S. 27/1-Debra McClinton; S. 27/3-E. Faure; S. 48-Mark Allan; S. 66/1-Handout; S. 66/2-David Kemmerly; S. 66/3; S. 66/4; S. 66/5-M. Loccisano; S. 66/6-F. Brown

Picture Allicance: S. 33/1-Hans Jürgen Wege; S. 47/5-Akg-images; S. 74/3-Sven Simon; S. 74/4-20th Century Fox; S. 79; S. 83-dpa; S. 103-Jochen Lübke

Ullstein-Bild: S. 47/3

Wildlife: S. 36-Martin Harvey/Peter Arnold

Mit freundlicher Unterstützung:
S. 7 www.theaward.org; S. 23/2-Dove; S. 28/1/2/3/4 und S. 32-Neue Visionen Filmverleih GmbH, Berlin; S. 38/3-SPT Glasgow; S. 71/1 www.cm-insight.com/guy-fielding; S. 86 The Votes at 16 Coalition

Landkarten:
Carlos Borrell, Berlin

TEXTQUELLEN

S. 7: http://www.theaward.org/youth/flash.html
S. 10: http://family.go.com/parenting/ms-learning/article-gs-17954-the-debate-over-dress-codes-and-uniforms-t/
S. 17: http://news.bbc.co.uk/1/hi/england/devon/4562737.stm
S. 21: http://teenink.com/Past/1999/10564.html
S. 24: http://news.bbc.co.uk/nolpda/ifs_news/hi/newsid_6335000/6335077.stm
S. 29: Neue Visionen Filmverleih GmbH, Berlin
S. 34: http://www.gap.org.uk/uwhat/uwhat.html
S. 39: "In Britain" Magazin, April/May 2005
S. 43/44: The Observer, 14. März 2004
S. 48: The Proclaimers, Chrysalis Records
S. 55: Bill Bryson, "The Lost Continent", Blackswan, 1999
S. 57: Jack Kerouac, "On the Road", London (Penguin) 1998
S. 61: John Philipps
S. 62/63: http://news.bbc.co.uk/2/hi/uk_news/magazine/4782118.stm
S. 66/67: The Economist, 13. April 2002
S. 70/71: http://www.ananova.com/news/story/sm_54806.html
S. 74: The R. Crumb Handbook, London 2005
S. 78: The Guardian, 13. Juni 2007
S. 79: The Sun, 13. Juni 2007
S. 83: http://news.bbc.co.uk/2/hi/in_depth/world/2003/reporters_log/2957699.stm
S. 86: http://www.votesat16.org.uk/news/5.html?PHPSESSID=291e9ec09f5c4e0578e15b44fb69cb5f
S. 91: http://www.ehow.com/how_136497_become-president-united.html
S. 94/95: http://www.historylearningsite.co.uk/first_past_the_post.htm
S. 98/99: The Independent, 12. Februar 2007
S. 102/103: Leo Hickman, "A Life Stripped Bare", 2005

European Union